NOT DRUNK ENOUGH

AN ONI PRESS PRODUCTION

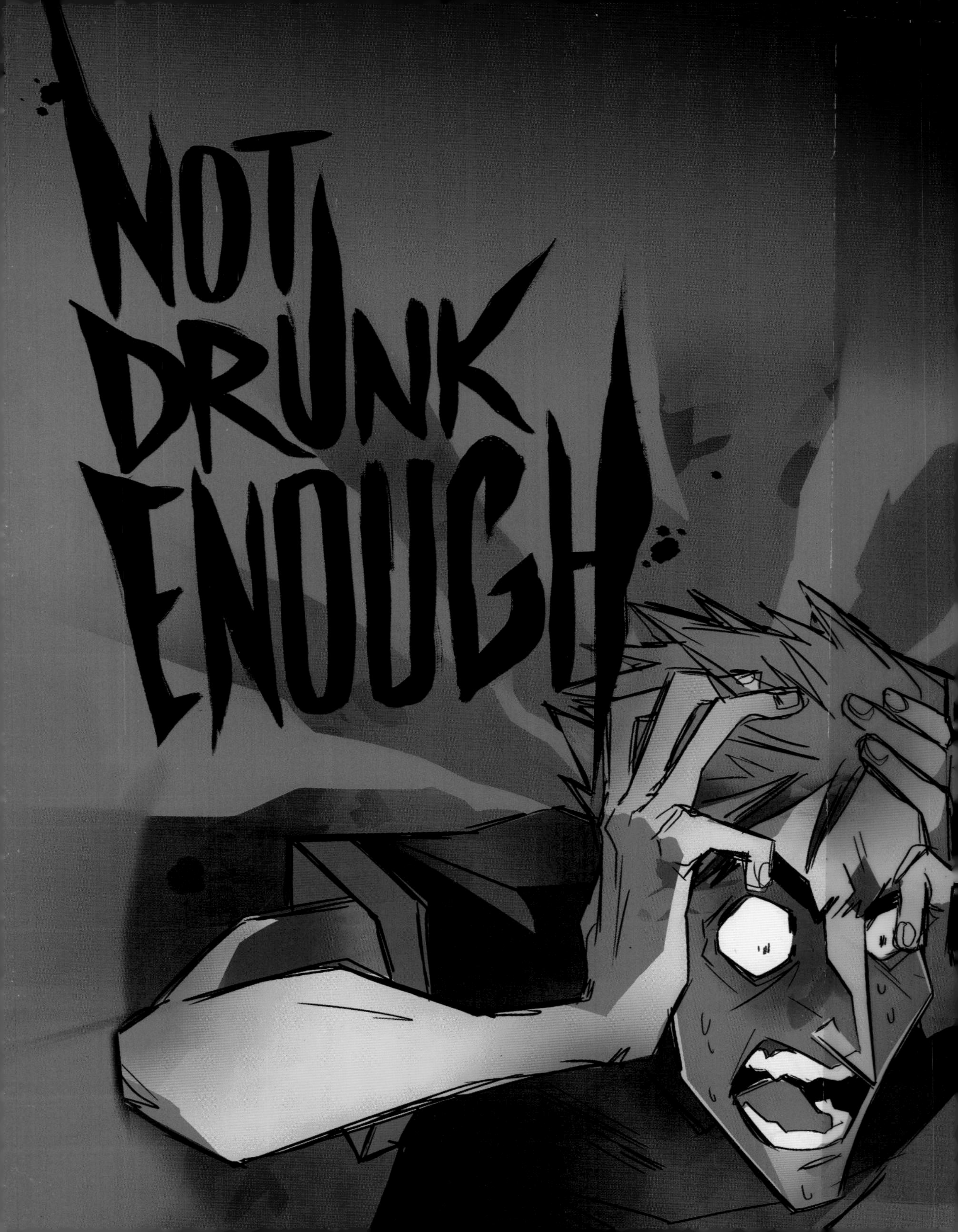
NOT DRUNK ENOUGH

BOOK TWO

WRITTEN, ILLUSTRATED, AND LETTERED BY

TESS STONE

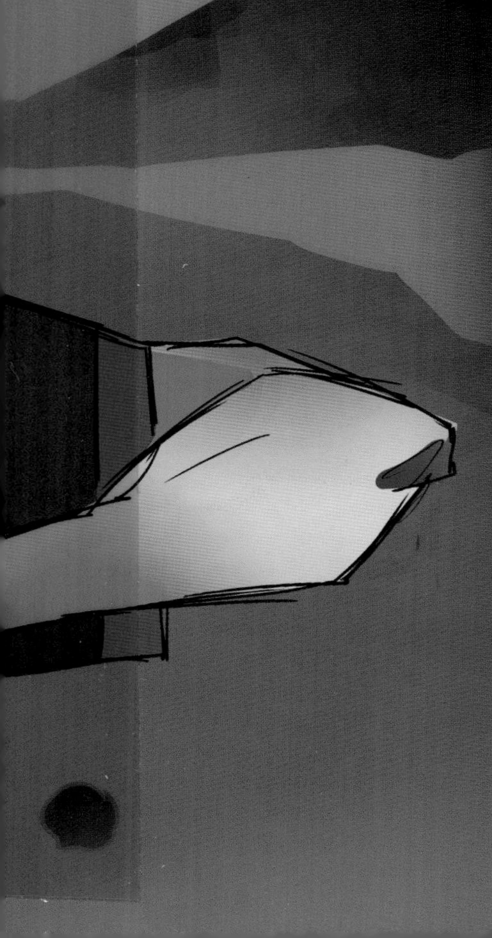

COLLECTION EDITED BY
ROBIN HERRERA

DESIGNED BY
SONJA SYNAK AND ROBERT ARMBRISTER

PUBLISHED BY ONI-LION FORGE PUBLISHING GROUP, LLC

JAMES LUCAS JONES, president & publisher • SARAH GAYDOS, editor in chief • CHARLIE CHU, e.v.p. of creative & business development
BRAD ROOKS, director of operations • AMBER O'NEILL, special projects manager • HARRIS FISH, events manager • MARGOT WOOD, director of marketing & sales
JEREMY ATKINS, director of brand communications • DEVIN FUNCHES, sales & marketing manager • TARA LEHMANN, marketing & publicity associate
TROY LOOK, director of design & production • KATE Z. STONE, senior graphic designer • SONJA SYNAK, graphic designer • HILARY THOMPSON, graphic designer
ANGIE KNOWLES, digital prepress lead • SHAWNA GORE, senior editor • ROBIN HERRERA, senior editor • AMANDA MEADOWS, senior editor
JASMINE AMIRI, editor • GRACE BORNHOFT, editor • ZACK SOTO, editor • STEVE ELLIS, vice president of games • BEN EISNER, game developer
MICHELLE NGUYEN, executive assistant • JUNG LEE, logistics coordinator

JOE NOZEMACK, publisher emeritus

Hiveworks Comics LLC
A creator owned publisher and studio
WWW.THEHIVEWORKS.COM

ONIPRESS.COM | LIONFORGE.COM
FACEBOOK.COM/ONIPRESS | FACEBOOK.COM/LIONFORGE
TWITTER.COM/ONIPRESS | TWITTER.COM/LIONFORGE
INSTAGRAM.COM/ONIPRESS | INSTAGRAM.COM/LIONFORGE

NOTDRUNKENOUGH.COM

First Edition: March 2020
ISBN 978-1-62010-688-4
eISBN 978-1-62010-700-3

1 3 5 7 9 10 8 6 4 2

Library of Congress Control Number: 2019940882

Printed in China.

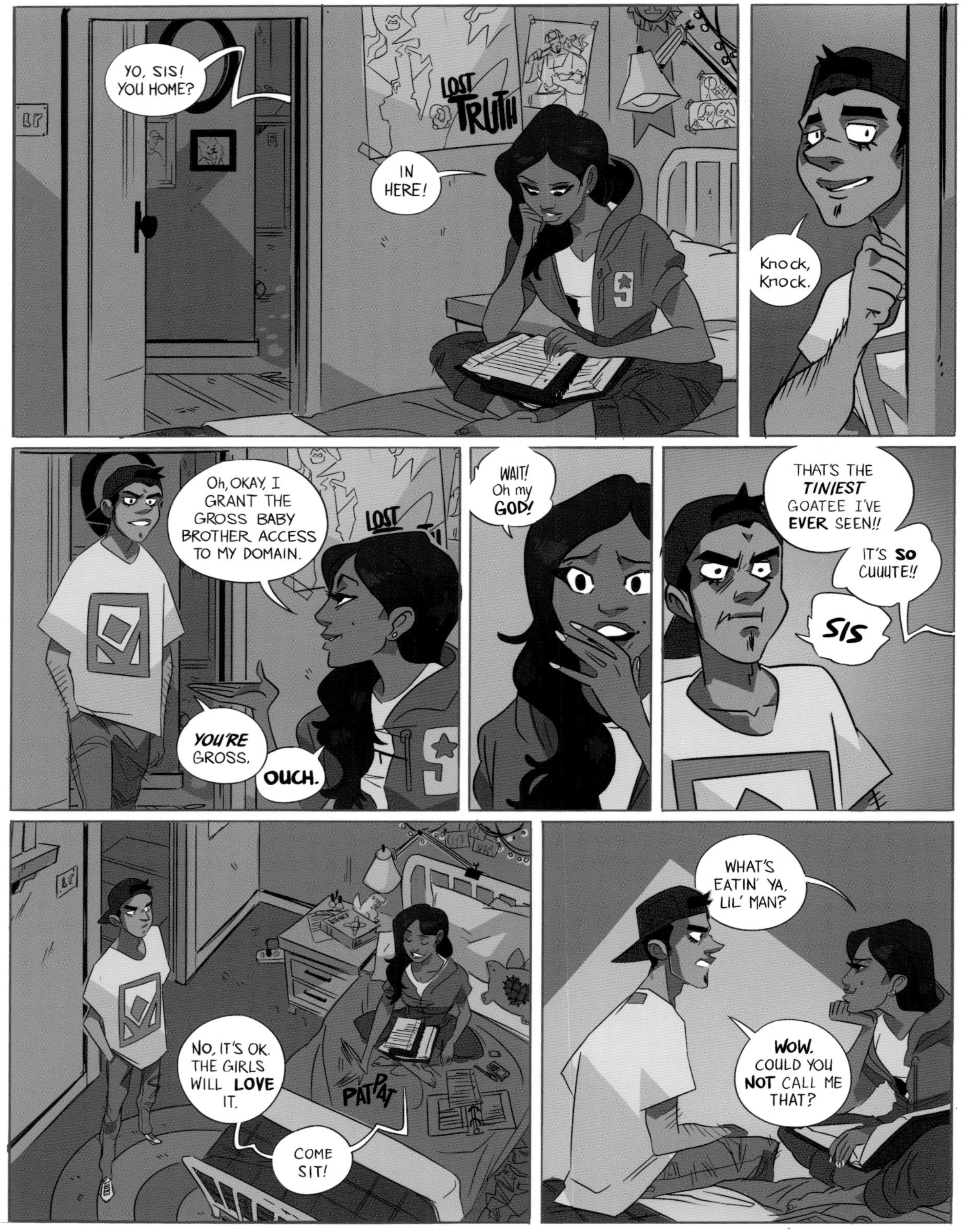
YO, SIS! YOU HOME?
IN HERE!
LOST TRUTH
Knock, Knock.
Oh, OKAY, I GRANT THE GROSS BABY BROTHER ACCESS TO MY DOMAIN.
YOU'RE GROSS.
OUCH.
WAIT! Oh my GOD!
THAT'S THE TINIEST GOATEE I'VE EVER SEEN!!
IT'S SO CUUUTE!!
SIS
NO, IT'S OK. THE GIRLS WILL LOVE IT.
PAT PAT
COME SIT!
WHAT'S EATIN' YA, LIL' MAN?
WOW. COULD YOU NOT CALL ME THAT?

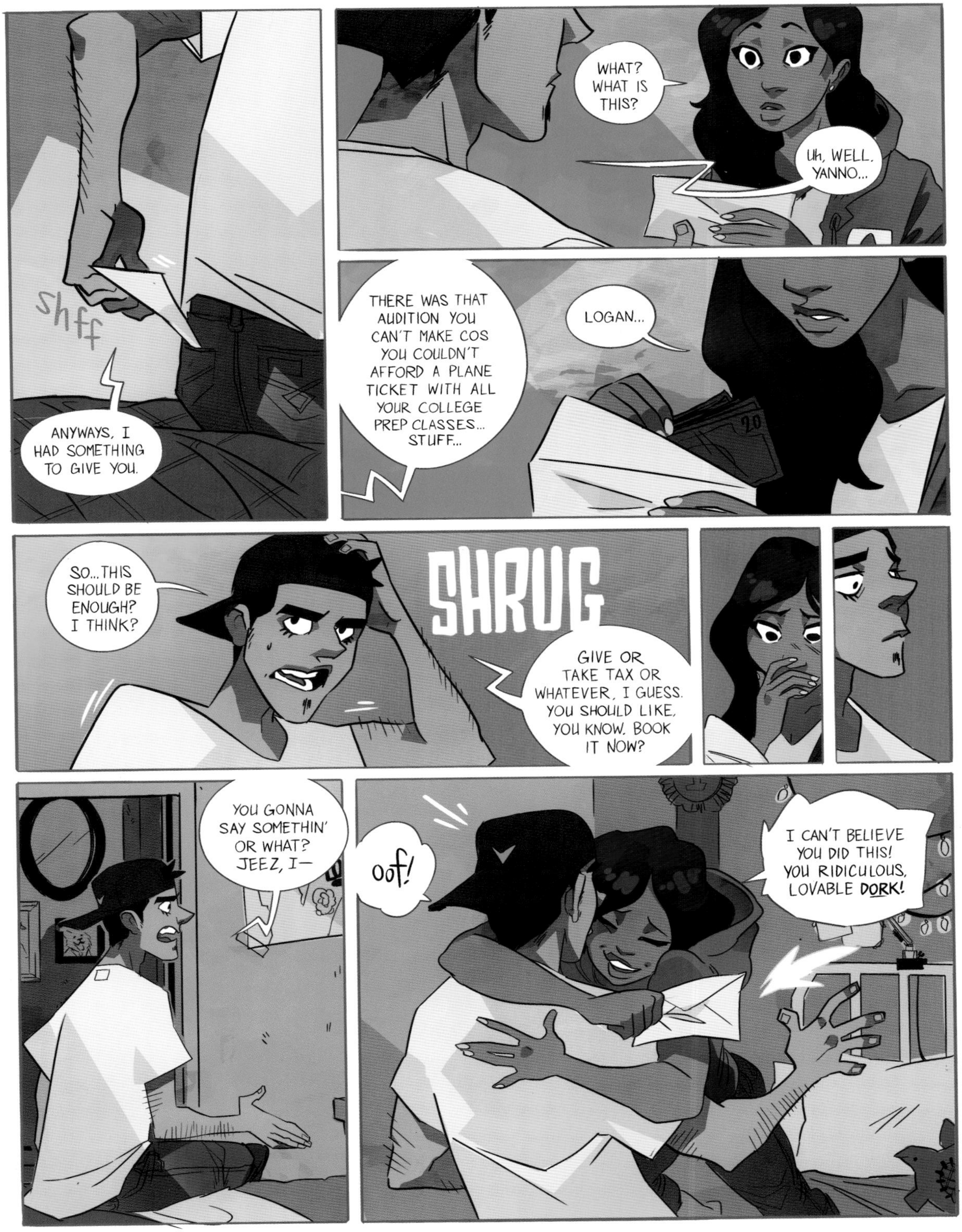
shff
ANYWAYS, I HAD SOMETHING TO GIVE YOU.
WHAT? WHAT IS THIS?
Uh, WELL, YANNO...
THERE WAS THAT AUDITION YOU CAN'T MAKE COS YOU COULDN'T AFFORD A PLANE TICKET WITH ALL YOUR COLLEGE PREP CLASSES... STUFF...
LOGAN...
SO... THIS SHOULD BE ENOUGH? I THINK?
SHRUG
GIVE OR TAKE TAX OR WHATEVER, I GUESS. YOU SHOULD LIKE, YOU KNOW. BOOK IT NOW?
YOU GONNA SAY SOMETHIN' OR WHAT? JEEZ, I—
oof!
I CAN'T BELIEVE YOU DID THIS! YOU RIDICULOUS, LOVABLE **DORK!**

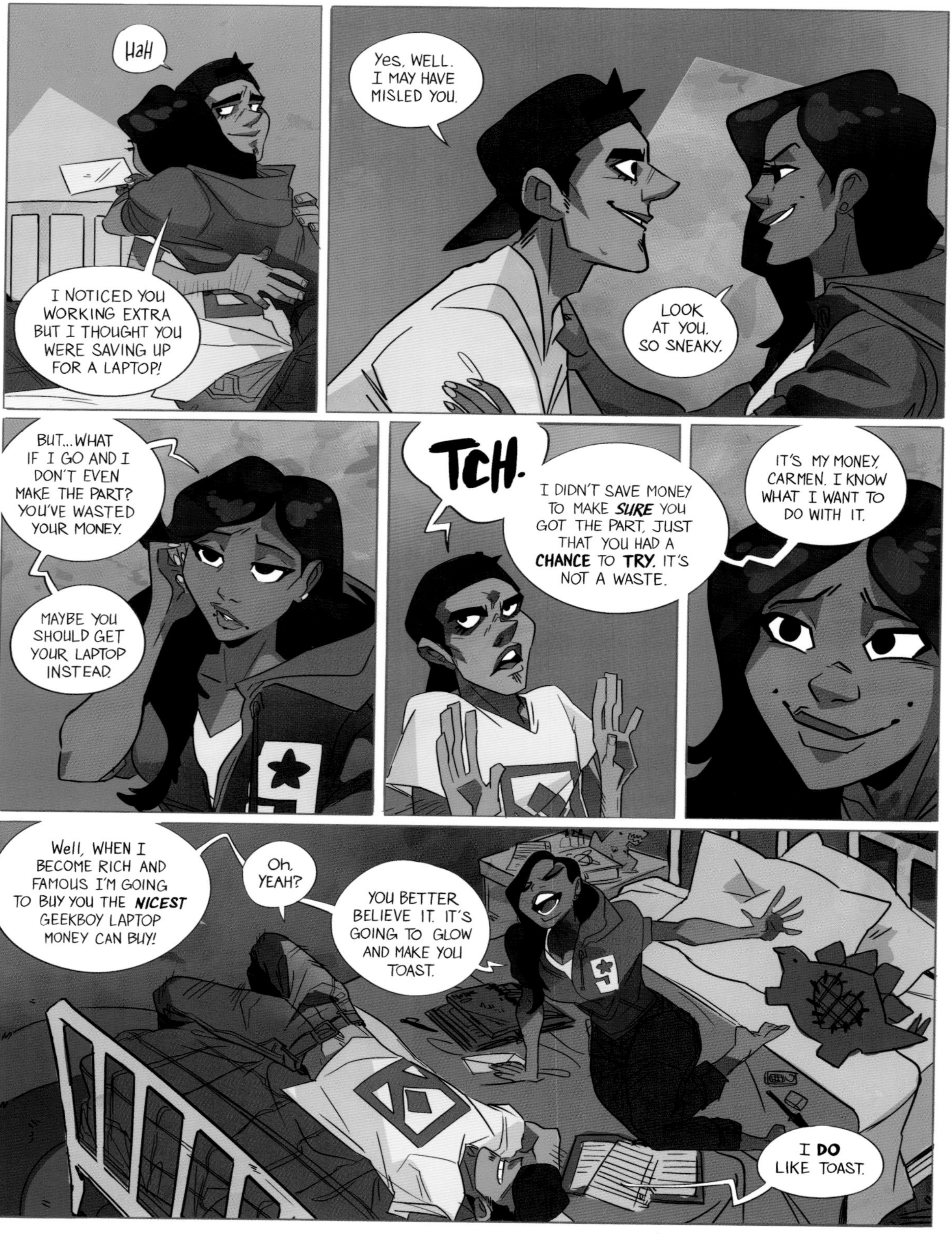
HaH
I NOTICED YOU WORKING EXTRA BUT I THOUGHT YOU WERE SAVING UP FOR A LAPTOP!
Yes, WELL. I MAY HAVE MISLED YOU.
LOOK AT YOU. SO SNEAKY.
BUT... WHAT IF I GO AND I DON'T EVEN MAKE THE PART? YOU'VE WASTED YOUR MONEY.
MAYBE YOU SHOULD GET YOUR LAPTOP INSTEAD.
TCH.
I DIDN'T SAVE MONEY TO MAKE SURE YOU GOT THE PART, JUST THAT YOU HAD A CHANCE TO TRY. IT'S NOT A WASTE.
IT'S MY MONEY, CARMEN. I KNOW WHAT I WANT TO DO WITH IT.
Well, WHEN I BECOME RICH AND FAMOUS I'M GOING TO BUY YOU THE NICEST GEEKBOY LAPTOP MONEY CAN BUY!
Oh, YEAH?
YOU BETTER BELIEVE IT. IT'S GOING TO GLOW AND MAKE YOU TOAST.
I DO LIKE TOAST.

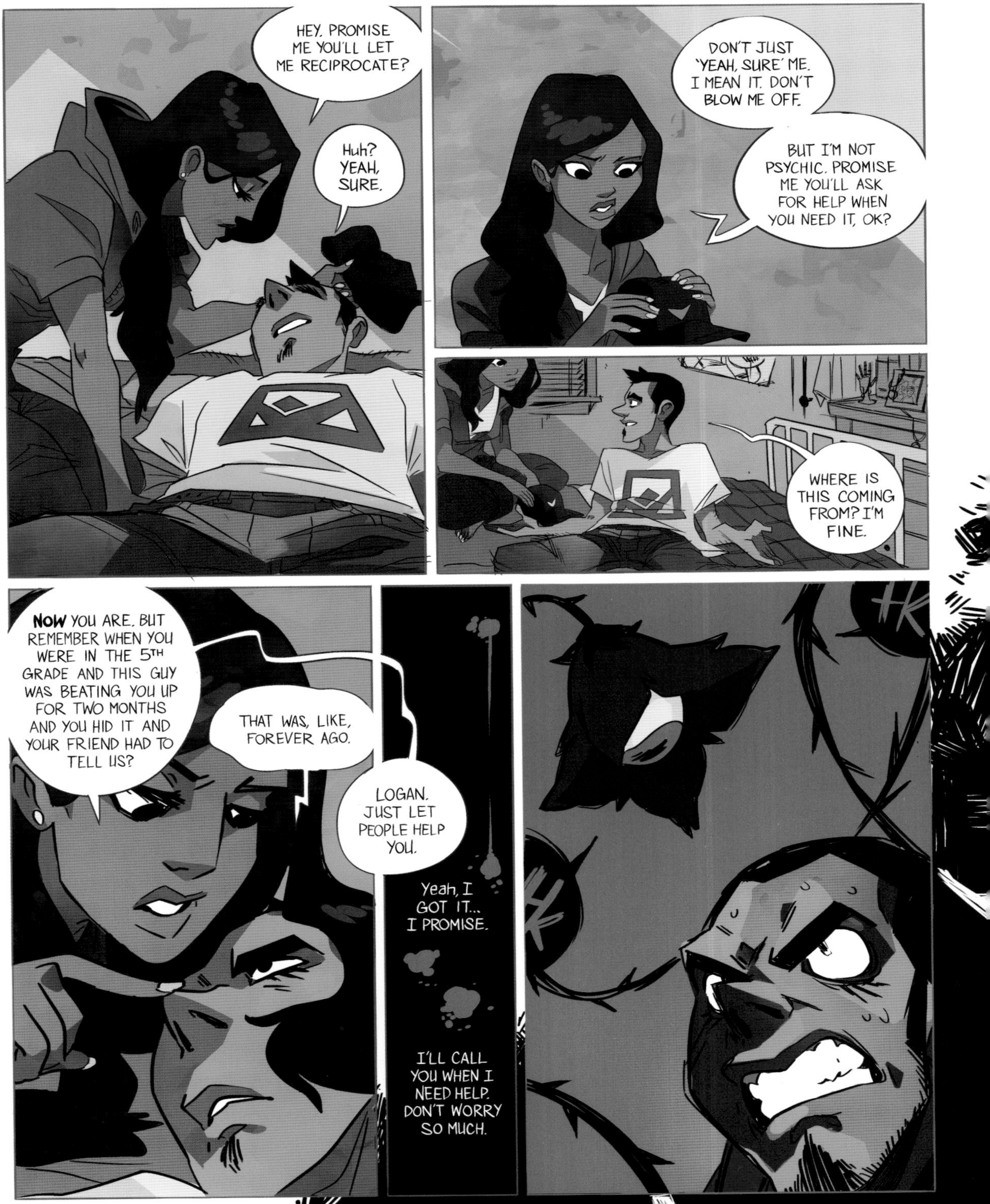
HEY, PROMISE ME YOU'LL LET ME RECIPROCATE?
Huh? YEAH, SURE.
DON'T JUST 'YEAH, SURE' ME. I MEAN IT. DON'T BLOW ME OFF.
BUT I'M NOT PSYCHIC. PROMISE ME YOU'LL ASK FOR HELP WHEN YOU NEED IT, OK?
WHERE IS THIS COMING FROM? I'M FINE.
NOW YOU ARE. BUT REMEMBER WHEN YOU WERE IN THE 5TH GRADE AND THIS GUY WAS BEATING YOU UP FOR TWO MONTHS AND YOU HID IT AND YOUR FRIEND HAD TO TELL US?
THAT WAS, LIKE, FOREVER AGO.
LOGAN. JUST LET PEOPLE HELP YOU.
Yeah, I GOT IT... I PROMISE.
I'LL CALL YOU WHEN I NEED HELP. DON'T WORRY SO MUCH.

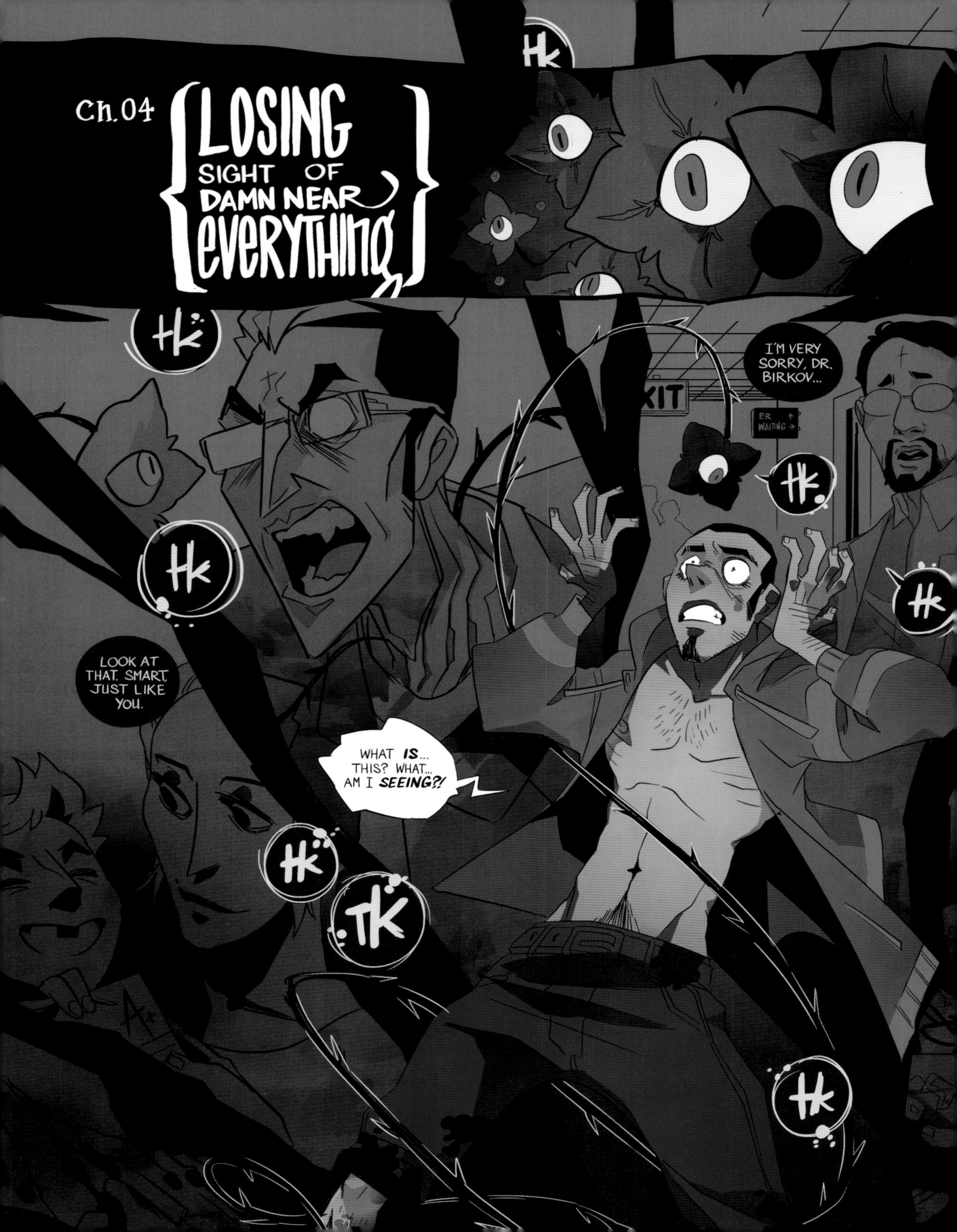

Ch.04 LOSING SIGHT OF DAMN NEAR EVERYTHING
TK
I'M VERY SORRY, DR. BIRKOV...
EXIT
ER ↑
WAITING →
LOOK AT THAT. SMART, JUST LIKE YOU.
WHAT IS... THIS? WHAT... AM I SEEING?!

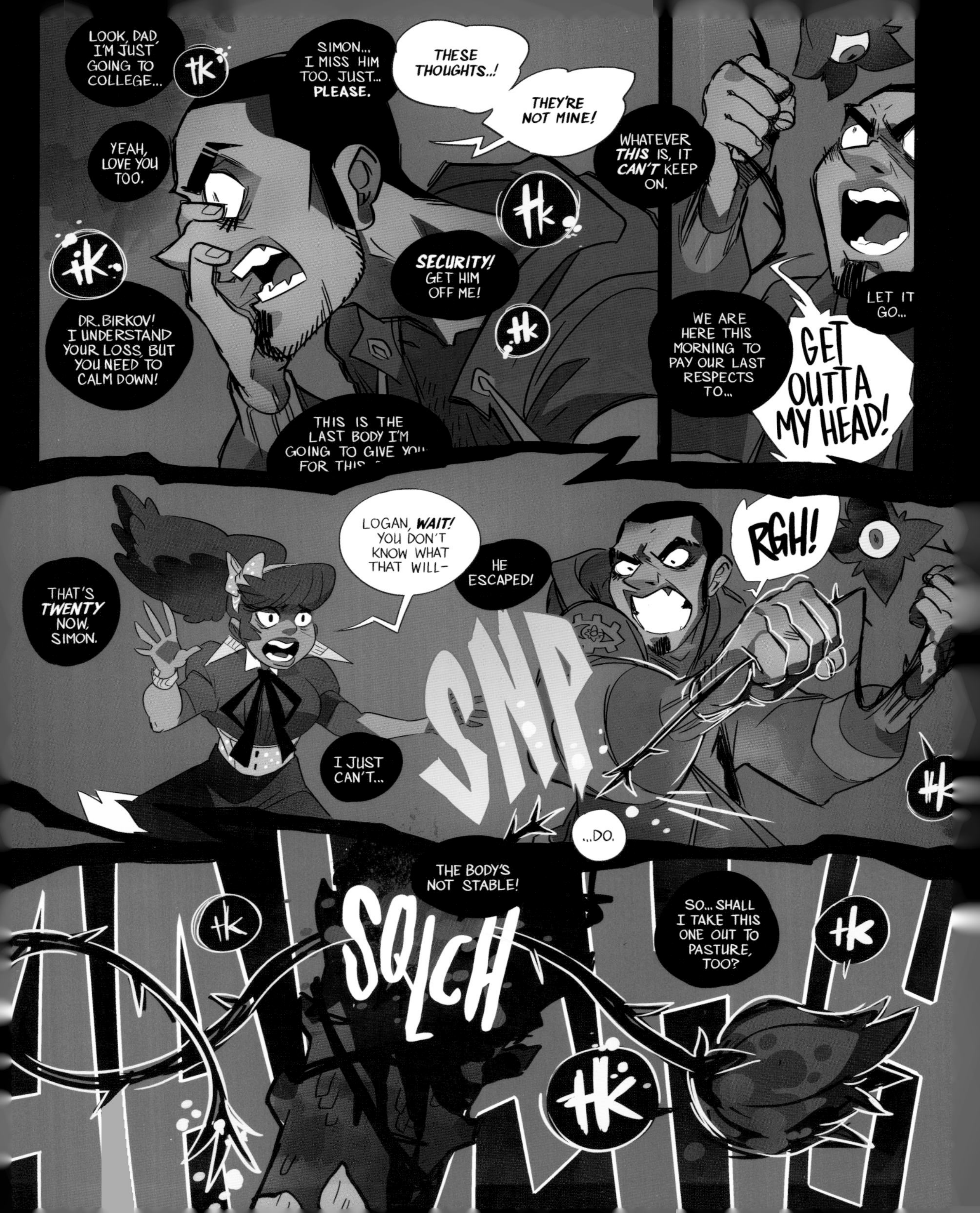
LOOK, DAD, I'M JUST GOING TO COLLEGE...
TK
SIMON... I MISS HIM TOO. JUST... **PLEASE.**
THESE THOUGHTS...!
THEY'RE NOT MINE!
YEAH, LOVE YOU TOO.
WHATEVER ***THIS*** IS, IT ***CAN'T*** KEEP ON.
TK
TK
SECURITY! GET HIM OFF ME!
DR. BIRKOV! I UNDERSTAND YOUR LOSS, BUT YOU NEED TO CALM DOWN!
TK
THIS IS THE LAST BODY I'M GOING TO GIVE YOU FOR THIS
LET IT GO...
WE ARE HERE THIS MORNING TO PAY OUR LAST RESPECTS TO...
GET OUTTA MY HEAD!
THAT'S ***TWENTY*** NOW, SIMON.
LOGAN, ***WAIT!*** YOU DON'T KNOW WHAT THAT WILL-
HE ESCAPED!
RGH!
I JUST CAN'T...
SNP
TK
...DO.
THE BODY'S NOT STABLE!
TK
SQLCH
SO... SHALL I TAKE THIS ONE OUT TO PASTURE, TOO?
TK
TK

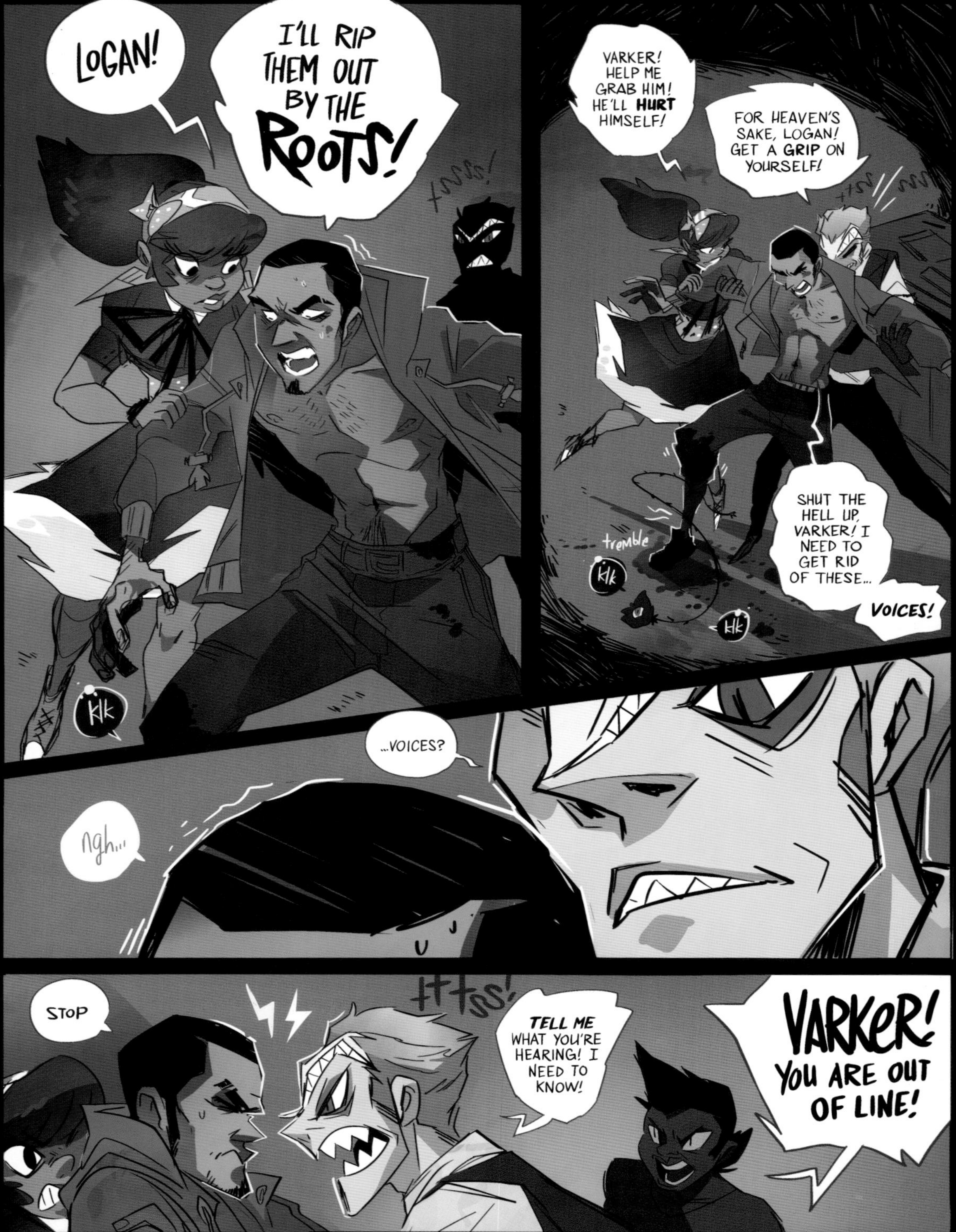
LOGAN!
I'LL RIP THEM OUT BY THE ROOTS!
tsssss!
klk
VARKER! HELP ME GRAB HIM! HE'LL HURT HIMSELF!
FOR HEAVEN'S SAKE, LOGAN! GET A GRIP ON YOURSELF!
tsss
tremble
klk
klk
SHUT THE HELL UP, VARKER! I NEED TO GET RID OF THESE...
VOICES!
...VOICES?
ngh...
STOP
ttss!
TELL ME WHAT YOU'RE HEARING! I NEED TO KNOW!
VARKER! YOU ARE OUT OF LINE!

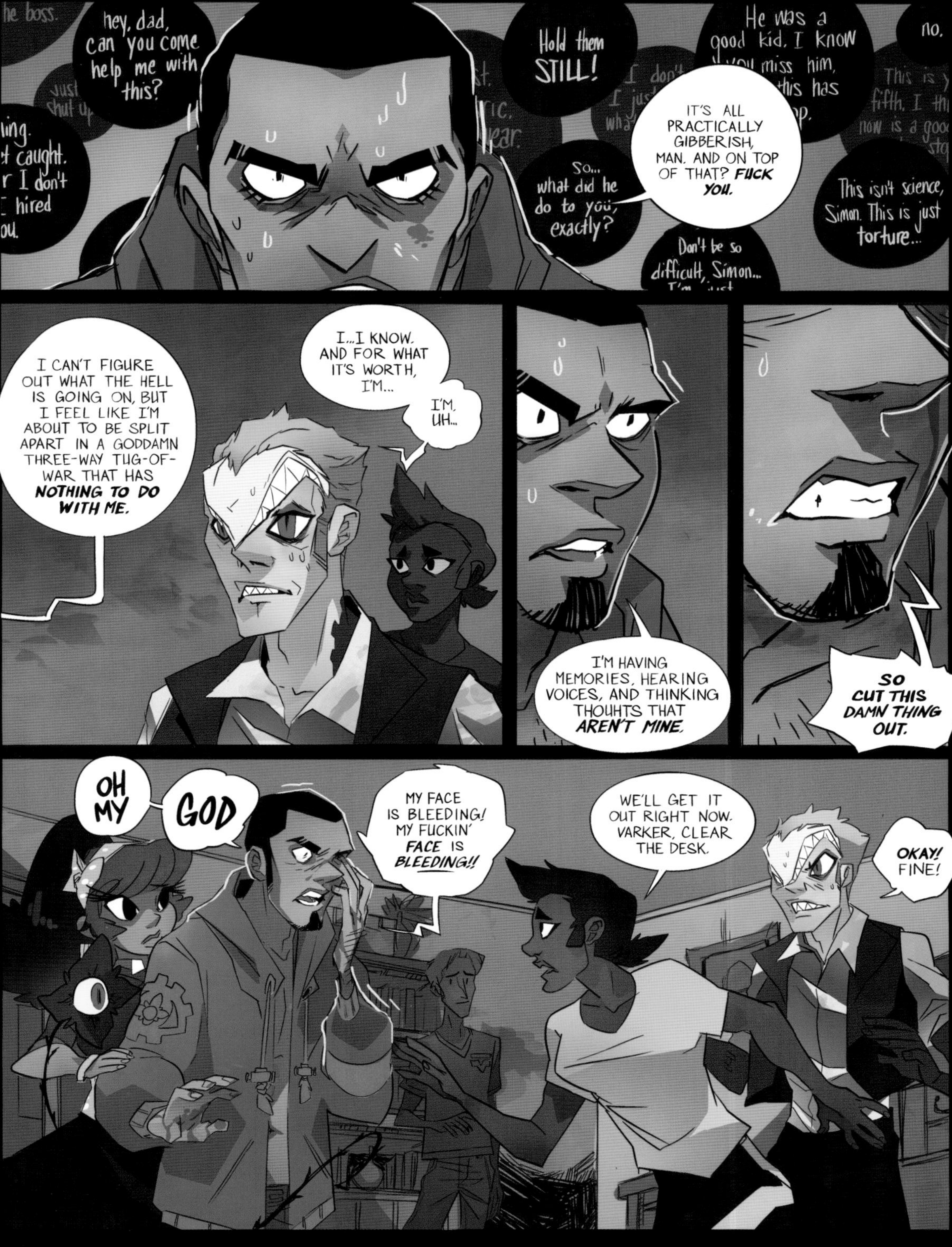

hey, dad, can you come help me with this?
Hold them STILL!
no.
So... what did he do to you, exactly?
IT'S ALL PRACTICALLY GIBBERISH, MAN. AND ON TOP OF THAT? **FUCK YOU.**
This isn't science, Simon. This is just torture...
Don't be so difficult, Simon...
I CAN'T FIGURE OUT WHAT THE HELL IS GOING ON, BUT I FEEL LIKE I'M ABOUT TO BE SPLIT APART IN A GODDAMN THREE-WAY TUG-OF-WAR THAT HAS **NOTHING TO DO WITH ME.**
I...I KNOW. AND FOR WHAT IT'S WORTH, I'M...
I'M, UH...
I'M HAVING MEMORIES, HEARING VOICES, AND THINKING THOUHTS THAT **AREN'T MINE.**
SO CUT THIS DAMN THING OUT.
OH MY
GOD
MY FACE IS BLEEDING! MY FUCKIN' *FACE* IS *BLEEDING!!*
WE'LL GET IT OUT RIGHT NOW. VARKER, CLEAR THE DESK.
OKAY! FINE!

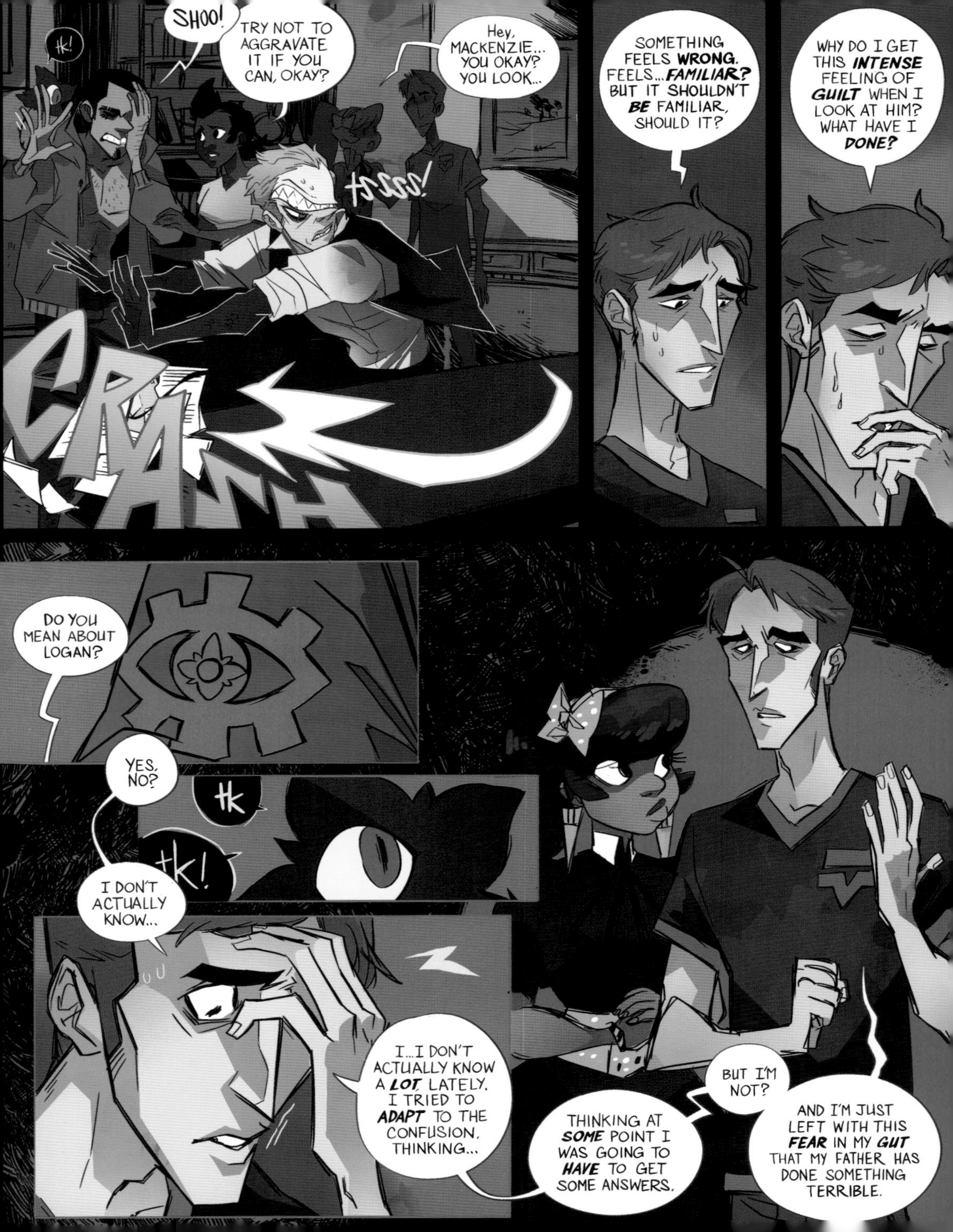
tk!
SHOO!
TRY NOT TO AGGRAVATE IT IF YOU CAN, OKAY?
Hey, MACKENZIE... YOU OKAY? YOU LOOK...
tssss!
CRASH
SOMETHING FEELS **WRONG.** FEELS... ***FAMILIAR?*** BUT IT SHOULDN'T ***BE*** FAMILIAR, SHOULD IT?
WHY DO I GET THIS ***INTENSE*** FEELING OF ***GUILT*** WHEN I LOOK AT HIM? WHAT HAVE I ***DONE?***
DO YOU MEAN ABOUT LOGAN?
YES, NO?
tk
tk!
I DON'T ACTUALLY KNOW...
I...I DON'T ACTUALLY KNOW A ***LOT,*** LATELY. I TRIED TO ***ADAPT*** TO THE CONFUSION, THINKING...
THINKING AT ***SOME*** POINT I WAS GOING TO ***HAVE*** TO GET SOME ANSWERS.
BUT I'M NOT?
AND I'M JUST LEFT WITH THIS ***FEAR*** IN MY ***GUT*** THAT MY FATHER HAS DONE SOMETHING TERRIBLE.

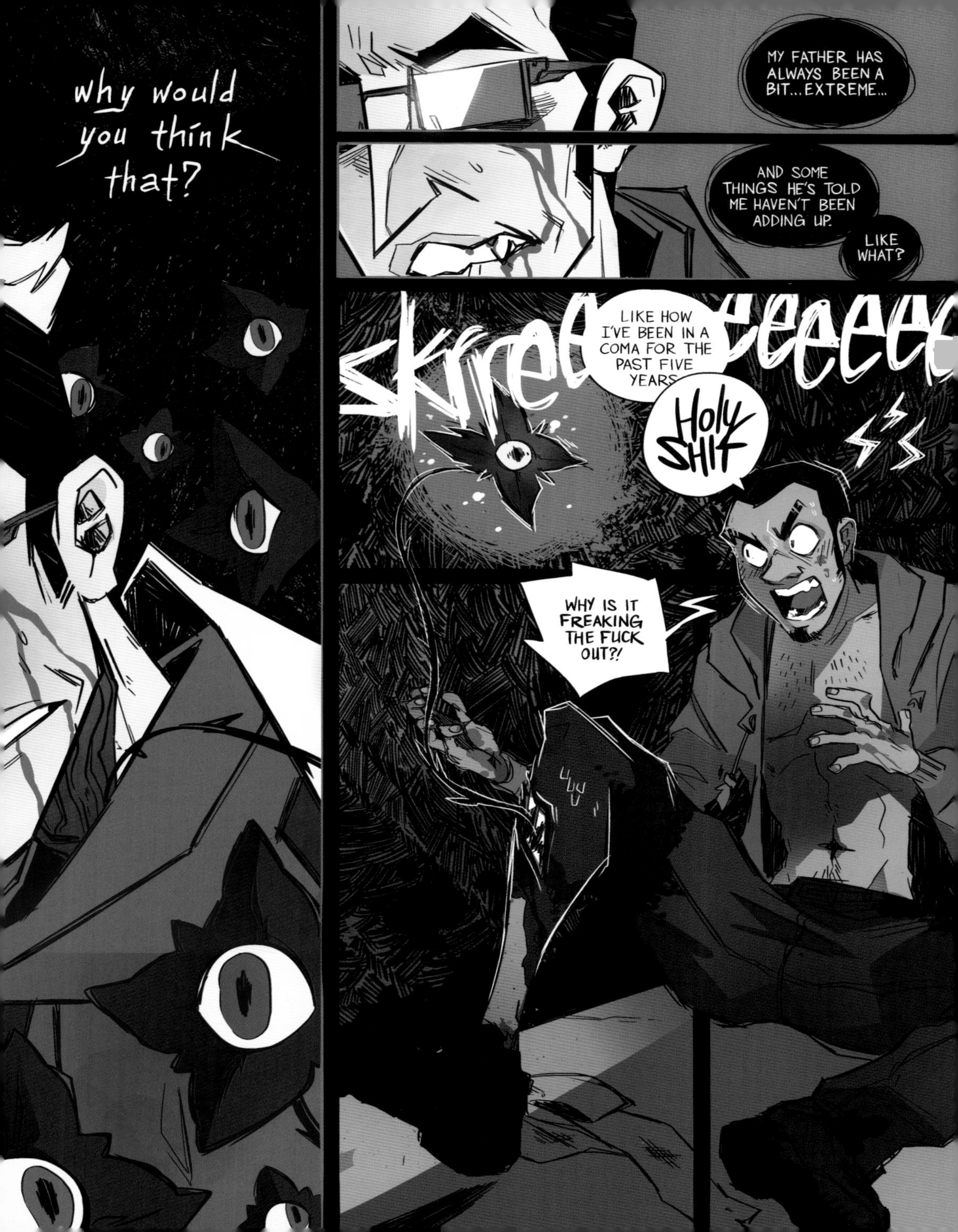
why would you think that?
MY FATHER HAS ALWAYS BEEN A BIT... EXTREME...
AND SOME THINGS HE'S TOLD ME HAVEN'T BEEN ADDING UP.
LIKE WHAT?
skreeeeeeee
LIKE HOW I'VE BEEN IN A COMA FOR THE PAST FIVE YEARS?
Holy SHIT
WHY IS IT FREAKING THE FUCK OUT?!

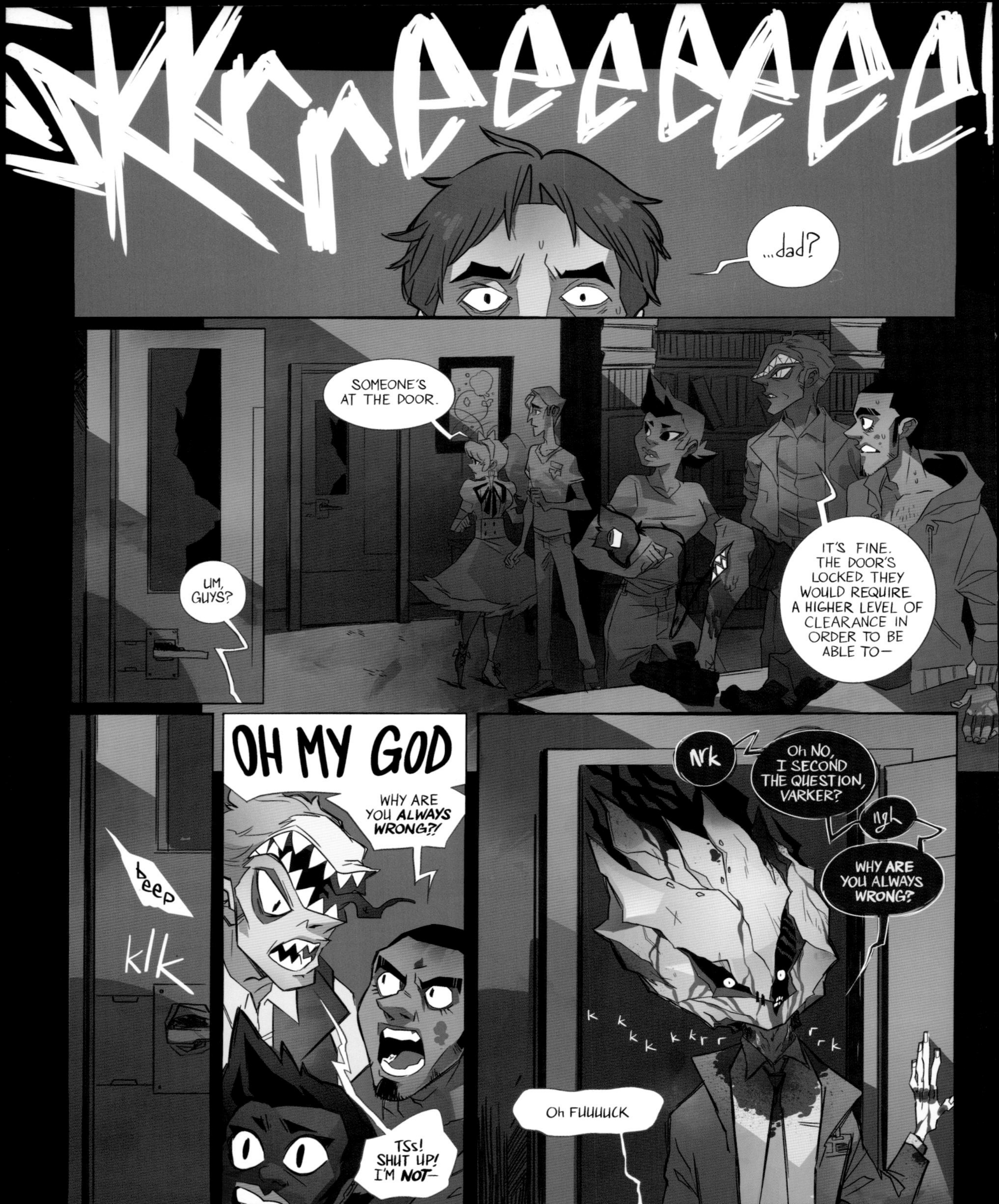

SKKREEEEEEE
...dad?
SOMEONE'S AT THE DOOR.
UM, GUYS?
IT'S FINE. THE DOOR'S LOCKED. THEY WOULD REQUIRE A HIGHER LEVEL OF CLEARANCE IN ORDER TO BE ABLE TO—
beep
klk
OH MY GOD
WHY ARE YOU ALWAYS WRONG?!
TSS! SHUT UP! I'M NOT—
Nrk
Oh NO, I SECOND THE QUESTION, VARKER?
ngh
WHY ARE YOU ALWAYS WRONG?
k kkk kkrr rrk
Oh FUUUUCK

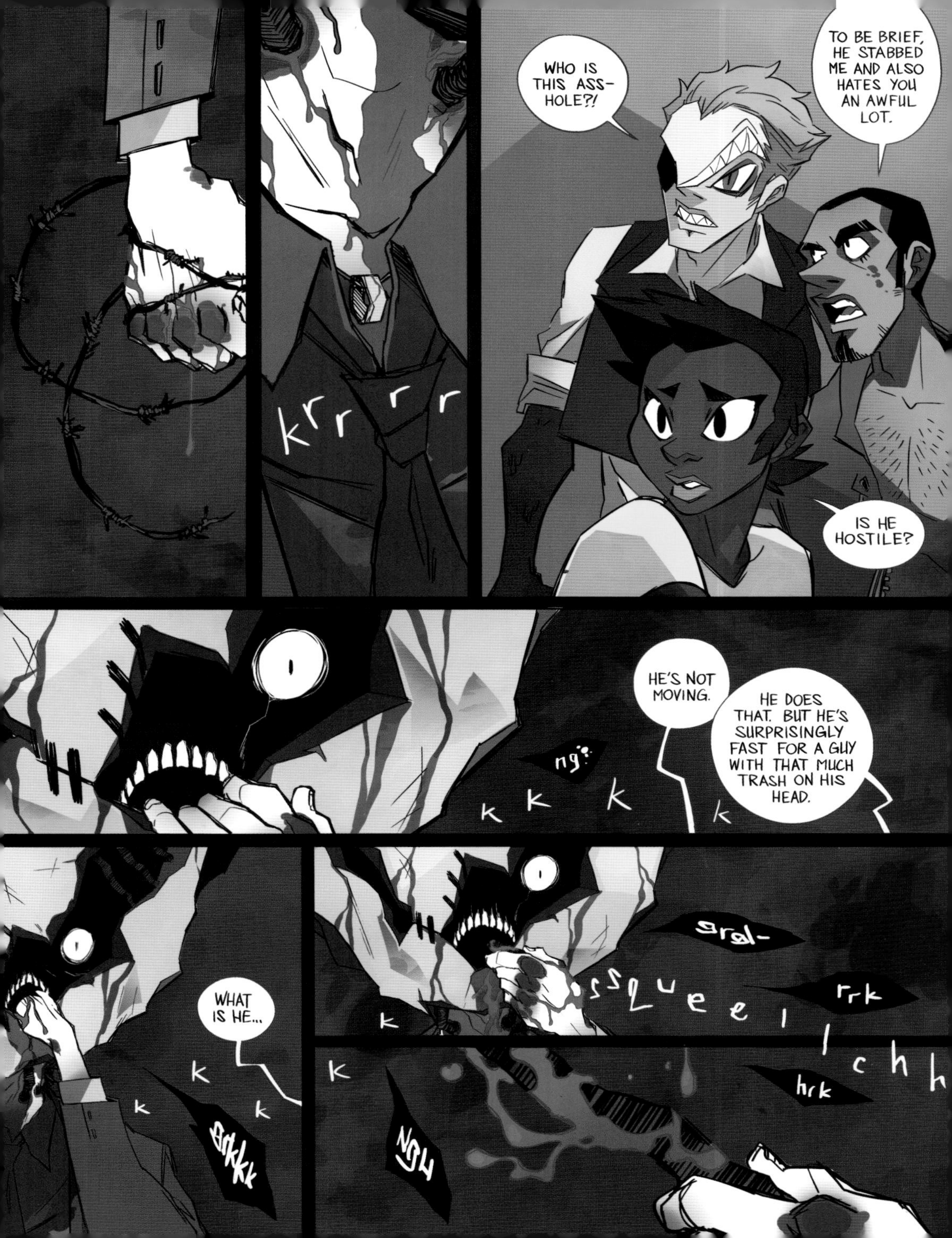
krrrr
WHO IS THIS ASS-HOLE?!
TO BE BRIEF, HE STABBED ME AND ALSO HATES YOU AN AWFUL LOT.
IS HE HOSTILE?
ng
HE'S NOT MOVING.
HE DOES THAT. BUT HE'S SURPRISINGLY FAST FOR A GUY WITH THAT MUCH TRASH ON HIS HEAD.
k k k k
WHAT IS HE...
k k k k
Brkkk
grgl-
ssqueeellchh
rrk
k
hrk
NGH

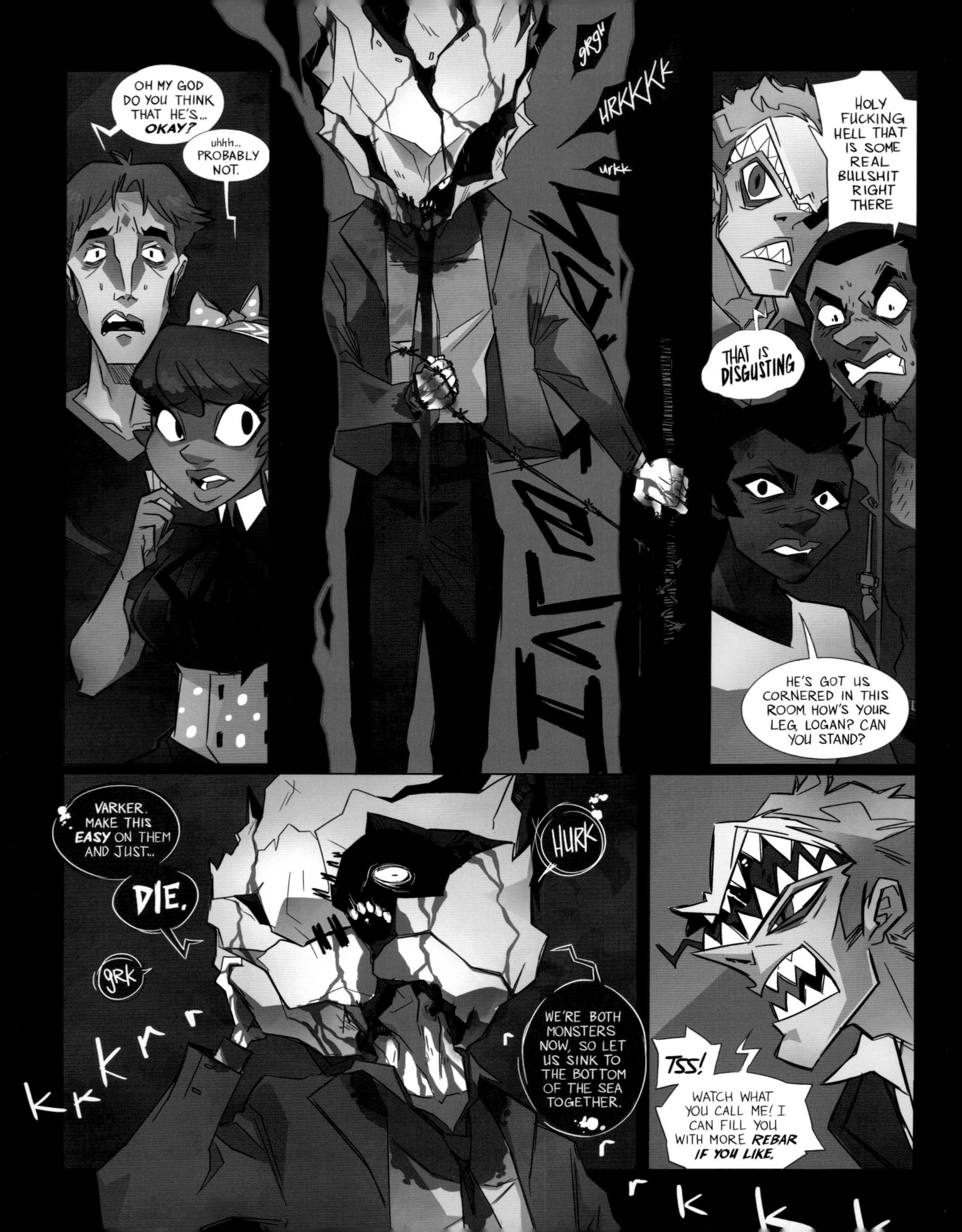
OH MY GOD DO YOU THINK THAT HE'S... **OKAY?**
uhhh... PROBABLY NOT.
grgh
HRKKKK
urkk
HOLY FUCKING HELL THAT IS SOME REAL BULLSHIT RIGHT THERE
THAT IS **DISGUSTING**
HE'S GOT US CORNERED IN THIS ROOM. HOW'S YOUR LEG, LOGAN? CAN YOU STAND?
VARKER. MAKE THIS **EASY** ON THEM AND JUST...
DIE.
grk
HURK
WE'RE BOTH MONSTERS NOW, SO LET US SINK TO THE BOTTOM OF THE SEA TOGETHER.
KkKrr
TSS!
WATCH WHAT YOU CALL ME! I CAN FILL YOU WITH MORE ***REBAR IF YOU LIKE.***
rkkk

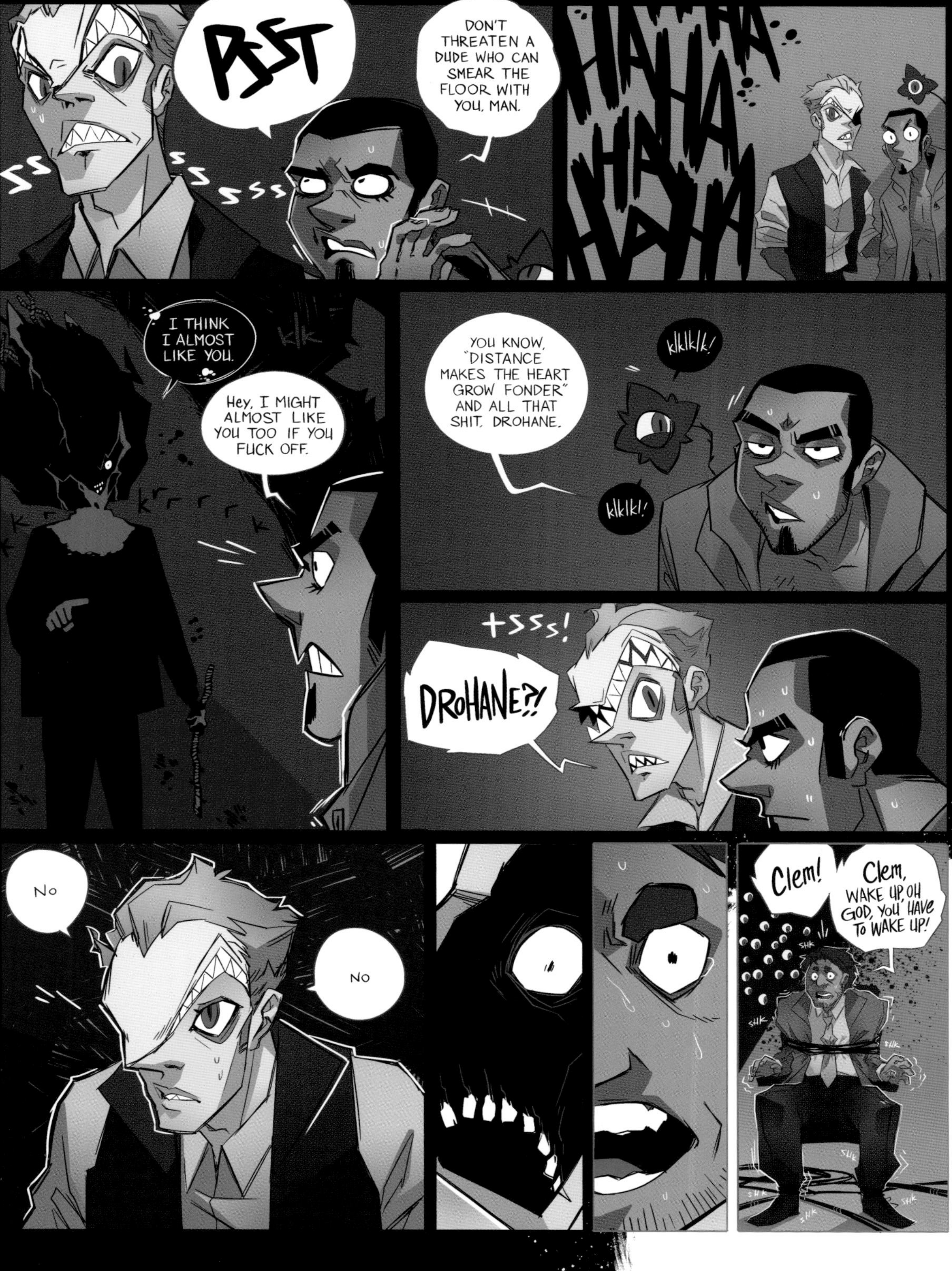

PST
ssssss
DON'T THREATEN A DUDE WHO CAN SMEAR THE FLOOR WITH YOU, MAN.
HAHA HAHA HAHA HAHA
I THINK I ALMOST LIKE YOU.
klk
Hey, I MIGHT ALMOST LIKE YOU TOO IF YOU FUCK OFF.
krrrrk
YOU KNOW, "DISTANCE MAKES THE HEART GROW FONDER" AND ALL THAT SHIT, DROHANE.
klklklk!
klklk!
tsss!
DROHANE?!
No
No
Clem!
Clem, WAKE UP, OH GOD, YOU HAVE TO WAKE UP!
SHK
SHK
SHK
SHK
SHK
SHK

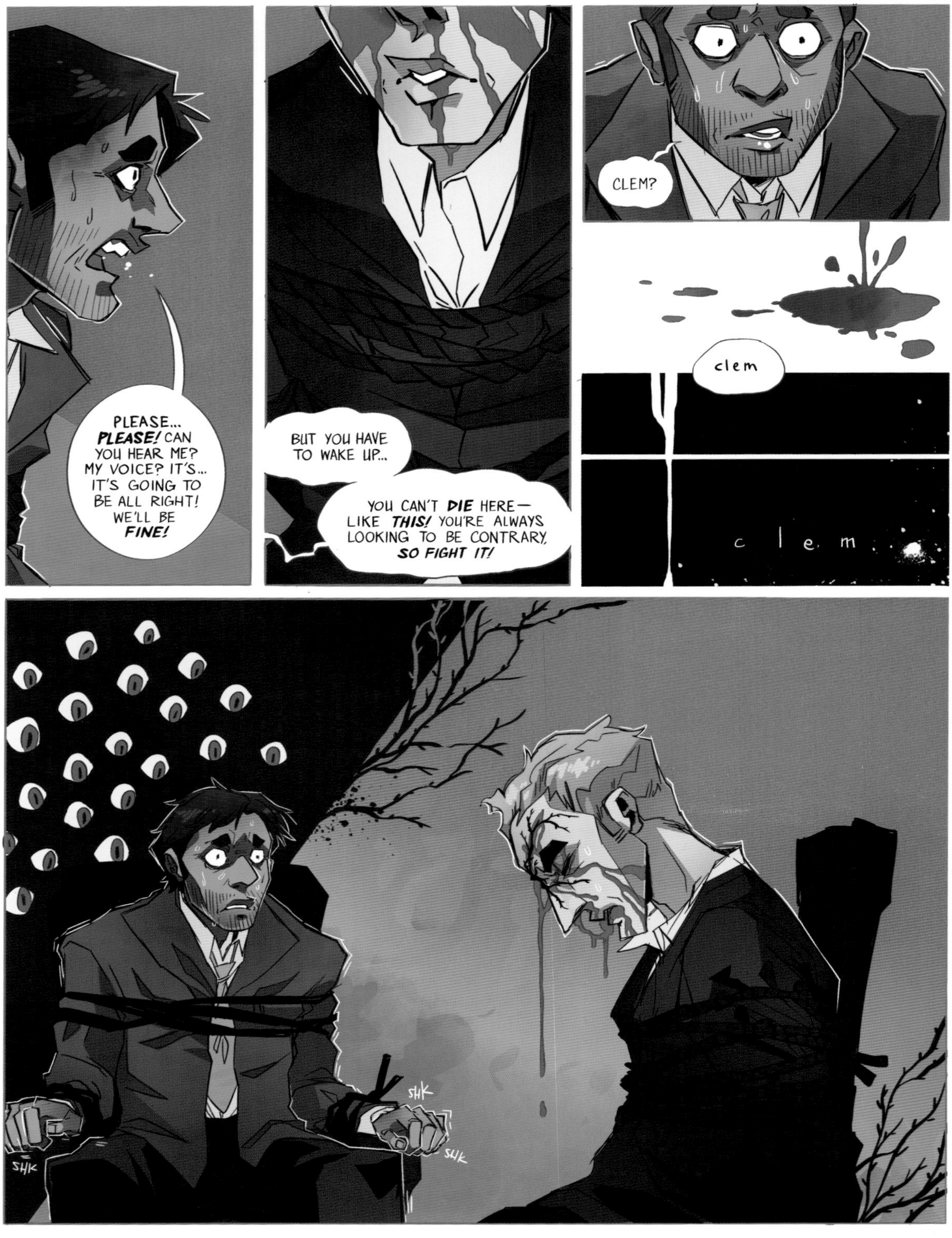
PLEASE... PLEASE! CAN YOU HEAR ME? MY VOICE? IT'S... IT'S GOING TO BE ALL RIGHT! WE'LL BE FINE!
BUT YOU HAVE TO WAKE UP...
YOU CAN'T DIE HERE— LIKE THIS! YOU'RE ALWAYS LOOKING TO BE CONTRARY, SO FIGHT IT!
CLEM?
clem
c l e m
SHK
SHK
SHK

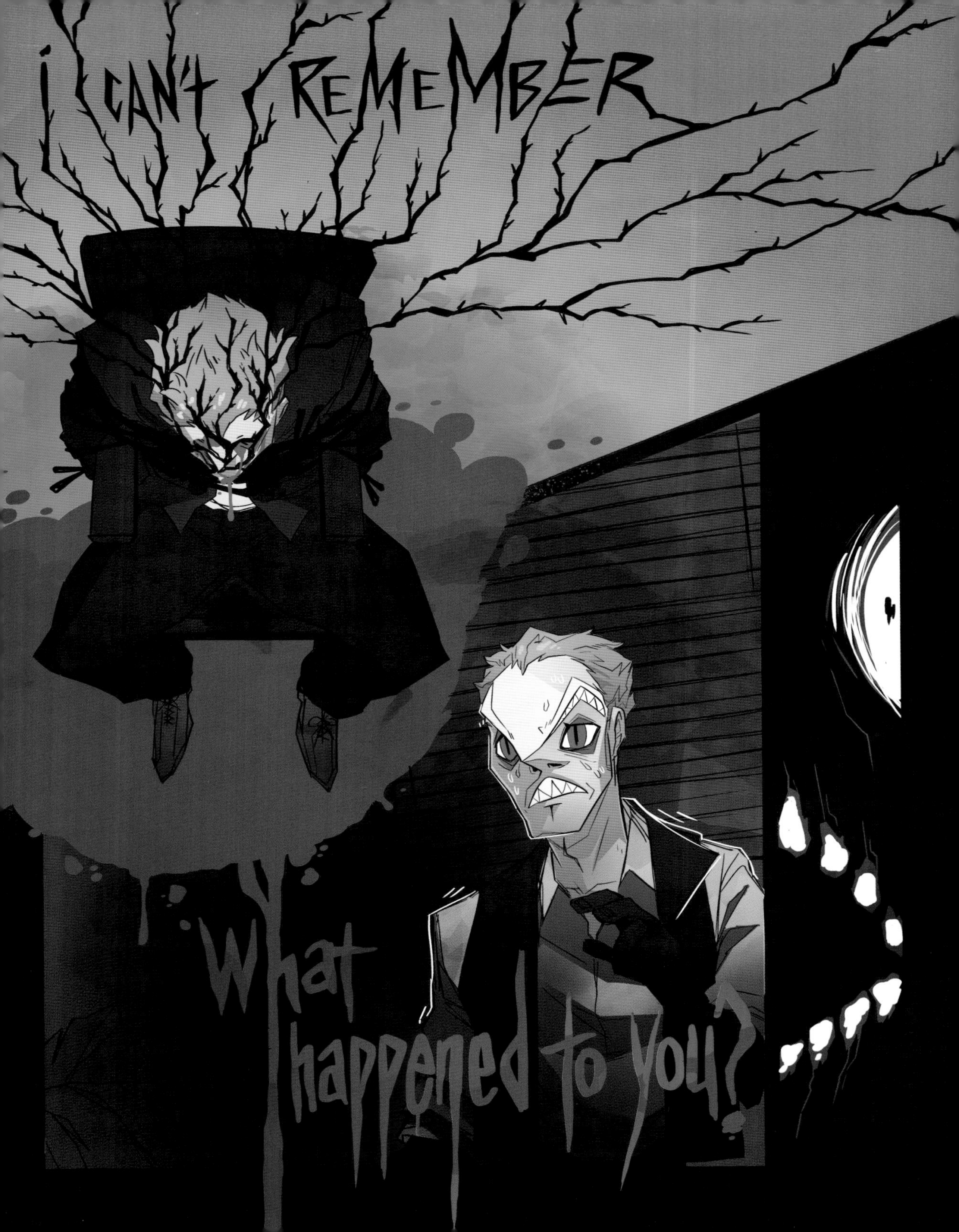
I CAN'T REMEMBER
What happened to you?

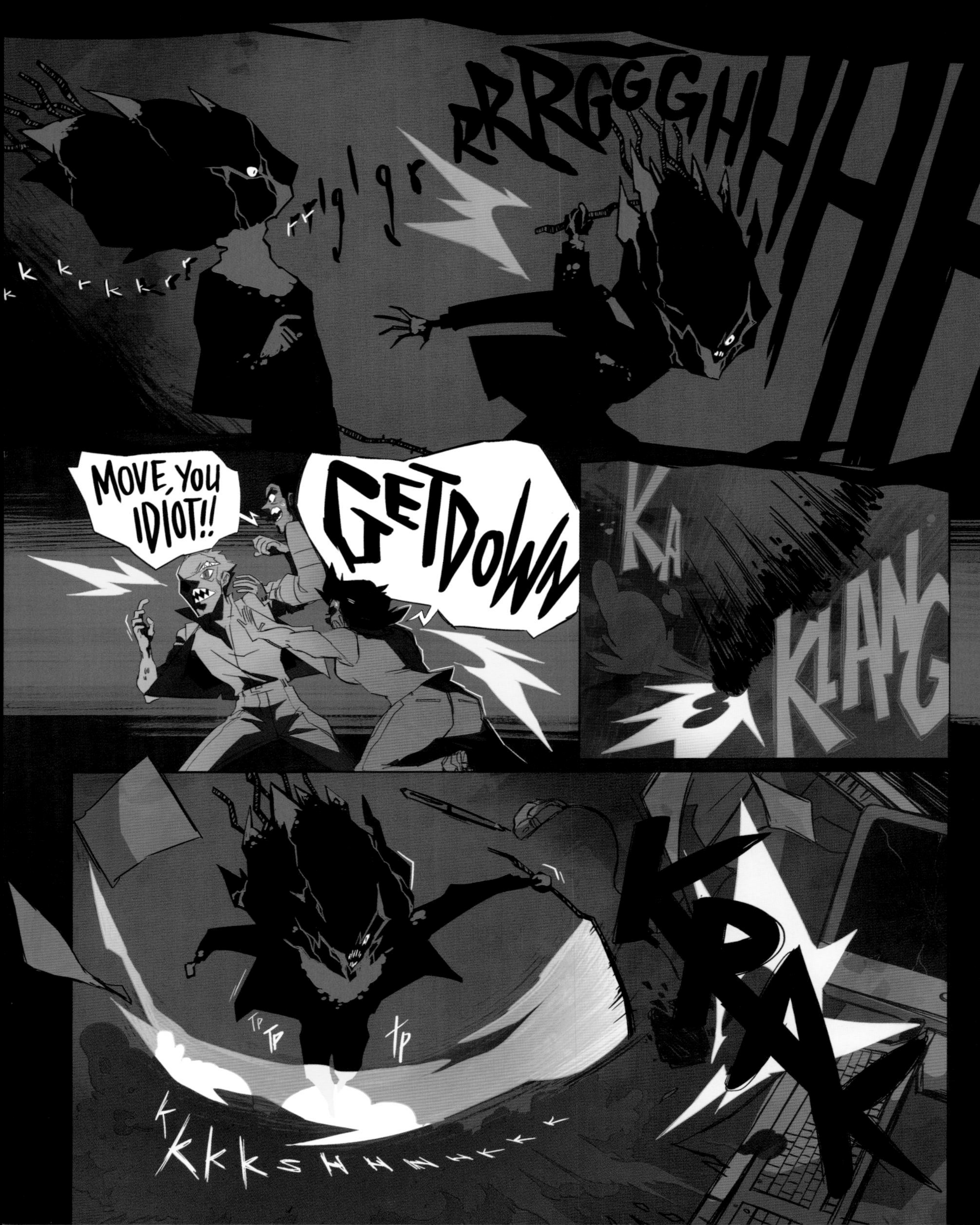

kkkrkkkrr
rr'g'gr
RRRGGGHHHH
MOVE, YOU IDIOT!!
GET DOWN
KA
KLANG
tp tp tp
KRAK
KKKKSHHHHKKK

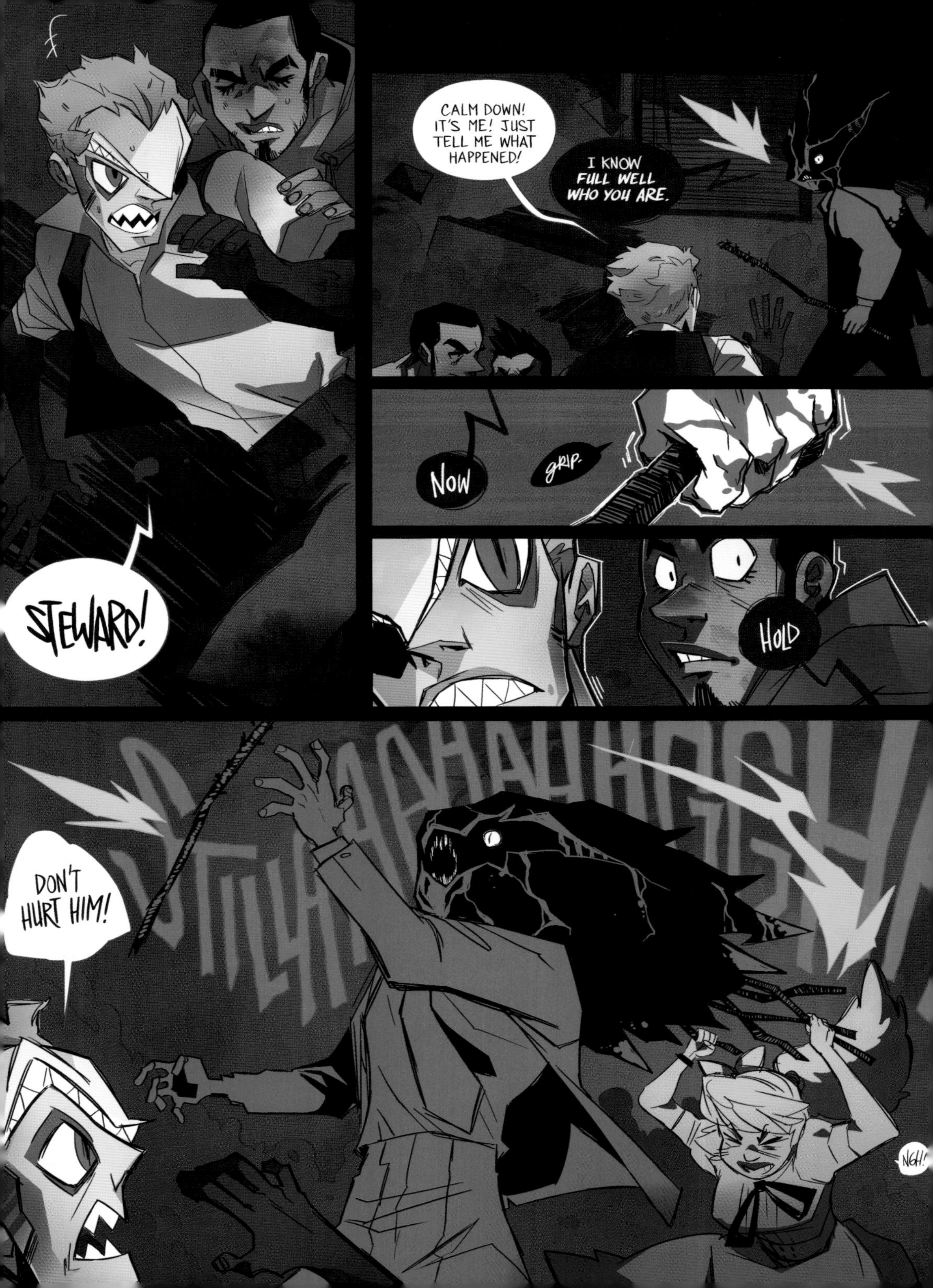
STEWARD!
CALM DOWN! IT'S ME! JUST TELL ME WHAT HAPPENED!
I KNOW **FULL WELL** WHO YOU ARE.
NOW
grip.
HOLD
DON'T HURT HIM!
NGH!

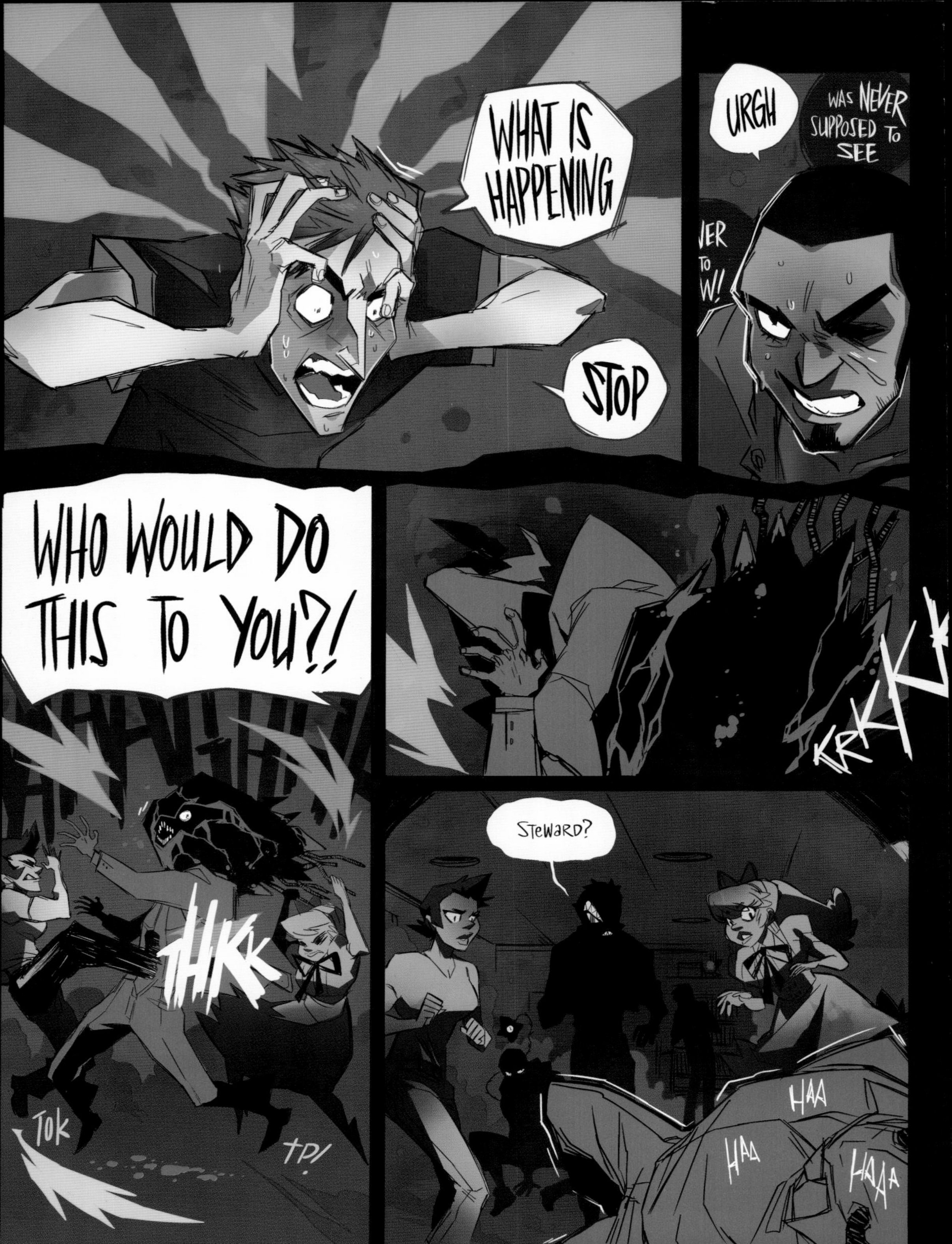
WHAT IS HAPPENING
STOP
URGH
WAS NEVER SUPPOSED TO SEE
WHO WOULD DO THIS TO YOU?!
THKK
TOK
TP!
KRKKK
STEWARD?
HAA
HAA
HAAA

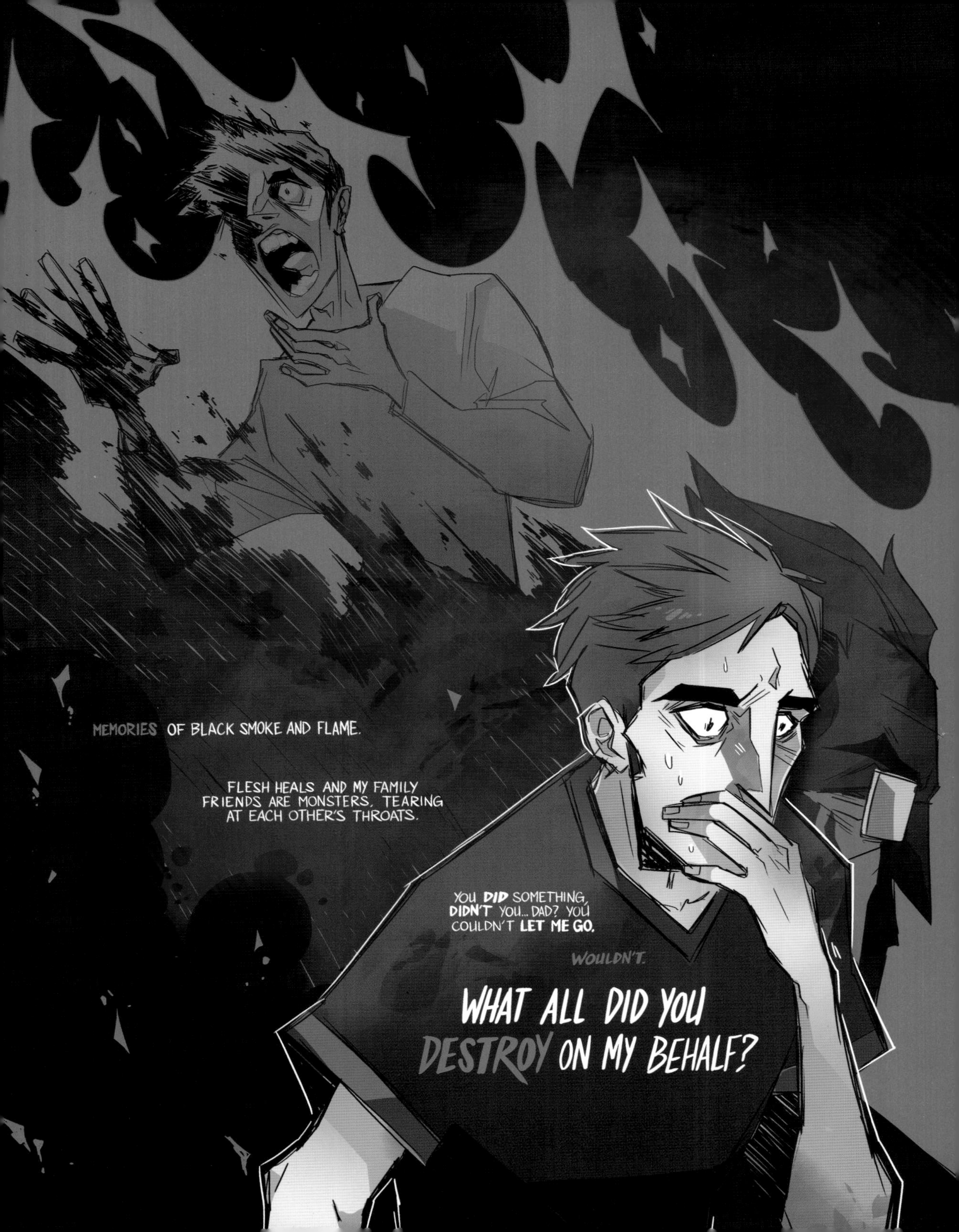
MEMORIES OF BLACK SMOKE AND FLAME.
FLESH HEALS AND MY FAMILY FRIENDS ARE MONSTERS, TEARING AT EACH OTHER'S THROATS.
YOU DID SOMETHING, DIDN'T YOU... DAD? YOU COULDN'T LET ME GO.
WOULDN'T.
WHAT ALL DID YOU DESTROY ON MY BEHALF?

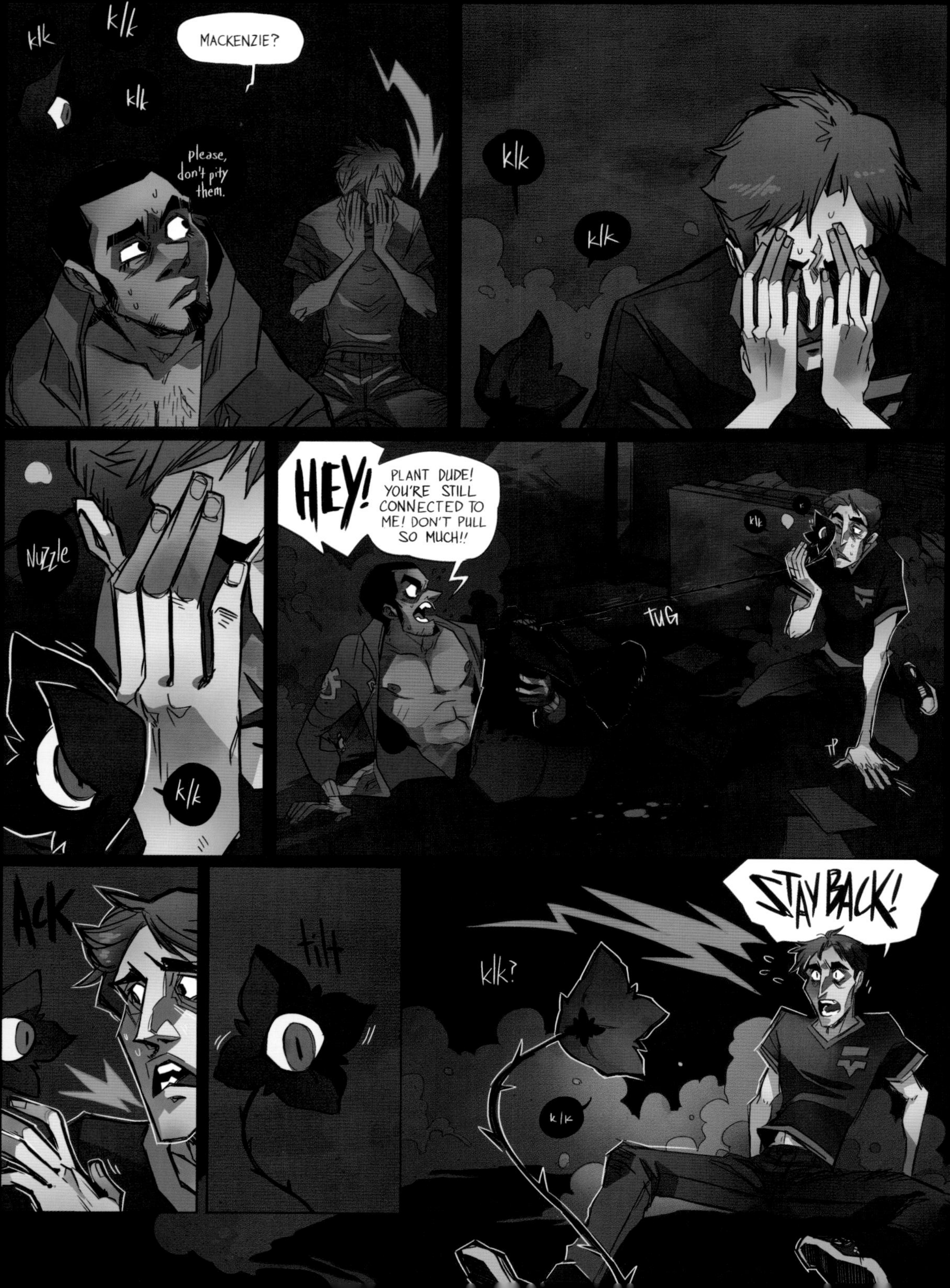

k/k
k/k
MACKENZIE?
k/k
please, don't pity them.
k/k
k/k
Nuzzle
k/k
HEY!
PLANT DUDE! YOU'RE STILL CONNECTED TO ME! DON'T PULL SO MUCH!!
k/k
TUG
TP
ACK
tilt
k/k?
STAY BACK!
k/k

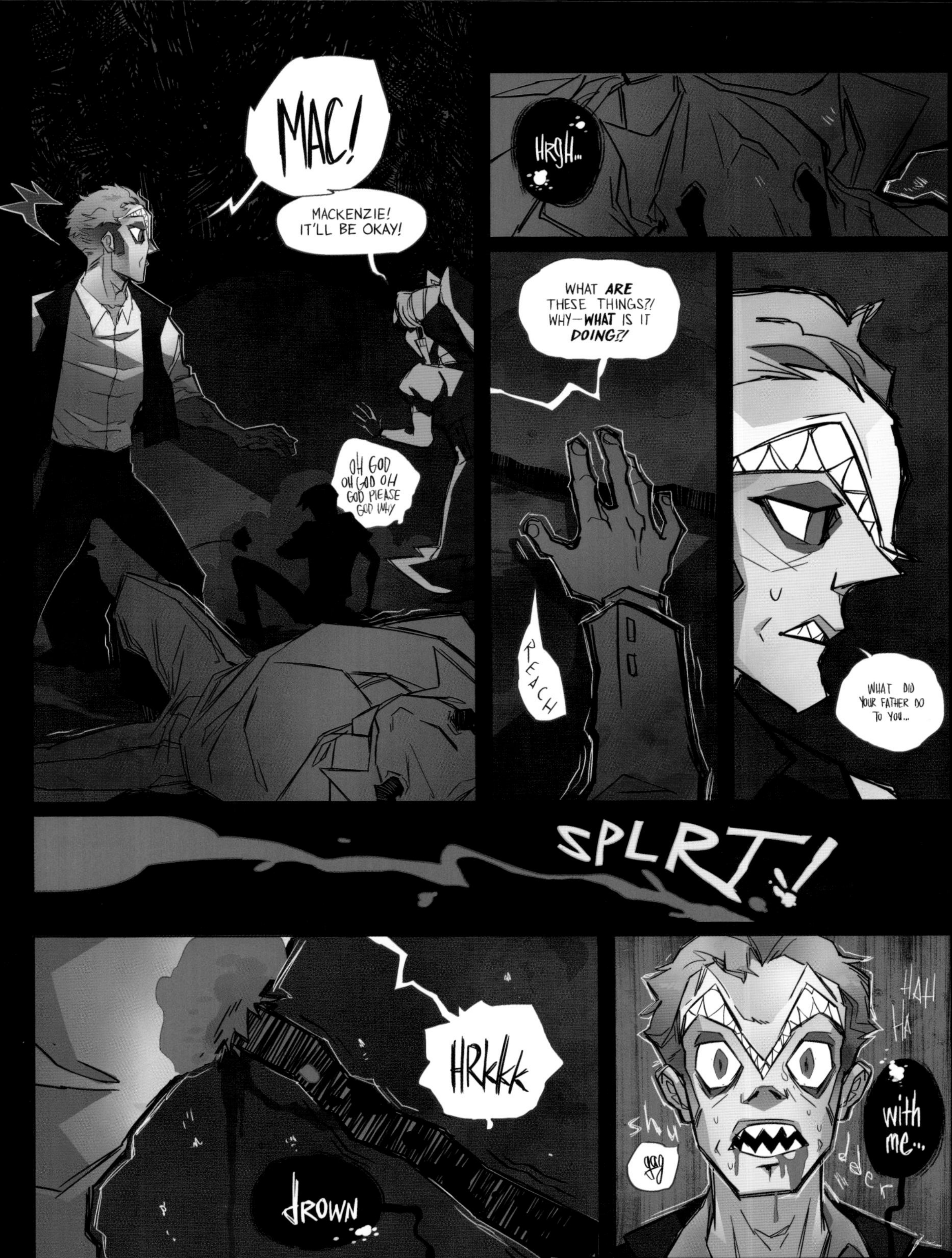
MAC!
MACKENZIE! IT'LL BE OKAY!
OH GOD OH GOD OH GOD PLEASE GOD WHY
HRGH...
WHAT **ARE** THESE THINGS?! WHY—**WHAT** IS IT **DOING**?!
REACH
WHAT DID YOUR FATHER DO TO YOU...
SPLRT!
HRKKK
DROWN
HAH HA
shudder
gag
with me...

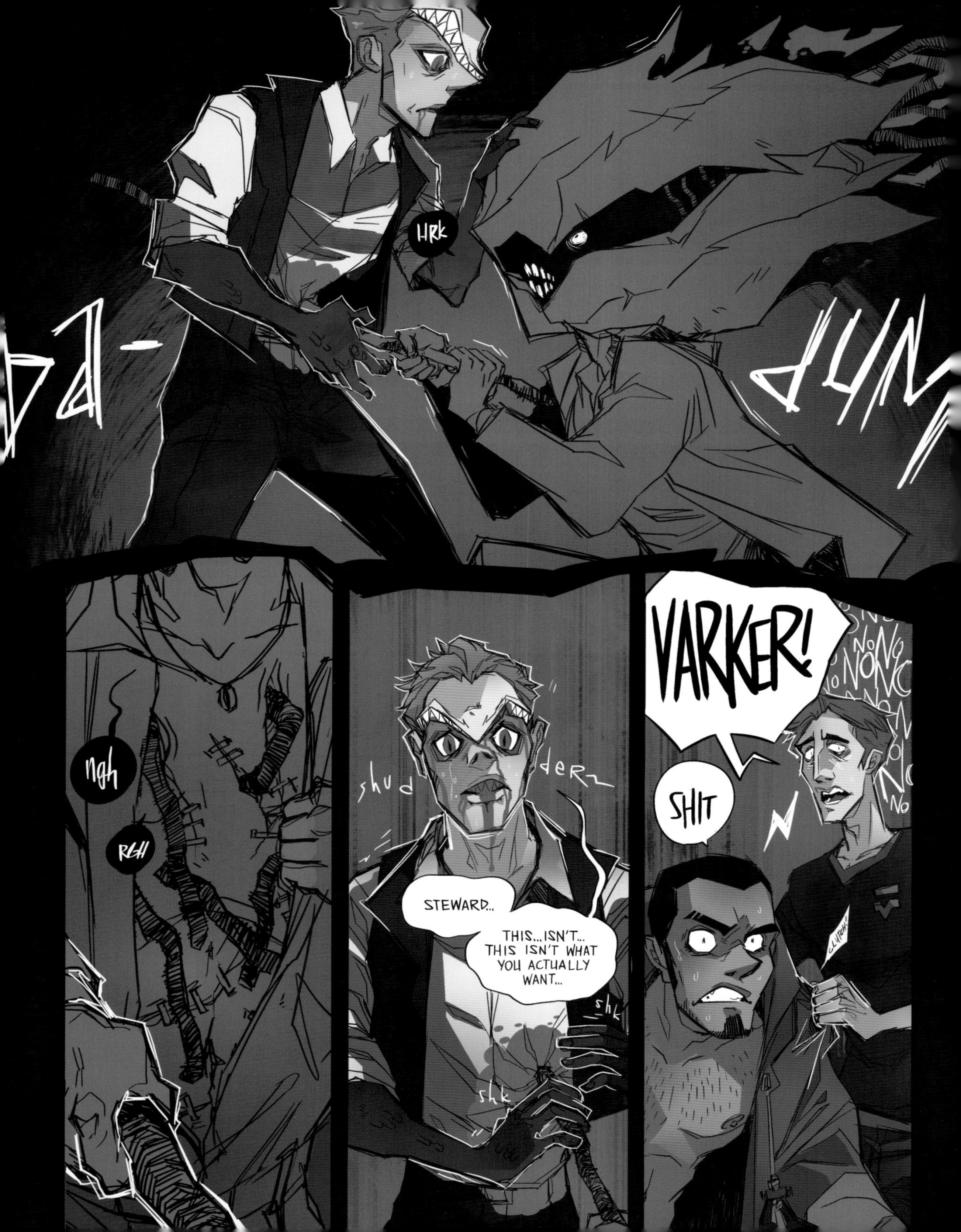

HRK
ba-
dum
ngh
RGH
shud
derr
STEWARD...
THIS... ISN'T... THIS ISN'T WHAT YOU ACTUALLY WANT...
shk
shk
VARKER!
SHIT
NO NO NO NO NO NO NO

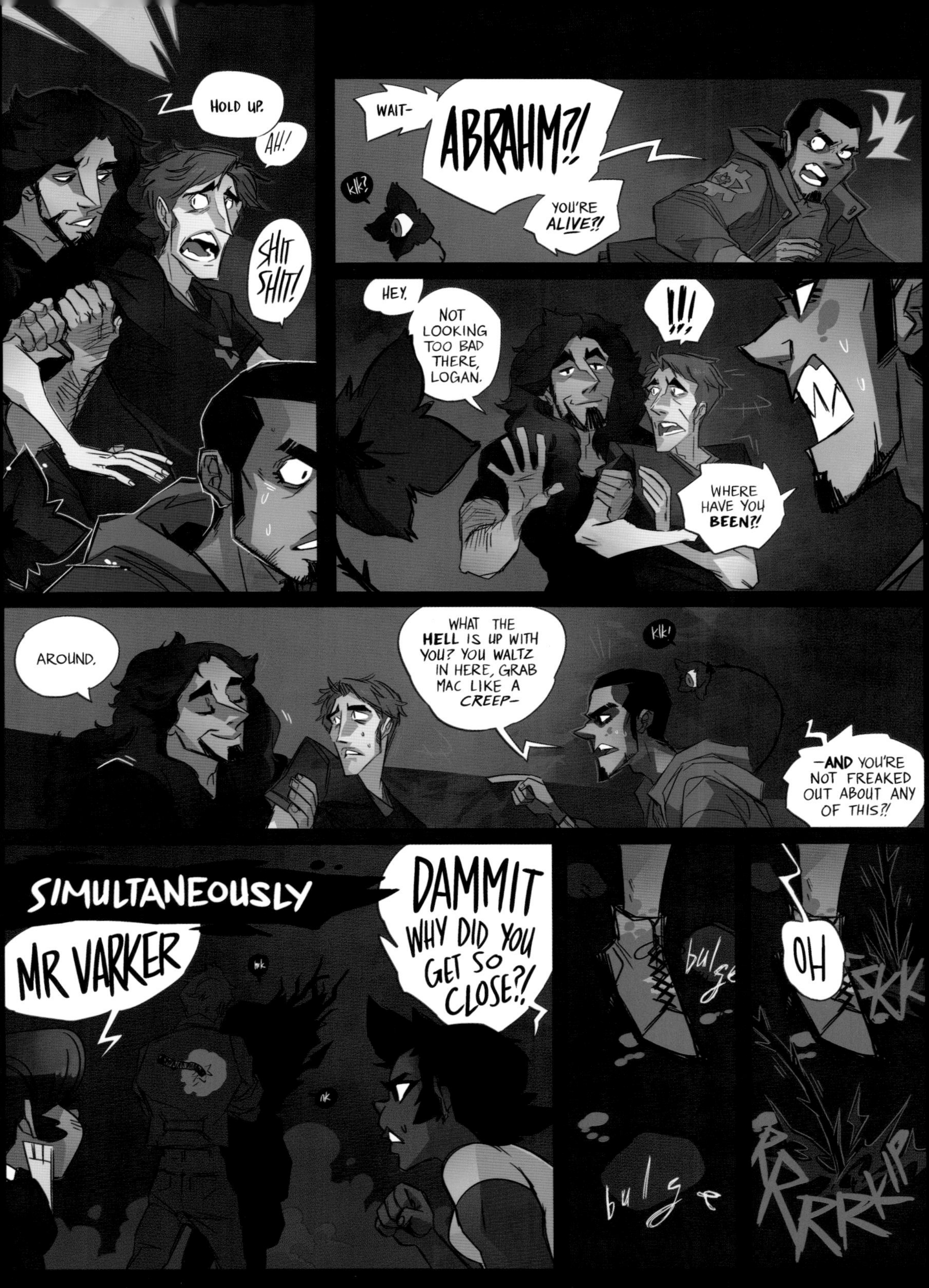

HOLD UP.
AH!
SHIT SHIT!
WAIT-
ABRAHM?!
klk?
YOU'RE ALIVE?!
HEY.
NOT LOOKING TOO BAD THERE, LOGAN.
!!!
WHERE HAVE YOU BEEN?!
AROUND.
WHAT THE HELL IS UP WITH YOU? YOU WALTZ IN HERE, GRAB MAC LIKE A CREEP-
klk!
-AND YOU'RE NOT FREAKED OUT ABOUT ANY OF THIS?!
SIMULTANEOUSLY
MR VARKER
DAMMIT WHY DID YOU GET SO CLOSE?!
bulge
bulge
OH
RRRRKIP

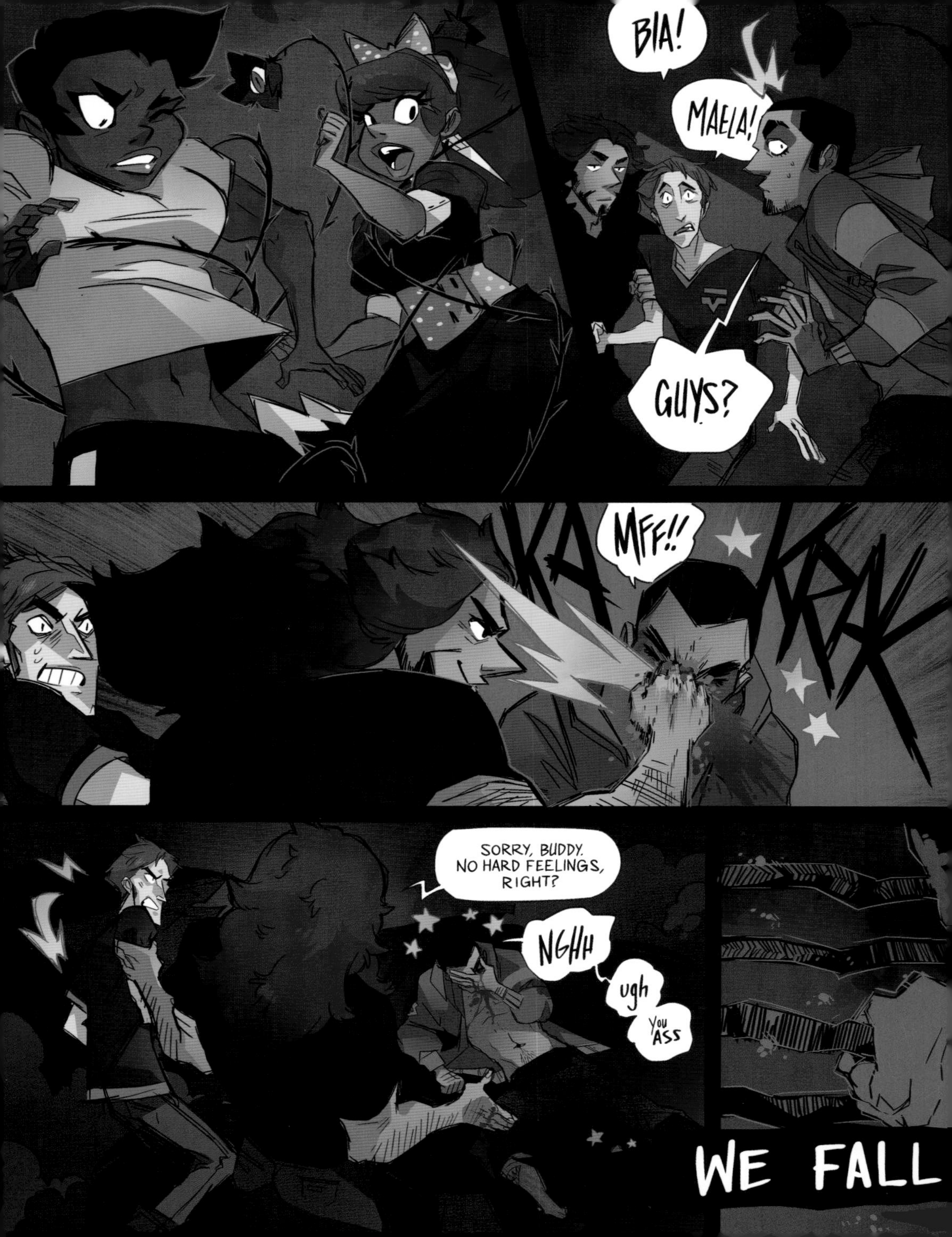
BIA!
MAELA!
GUYS?
MFF!!
KA KRAK
SORRY, BUDDY. NO HARD FEELINGS, RIGHT?
NGHH
ugh
You ASS
WE FALL

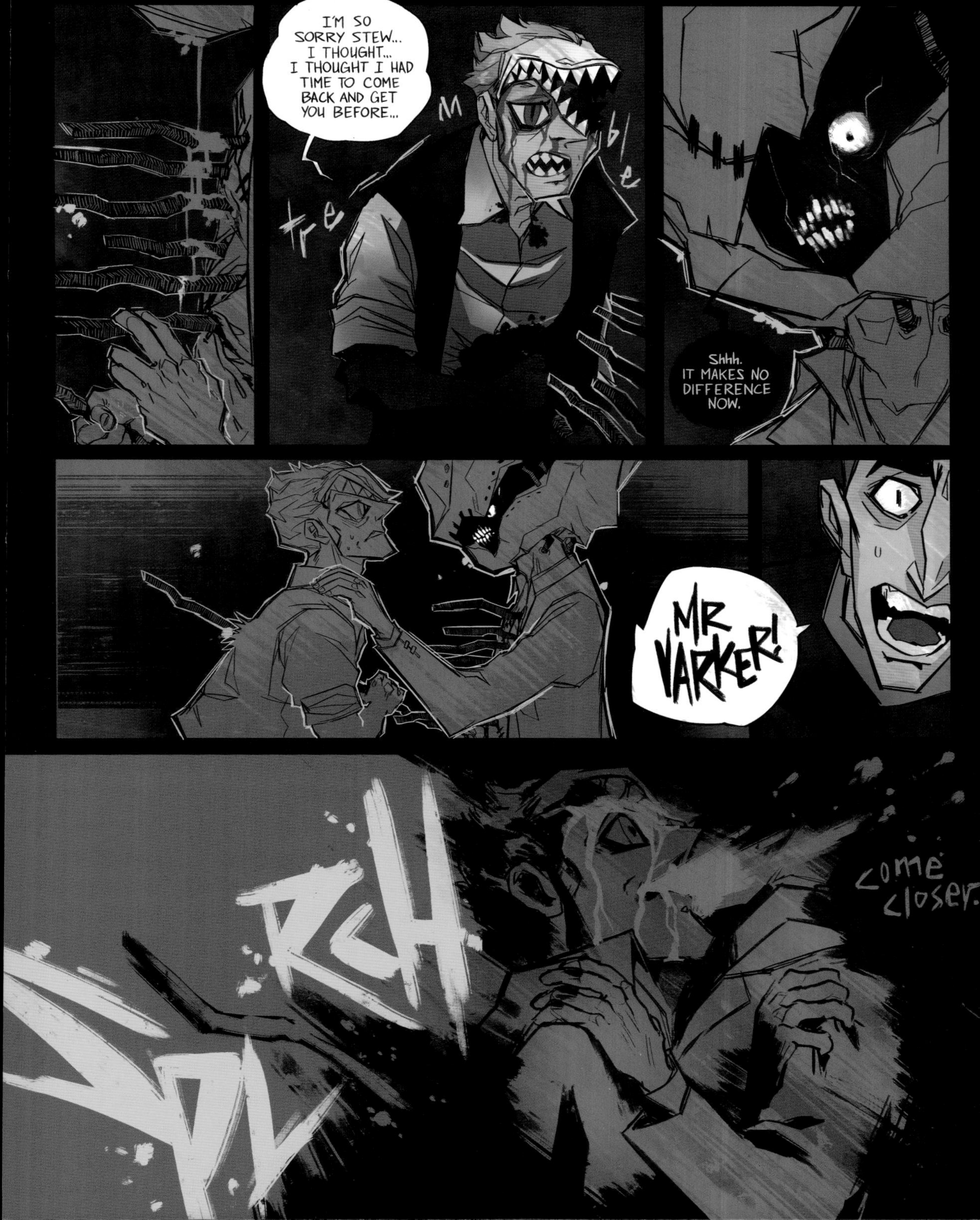
I'M SO SORRY STEW... I THOUGHT... I THOUGHT I HAD TIME TO COME BACK AND GET YOU BEFORE...
tre
m
ble
Shhh. IT MAKES NO DIFFERENCE NOW.
MR VARKER!
come closer.

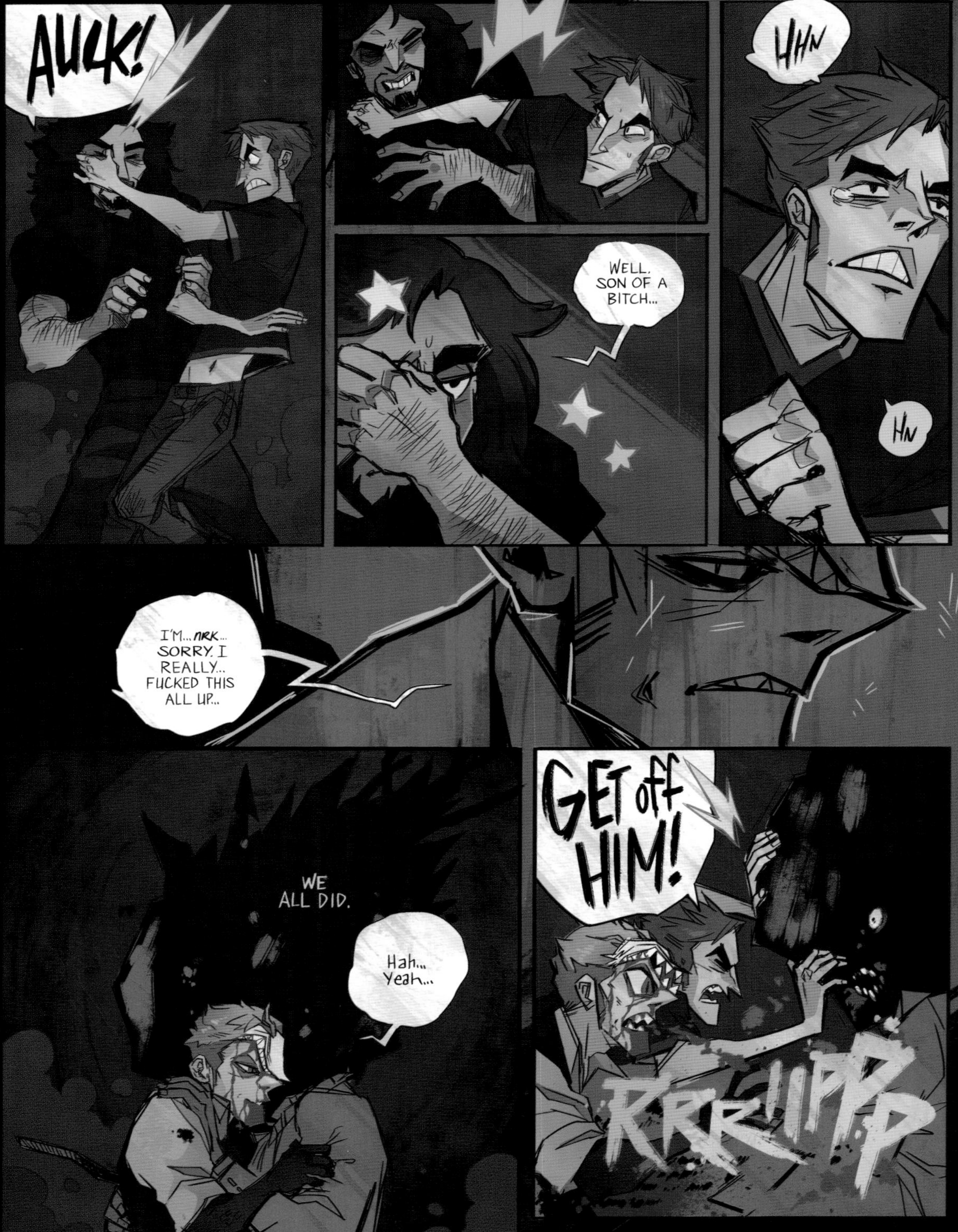
AUCK!
HHN
WELL. SON OF A BITCH...
HN
I'M... NRK... SORRY. I REALLY... FUCKED THIS ALL UP...
WE ALL DID.
Hah... Yeah...
GET off HIM!
RRRIIPP.P

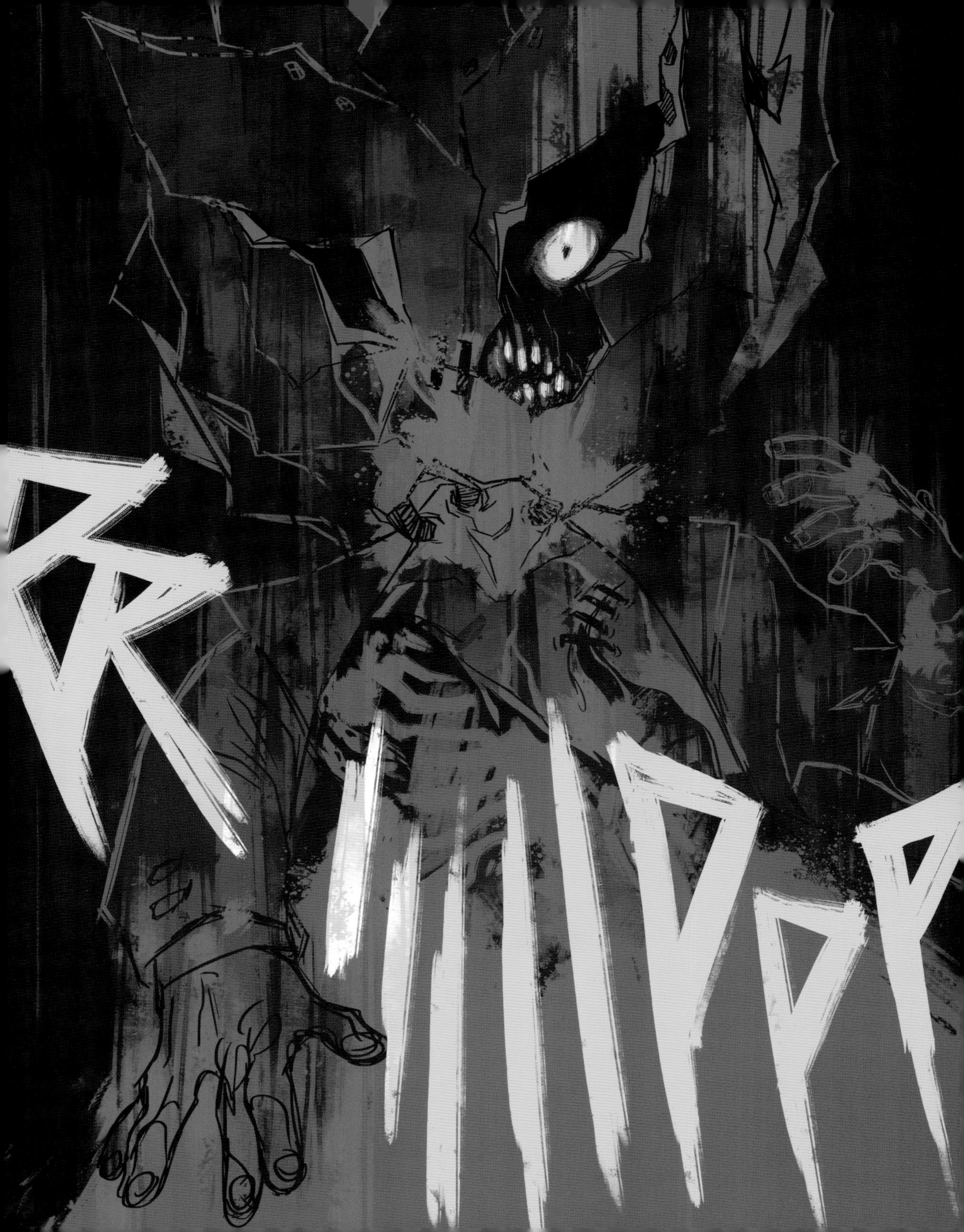
RIIIIPP

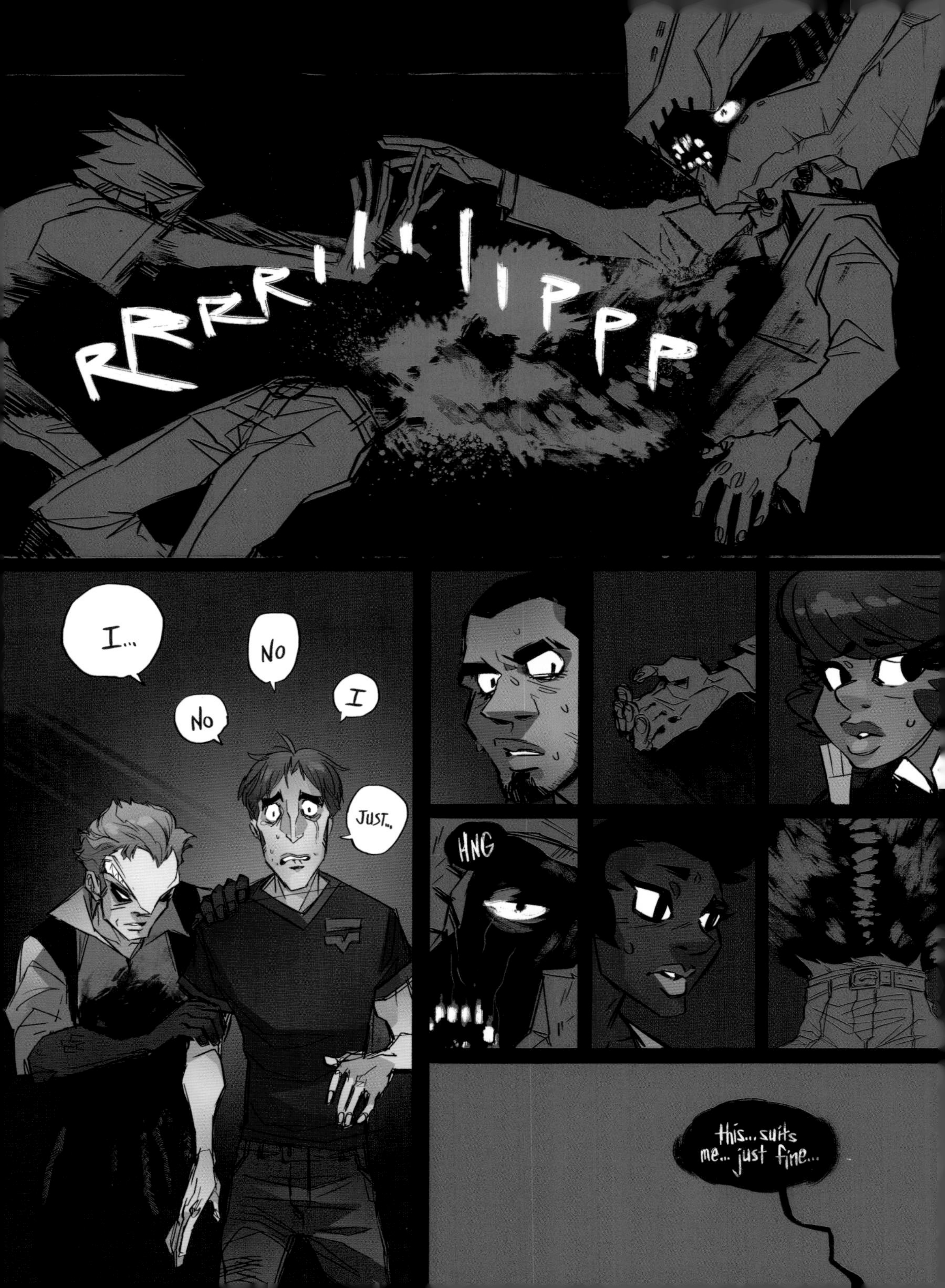
RRRRRIIIIIIPPP
I...
NO
NO
I
JUST...
HNG
this... suits me... just fine...

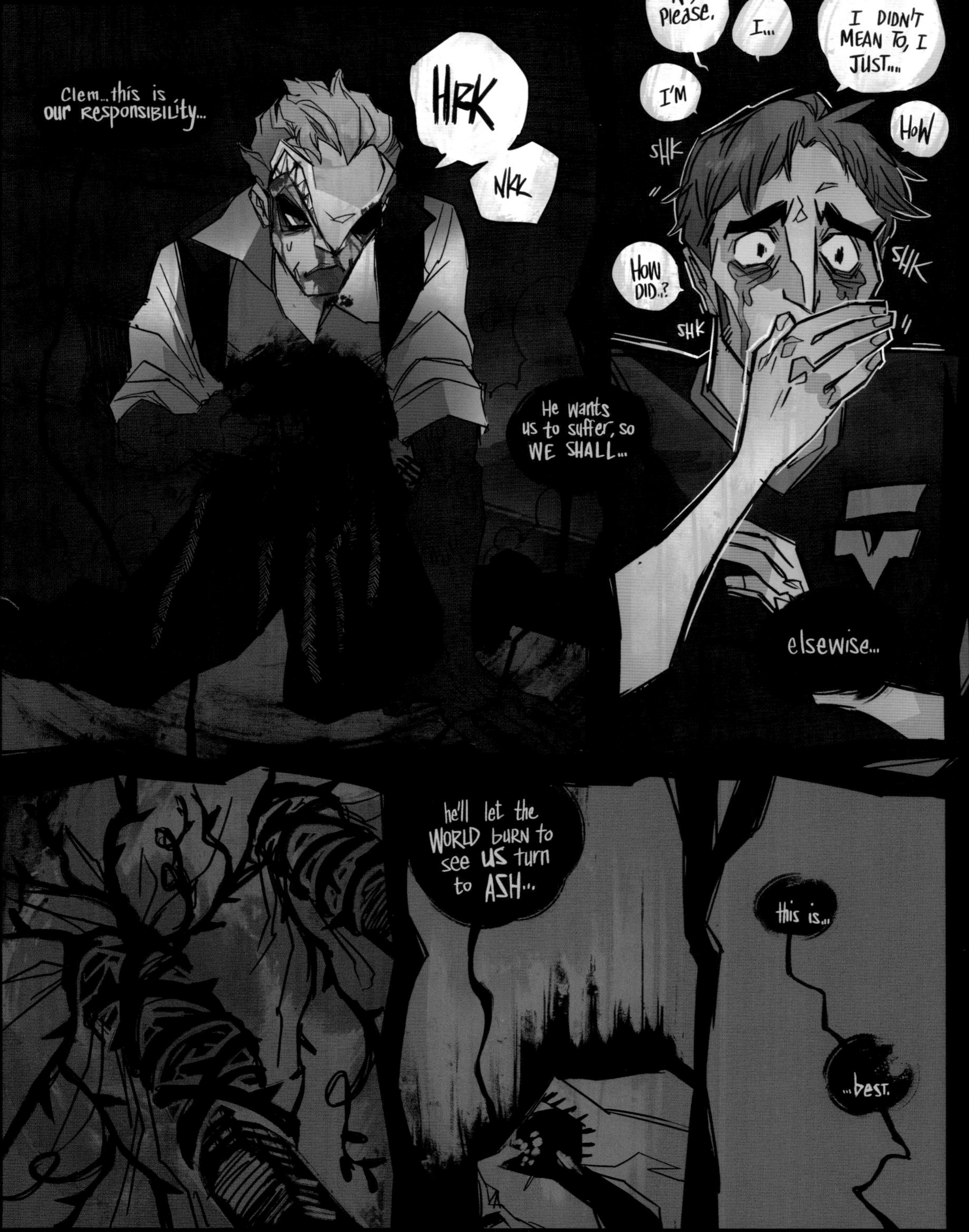
Clem... this is our RESPONSIBILITY...
HRK
NKK
He wants us to suffer, so WE SHALL...
No, please.
I...
I DIDN'T MEAN TO, I JUST...
I'M
HOW
SHK
HOW DID..?
SHK
SHK
elsewise...
he'll let the WORLD burn to see US turn to ASH...
this is...
...best.

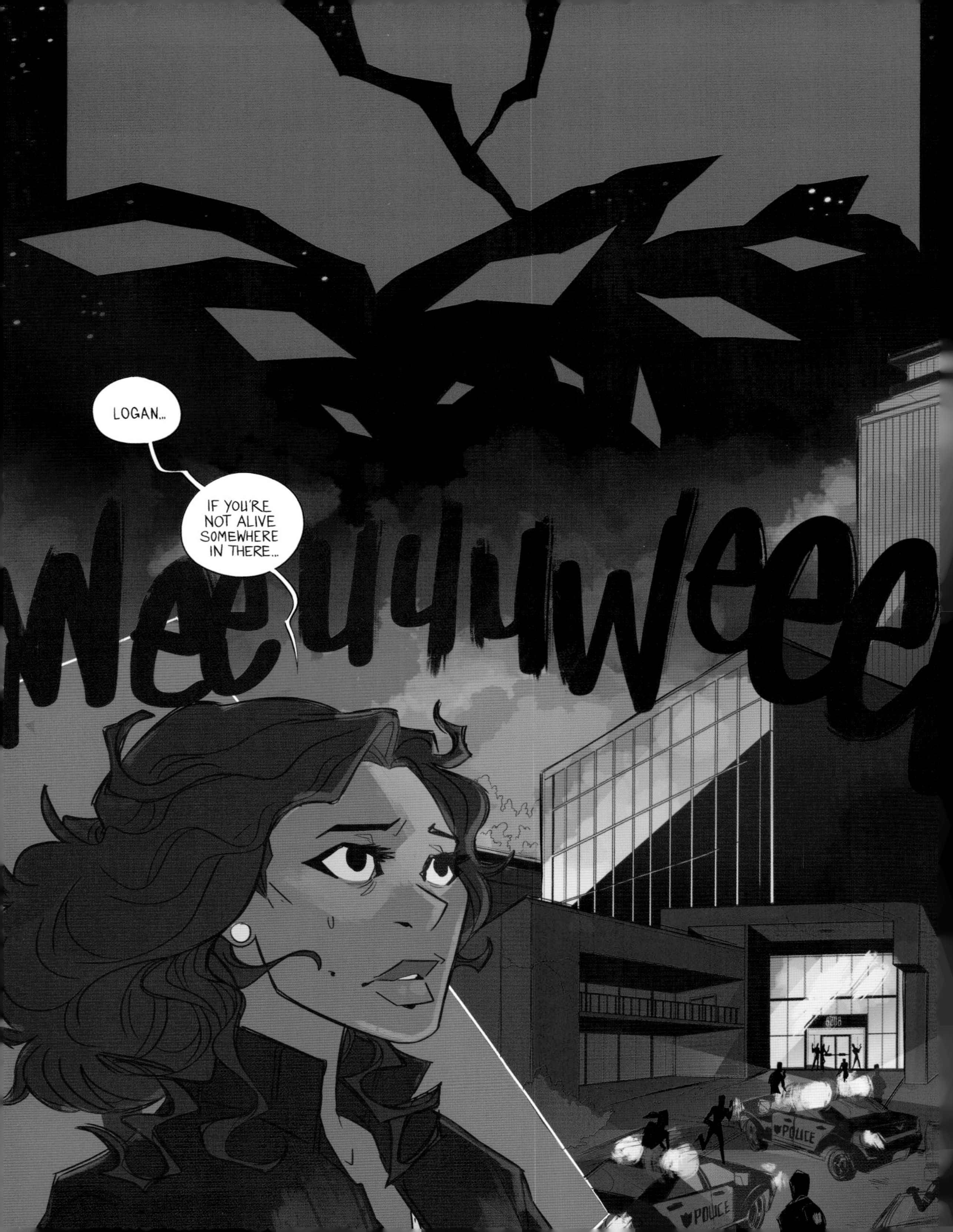

LOGAN...
IF YOU'RE NOT ALIVE SOMEWHERE IN THERE...
WEEUUUWEEE
POLICE
POLICE

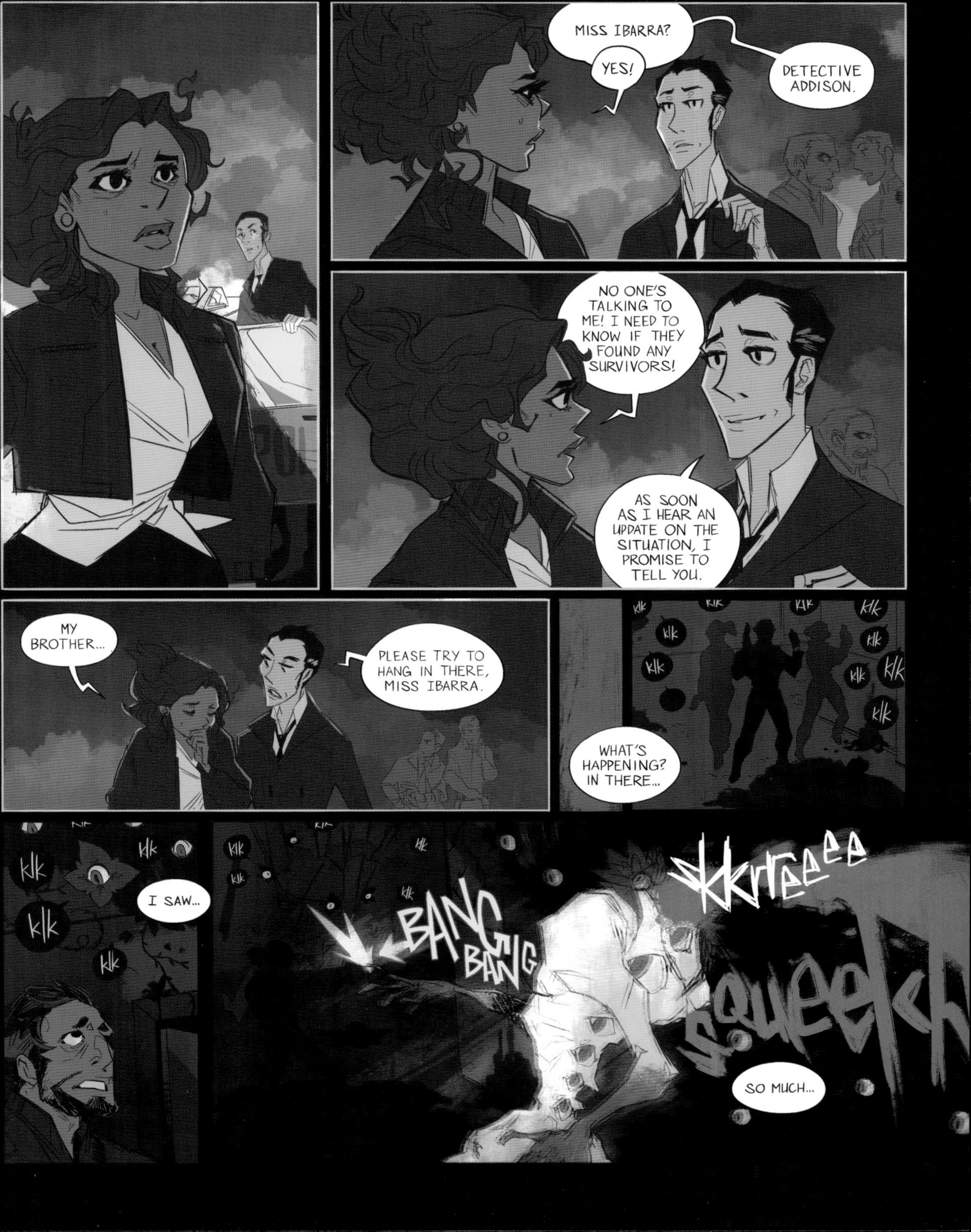
MISS IBARRA?
YES!
DETECTIVE ADDISON.
NO ONE'S TALKING TO ME! I NEED TO KNOW IF THEY FOUND ANY SURVIVORS!
AS SOON AS I HEAR AN UPDATE ON THE SITUATION, I PROMISE TO TELL YOU.
MY BROTHER...
PLEASE TRY TO HANG IN THERE, MISS IBARRA.
klk
WHAT'S HAPPENING? IN THERE...
klk
I SAW...
BANG BANG
SKKREEEE
SQUEELCH
SO MUCH...

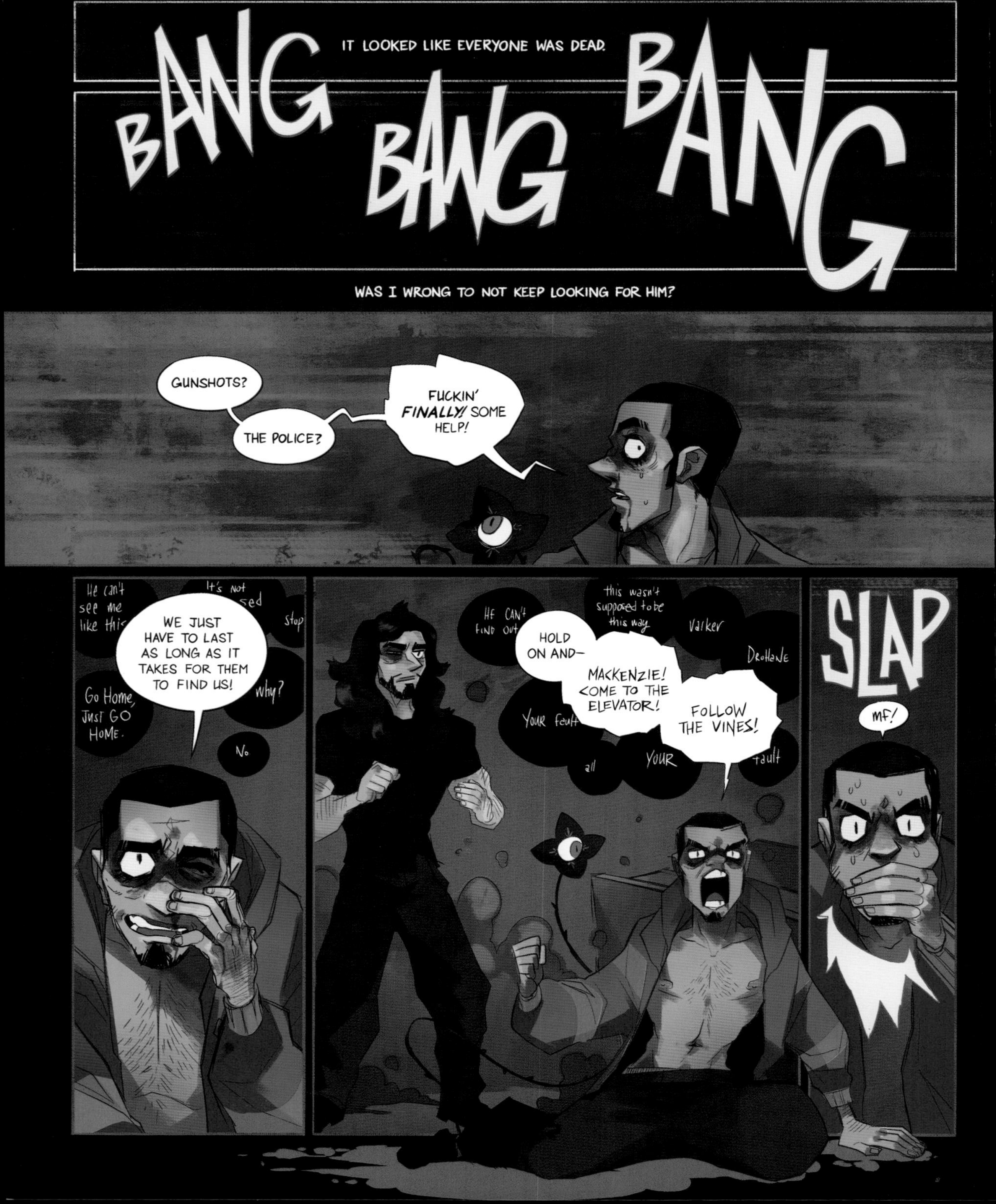

IT LOOKED LIKE EVERYONE WAS DEAD.
BANG BANG BANG
WAS I WRONG TO NOT KEEP LOOKING FOR HIM?
GUNSHOTS?
THE POLICE?
FUCKIN' *FINALLY!* SOME HELP!
He can't see me like this
It's not
sed
Stop
WE JUST HAVE TO LAST AS LONG AS IT TAKES FOR THEM TO FIND US!
Go Home, Just GO HOME.
why?
No.
HE CAN'T FIND OUT
this wasn't supposed to be this way
Varker
DroHaNe
HOLD ON AND—
MACKENZIE! COME TO THE ELEVATOR!
FOLLOW THE VINES!
YOUR fault
all
YOUR
fault
SLAP
MF!

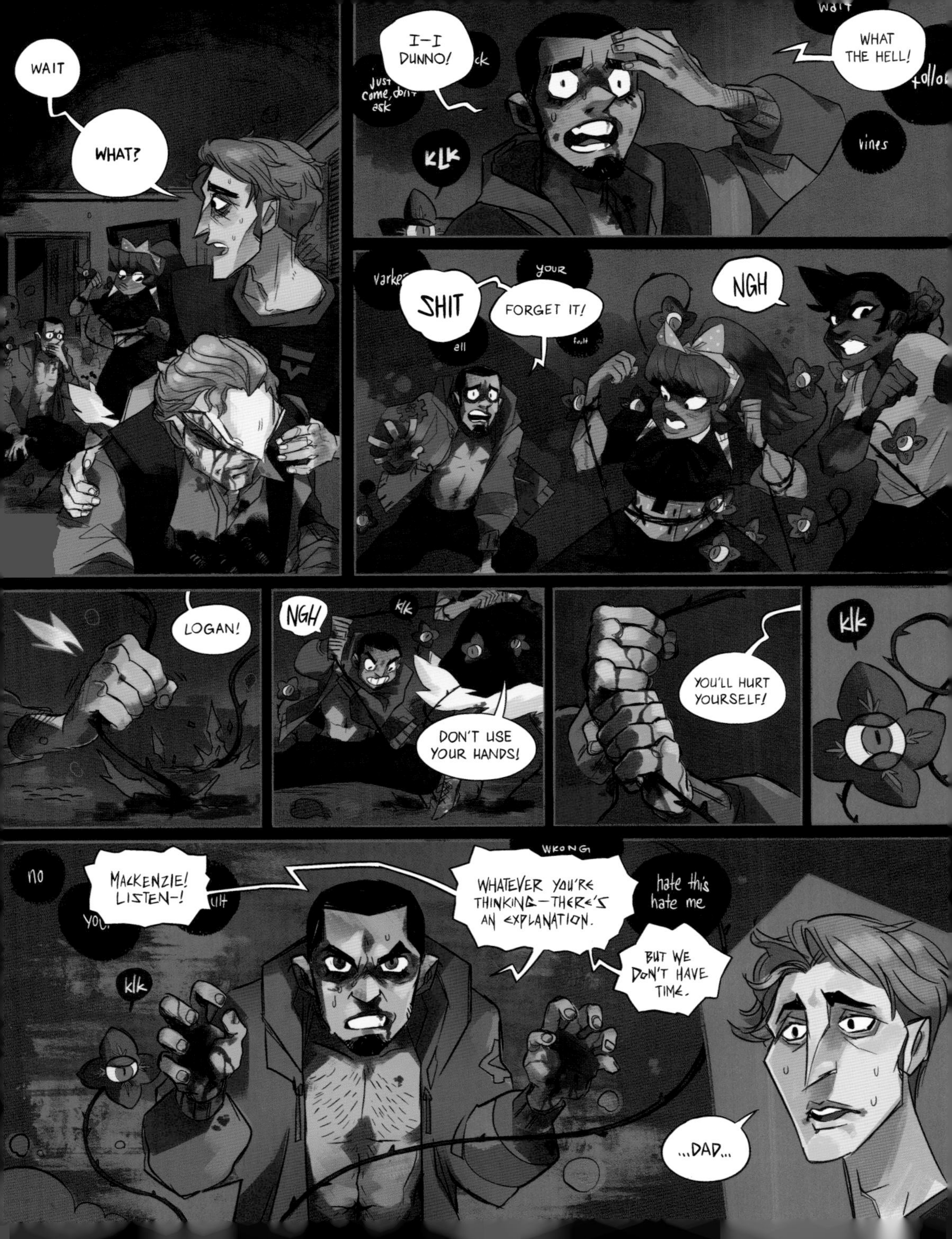
WAIT
WHAT?
I–I DUNNO!
just come, don't ask
KLK
wait
WHAT THE HELL!
vines
SHIT
your
FORGET IT!
ell
fault
NGH
LOGAN!
NGH
klk
DON'T USE YOUR HANDS!
YOU'LL HURT YOURSELF!
klk
no
MACKENZIE! LISTEN–!
WRONG
WHATEVER YOU'RE THINKING—THERE'S AN EXPLANATION.
hate this
hate me
BUT WE DON'T HAVE TIME.
klk
...DAD...

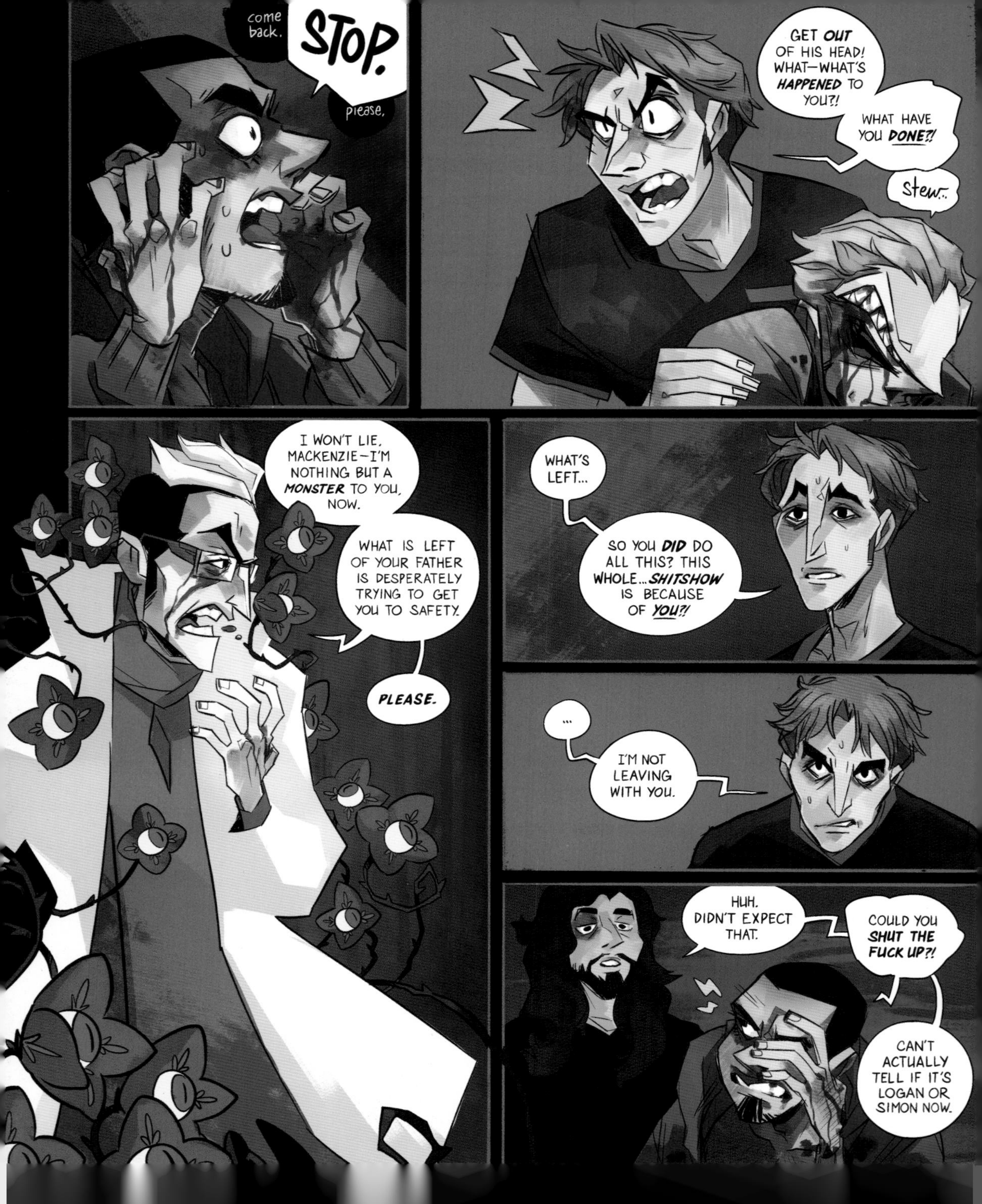
come back.
STOP.
please.
GET OUT OF HIS HEAD! WHAT—WHAT'S HAPPENED TO YOU?!
WHAT HAVE YOU DONE?!
Stew...
I WON'T LIE, MACKENZIE—I'M NOTHING BUT A MONSTER TO YOU, NOW.
WHAT IS LEFT OF YOUR FATHER IS DESPERATELY TRYING TO GET YOU TO SAFETY.
PLEASE.
WHAT'S LEFT...
SO YOU DID DO ALL THIS? THIS WHOLE...SHITSHOW IS BECAUSE OF YOU?!
...
I'M NOT LEAVING WITH YOU.
HUH. DIDN'T EXPECT THAT.
COULD YOU SHUT THE FUCK UP?!
CAN'T ACTUALLY TELL IF IT'S LOGAN OR SIMON NOW.

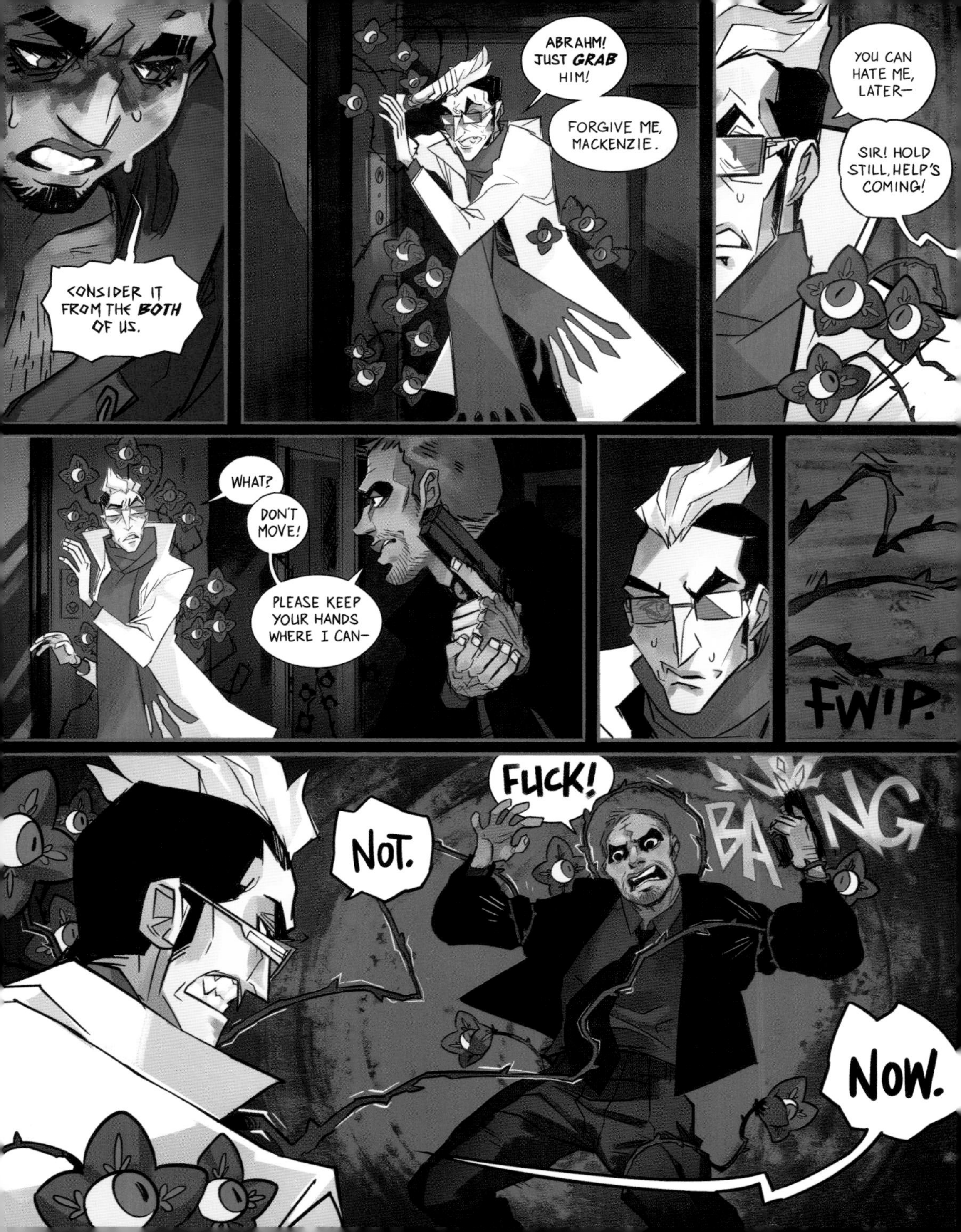
CONSIDER IT FROM THE BOTH OF US.
ABRAHM! JUST GRAB HIM!
FORGIVE ME, MACKENZIE.
YOU CAN HATE ME, LATER—
SIR! HOLD STILL, HELP'S COMING!
WHAT?
DON'T MOVE!
PLEASE KEEP YOUR HANDS WHERE I CAN-
FWIP.
NOT.
FUCK!
BANG
NOW.

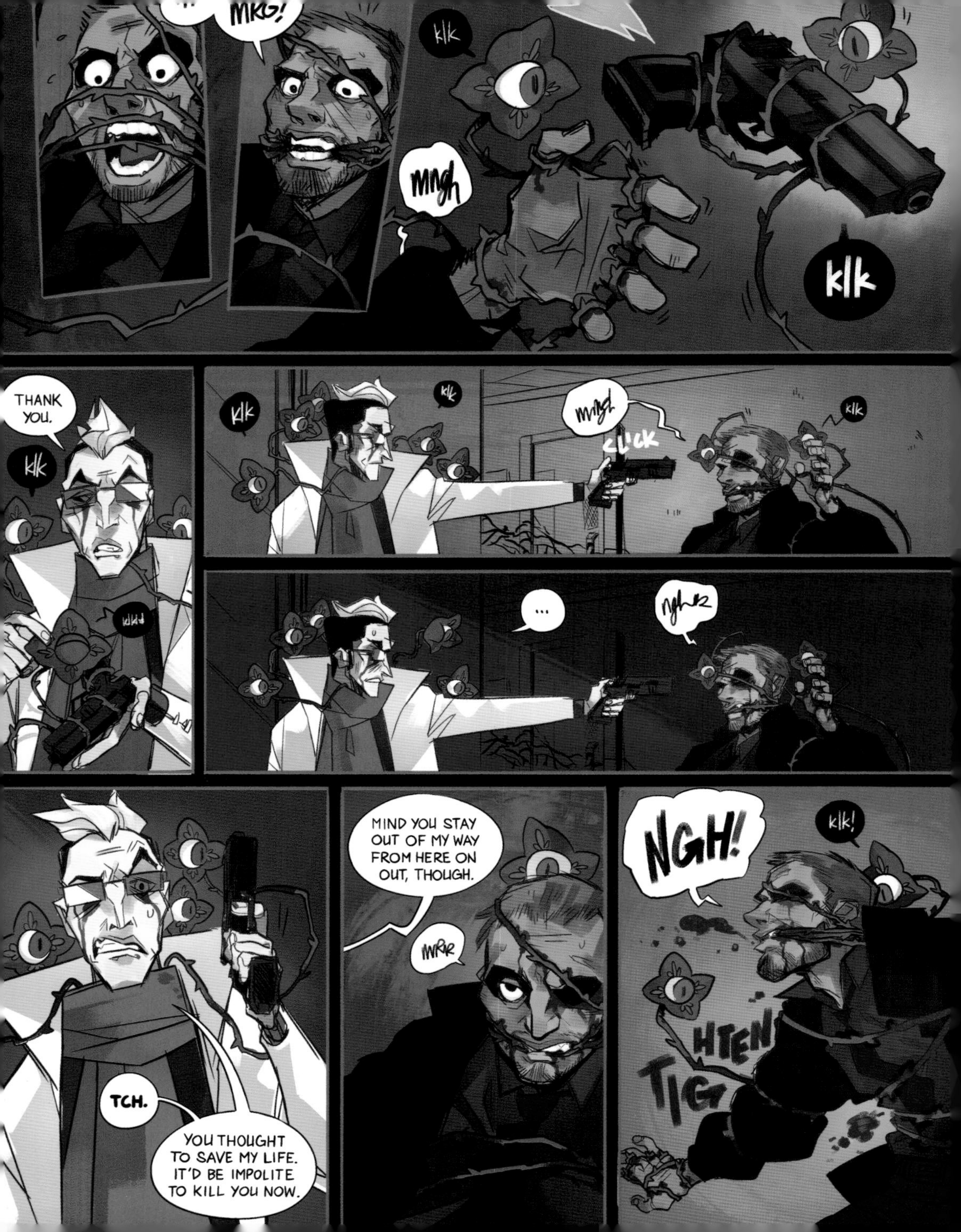
MKG!
klk
mngh
klk
THANK YOU.
klk
klk
klk
CLICK
klk
...
TCH.
YOU THOUGHT TO SAVE MY LIFE. IT'D BE IMPOLITE TO KILL YOU NOW.
MIND YOU STAY OUT OF MY WAY FROM HERE ON OUT, THOUGH.
MRR
NGH!
klk!
TIGHTEN

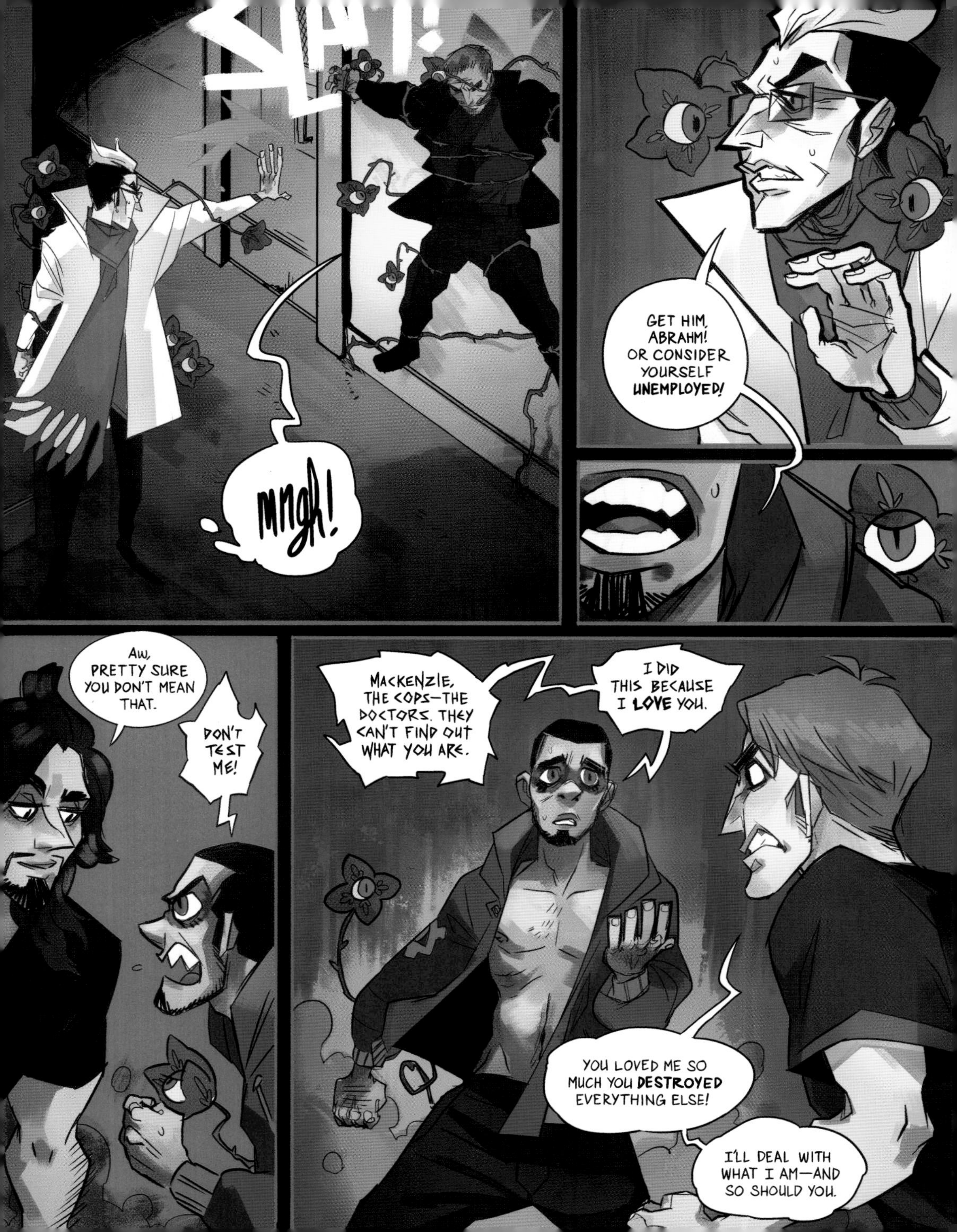
mngh!
GET HIM, ABRAHM! OR CONSIDER YOURSELF **UNEMPLOYED!**
Aw, PRETTY SURE YOU DON'T MEAN THAT.
DON'T TEST ME!
MACKENZIE, THE COPS—THE DOCTORS. THEY CAN'T FIND OUT WHAT YOU ARE.
I DID THIS BECAUSE I **LOVE** YOU.
YOU LOVED ME SO MUCH YOU **DESTROYED** EVERYTHING ELSE!
I'LL DEAL WITH WHAT I AM—AND SO SHOULD YOU.

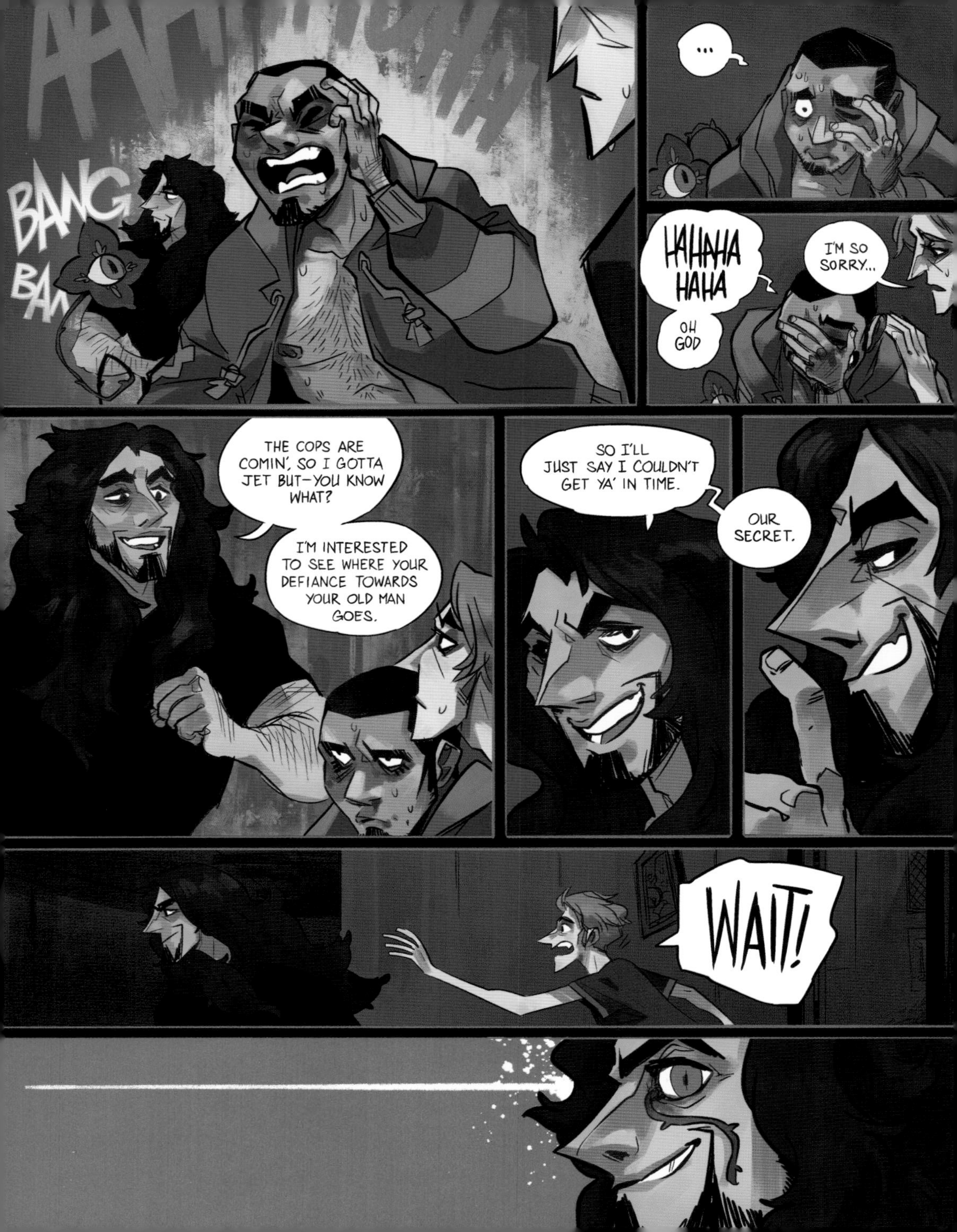
BANG
BAN
...
HAHAHA HAHA
OH GOD
I'M SO SORRY...
THE COPS ARE COMIN', SO I GOTTA JET BUT—YOU KNOW WHAT?
I'M INTERESTED TO SEE WHERE YOUR DEFIANCE TOWARDS YOUR OLD MAN GOES.
SO I'LL JUST SAY I COULDN'T GET YA' IN TIME.
OUR SECRET.
WAIT!

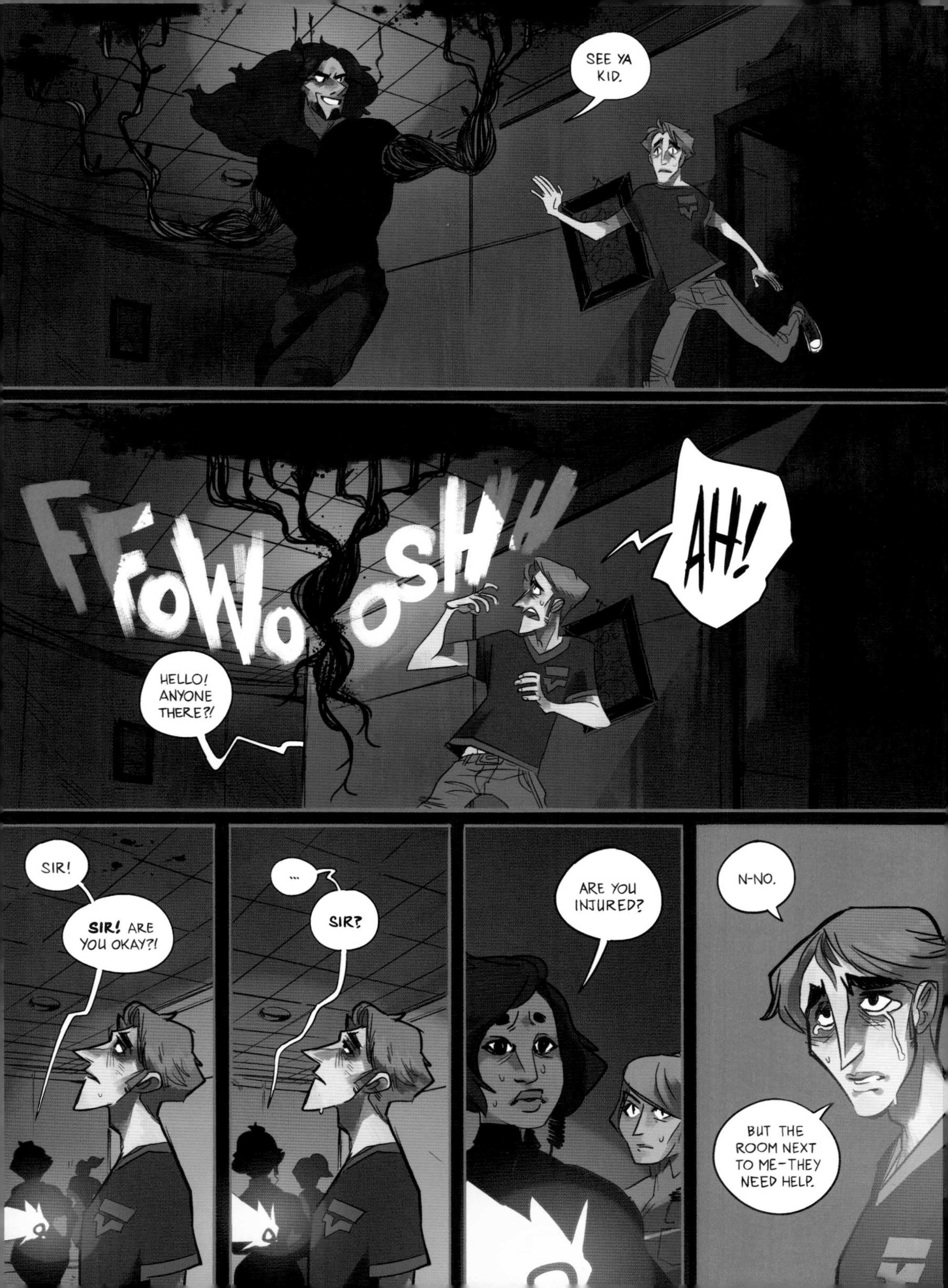
SEE YA KID.
FFOWOOSHHH
AH!
HELLO! ANYONE THERE?!
SIR!
SIR! ARE YOU OKAY?!
...
SIR?
ARE YOU INJURED?
N-NO.
BUT THE ROOM NEXT TO ME—THEY NEED HELP.

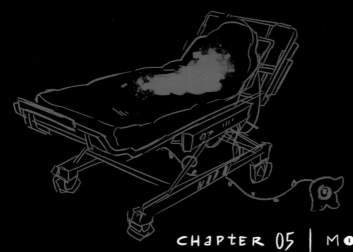

CHAPTER 05 | MONSTER INSIDE

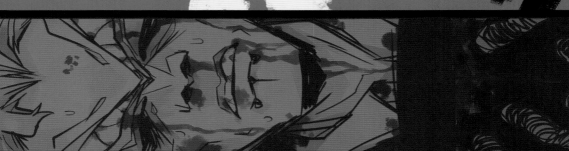

Weeuuu Weeuu

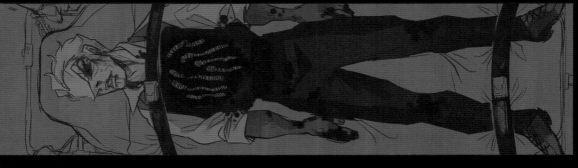

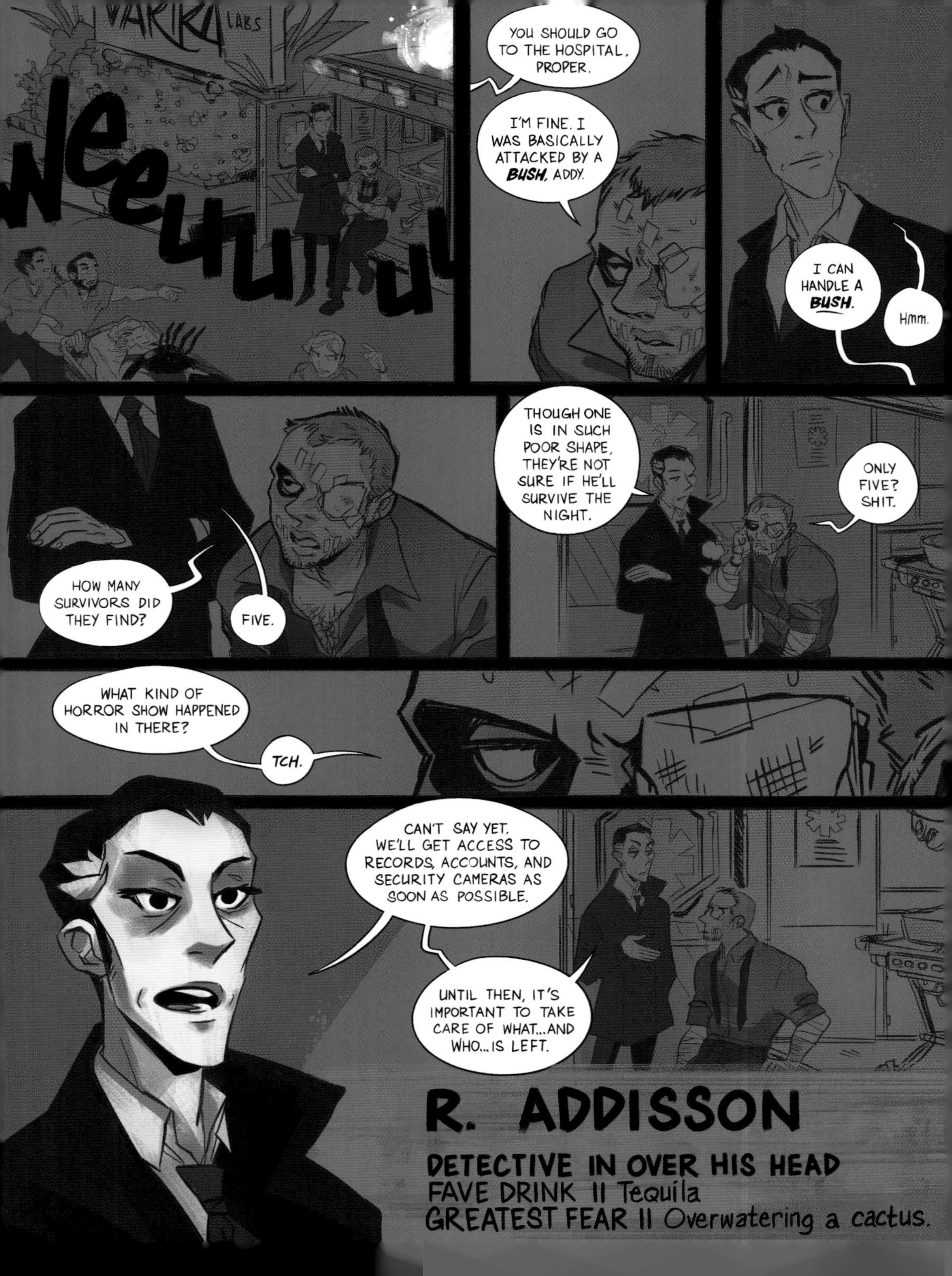
VARIKA LABS
WEEUUUUU
YOU SHOULD GO TO THE HOSPITAL, PROPER.
I'M FINE. I WAS BASICALLY ATTACKED BY A BUSH, ADDY.
I CAN HANDLE A BUSH.
Hmm.
HOW MANY SURVIVORS DID THEY FIND?
FIVE.
THOUGH ONE IS IN SUCH POOR SHAPE, THEY'RE NOT SURE IF HE'LL SURVIVE THE NIGHT.
ONLY FIVE? SHIT.
WHAT KIND OF HORROR SHOW HAPPENED IN THERE?
TCH.
CAN'T SAY YET. WE'LL GET ACCESS TO RECORDS, ACCOUNTS, AND SECURITY CAMERAS AS SOON AS POSSIBLE.
UNTIL THEN, IT'S IMPORTANT TO TAKE CARE OF WHAT...AND WHO...IS LEFT.
R. ADDISSON
DETECTIVE IN OVER HIS HEAD
FAVE DRINK II Tequila
GREATEST FEAR II Overwatering a cactus.

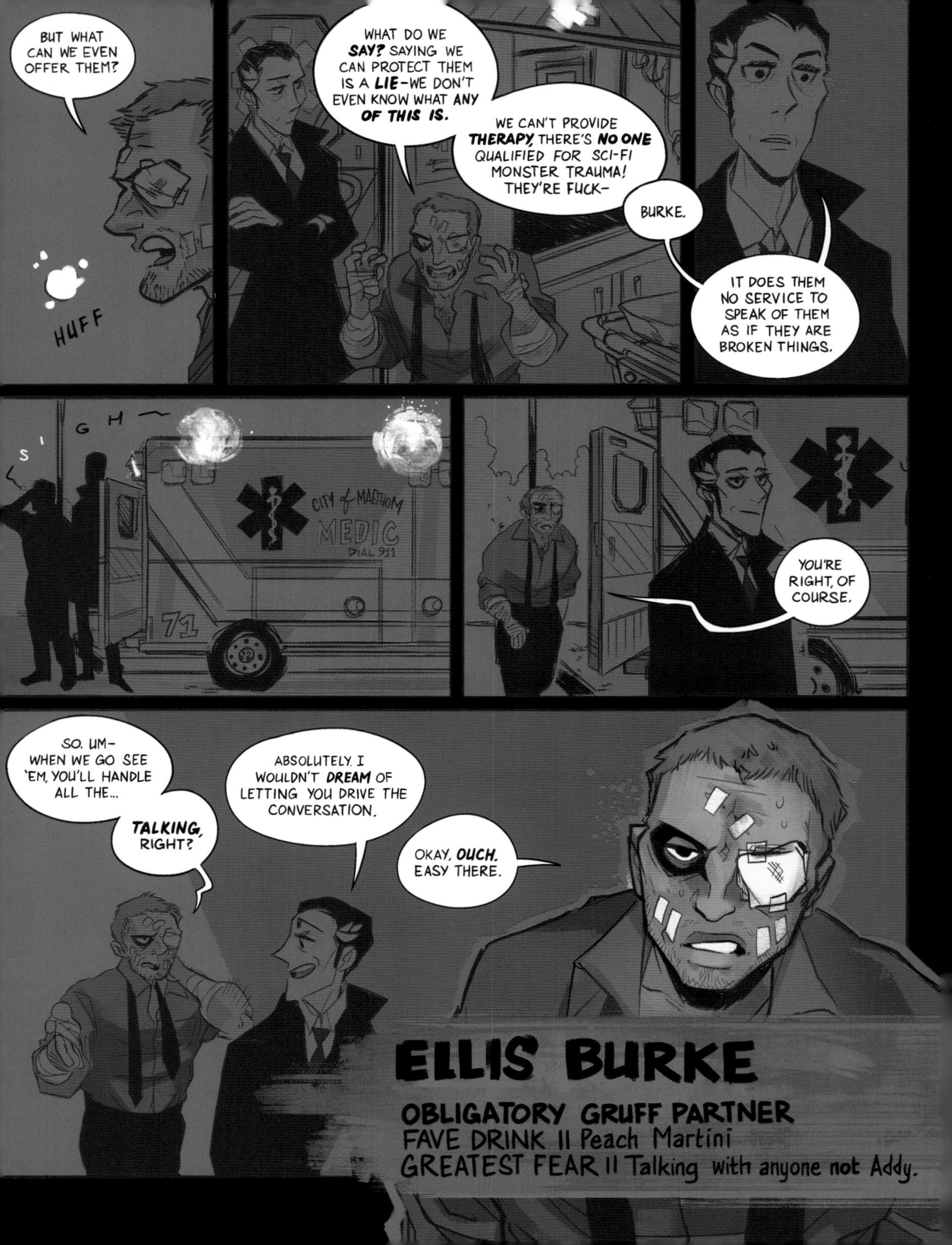
BUT WHAT CAN WE EVEN OFFER THEM?
HUFF
WHAT DO WE SAY? SAYING WE CAN PROTECT THEM IS A LIE—WE DON'T EVEN KNOW WHAT ANY OF THIS IS.
WE CAN'T PROVIDE THERAPY, THERE'S NO ONE QUALIFIED FOR SCI-FI MONSTER TRAUMA! THEY'RE FUCK—
BURKE.
IT DOES THEM NO SERVICE TO SPEAK OF THEM AS IF THEY ARE BROKEN THINGS.
SIGH—
CITY of MAETHOM
MEDIC
DIAL 911
71
YOU'RE RIGHT, OF COURSE.
SO. UM— WHEN WE GO SEE 'EM, YOU'LL HANDLE ALL THE...
TALKING, RIGHT?
ABSOLUTELY. I WOULDN'T DREAM OF LETTING YOU DRIVE THE CONVERSATION.
OKAY, OUCH. EASY THERE.
ELLIS BURKE
OBLIGATORY GRUFF PARTNER
FAVE DRINK II Peach Martini
GREATEST FEAR II Talking with anyone not Addy.

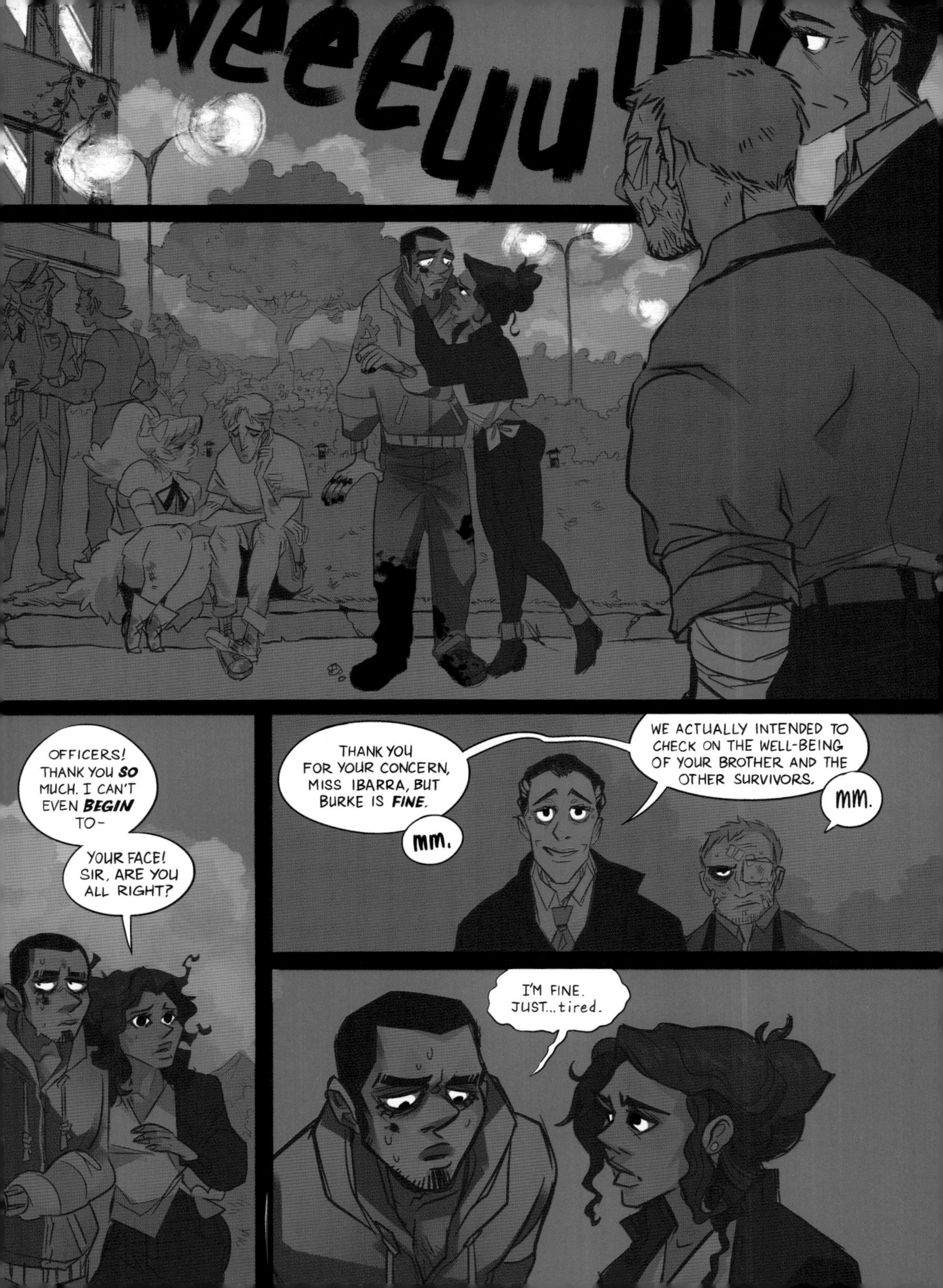
WEEEUUUU
OFFICERS! THANK YOU **SO** MUCH. I CAN'T EVEN **BEGIN** TO-
YOUR FACE! SIR, ARE YOU ALL RIGHT?
THANK YOU FOR YOUR CONCERN, MISS IBARRA, BUT BURKE IS **FINE**.
MM.
WE ACTUALLY INTENDED TO CHECK ON THE WELL-BEING OF YOUR BROTHER AND THE OTHER SURVIVORS.
MM.
I'M FINE. JUST...tired.

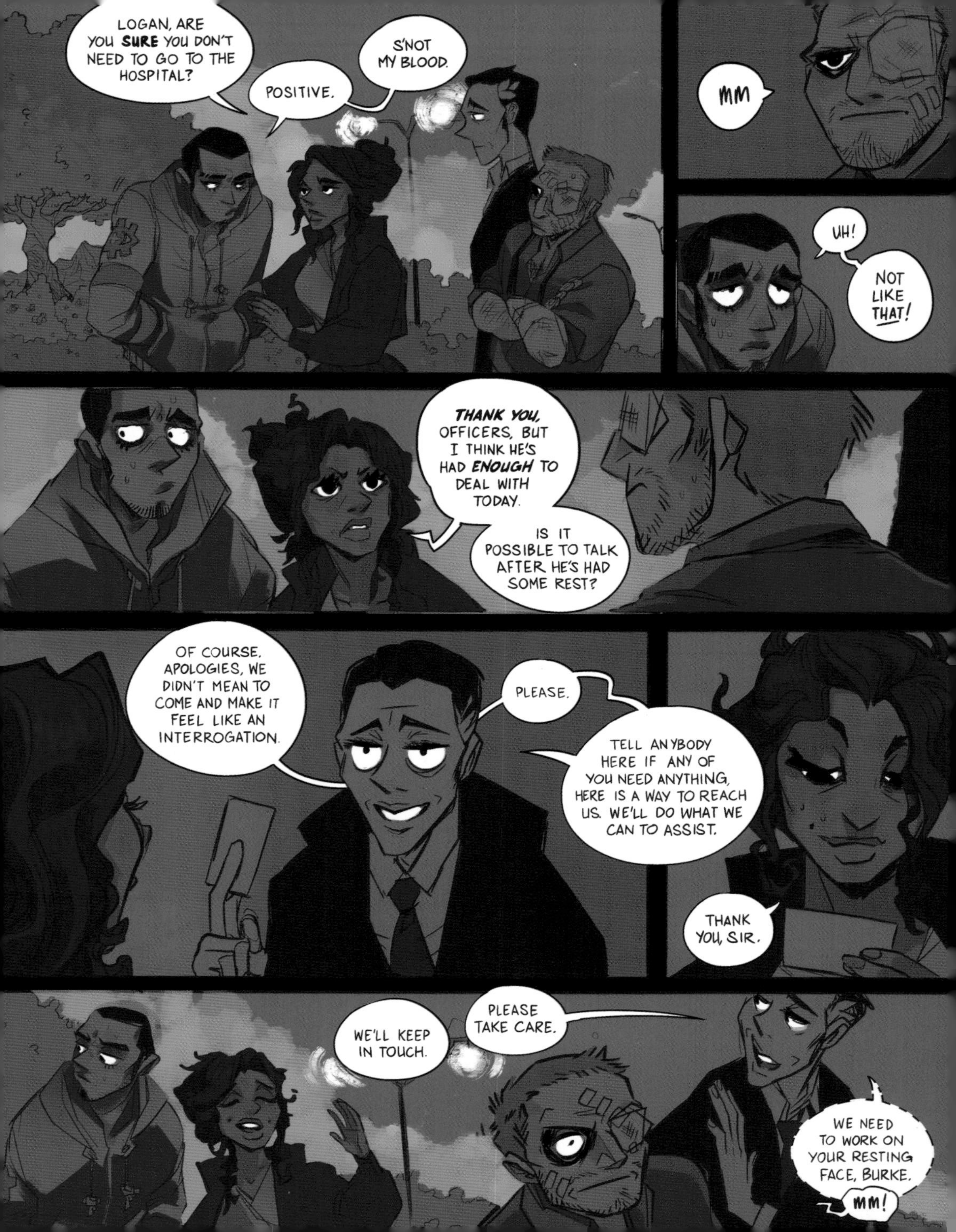
LOGAN, ARE YOU **SURE** YOU DON'T NEED TO GO TO THE HOSPITAL?
POSITIVE.
S'NOT MY BLOOD.
MM
UH!
NOT LIKE THAT!
THANK YOU, OFFICERS, BUT I THINK HE'S HAD **ENOUGH** TO DEAL WITH TODAY.
IS IT POSSIBLE TO TALK AFTER HE'S HAD SOME REST?
OF COURSE. APOLOGIES, WE DIDN'T MEAN TO COME AND MAKE IT FEEL LIKE AN INTERROGATION.
PLEASE.
TELL ANYBODY HERE IF ANY OF YOU NEED ANYTHING, HERE IS A WAY TO REACH US. WE'LL DO WHAT WE CAN TO ASSIST.
THANK YOU, SIR.
WE'LL KEEP IN TOUCH.
PLEASE TAKE CARE.
WE NEED TO WORK ON YOUR RESTING FACE, BURKE.
MM!

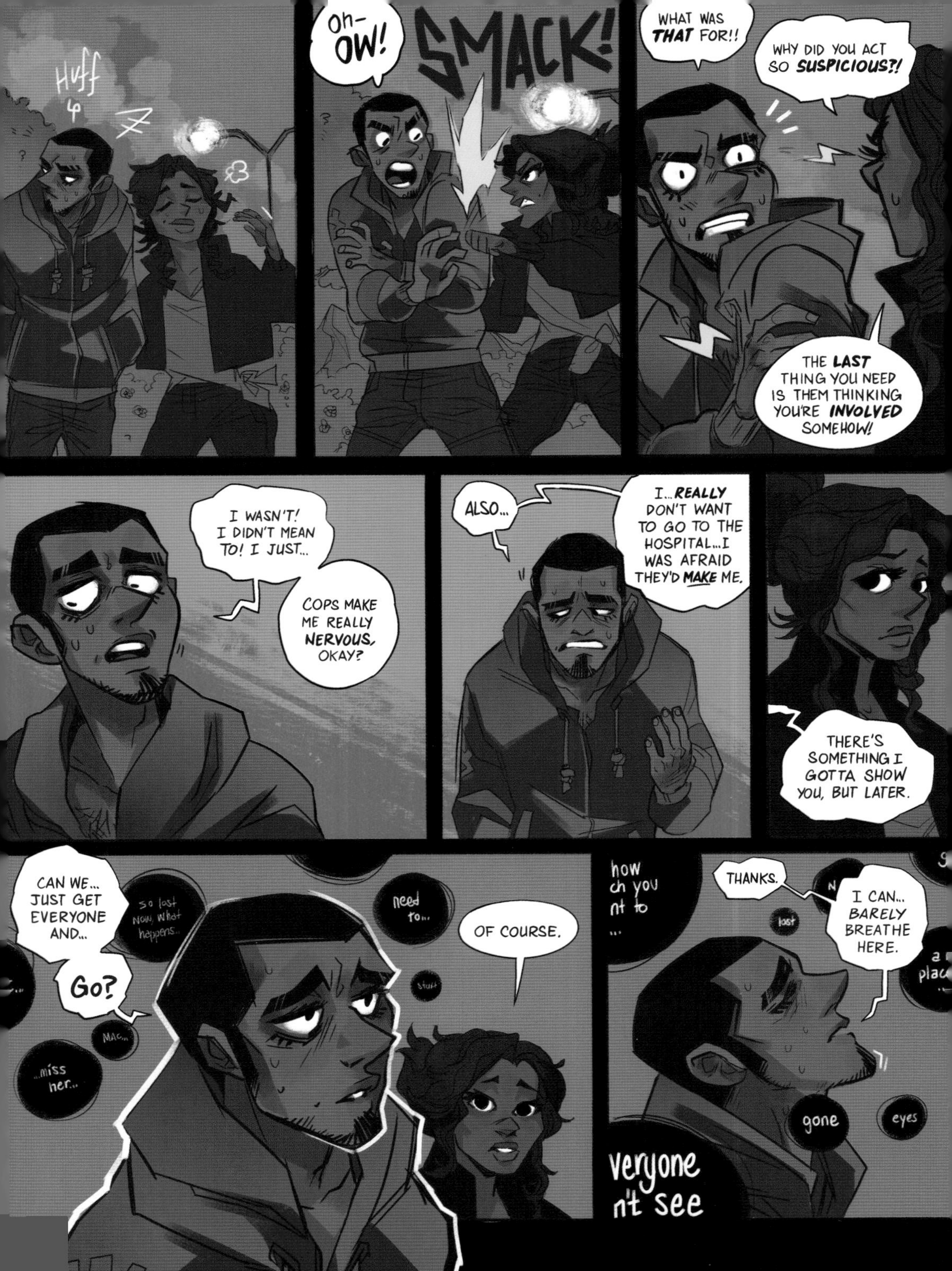

Huff
Huff
Oh-OW!
SMACK!
WHAT WAS THAT FOR!!
WHY DID YOU ACT SO SUSPICIOUS?!
THE LAST THING YOU NEED IS THEM THINKING YOU'RE INVOLVED SOMEHOW!
I WASN'T! I DIDN'T MEAN TO! I JUST...
COPS MAKE ME REALLY NERVOUS, OKAY?
ALSO...
I...REALLY DON'T WANT TO GO TO THE HOSPITAL...I WAS AFRAID THEY'D MAKE ME.
THERE'S SOMETHING I GOTTA SHOW YOU, BUT LATER.
CAN WE... JUST GET EVERYONE AND...
so lost Now, What happens...
need to...
GO?
stuff
MAC...
...miss her...
OF COURSE.
how
ch you
nt to
...
THANKS.
lost
I CAN... BARELY BREATHE HERE.
gone
eyes
veryone
n't see

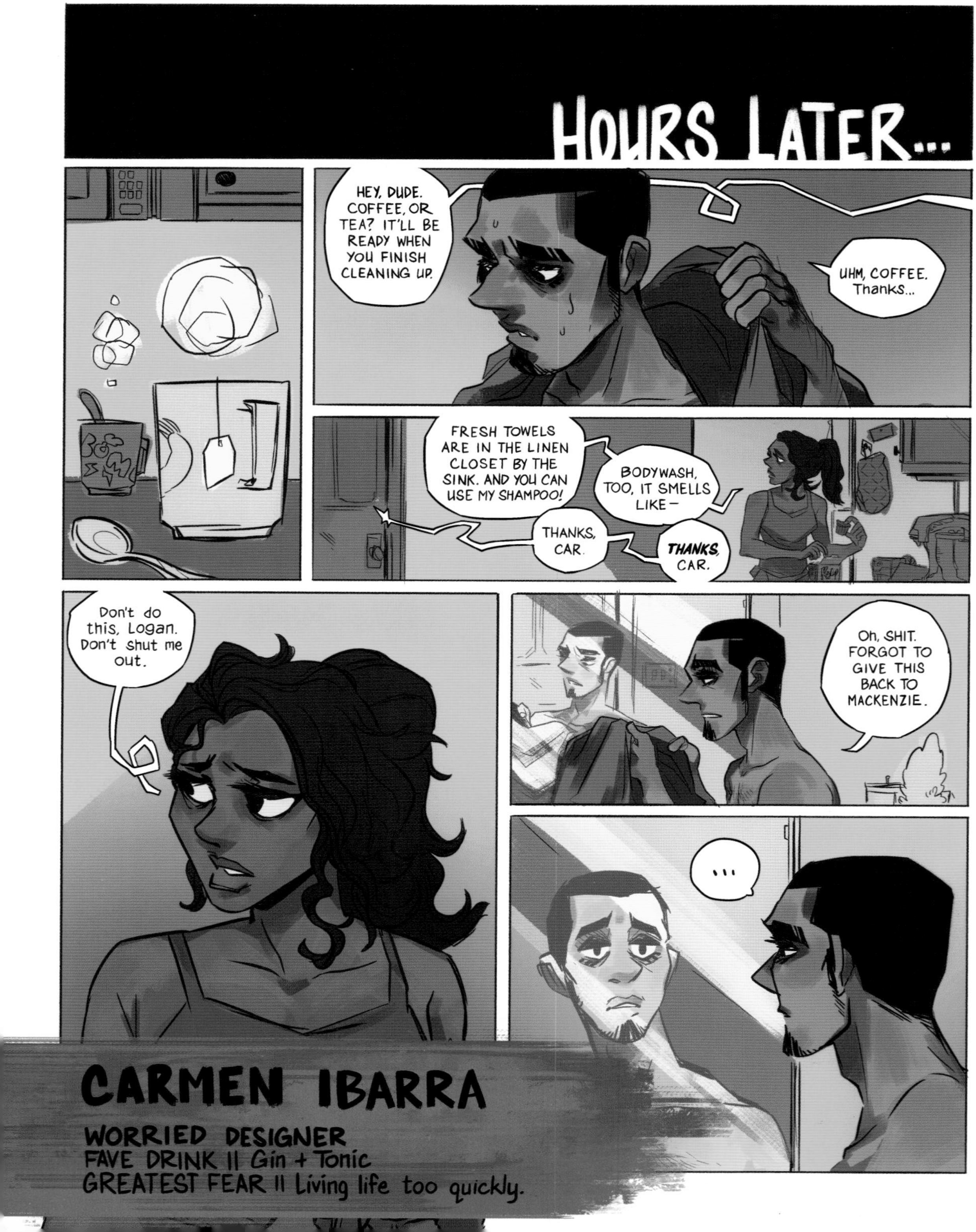
HOURS LATER...
HEY, DUDE. COFFEE, OR TEA? IT'LL BE READY WHEN YOU FINISH CLEANING UP.
UHM, COFFEE. Thanks...
FRESH TOWELS ARE IN THE LINEN CLOSET BY THE SINK. AND YOU CAN USE MY SHAMPOO!
BODYWASH, TOO, IT SMELLS LIKE—
THANKS, CAR.
THANKS, CAR.
Don't do this, Logan. Don't shut me out.
Oh, SHIT. FORGOT TO GIVE THIS BACK TO MACKENZIE.
...
CARMEN IBARRA
WORRIED DESIGNER
FAVE DRINK || Gin + Tonic
GREATEST FEAR || Living life too quickly.

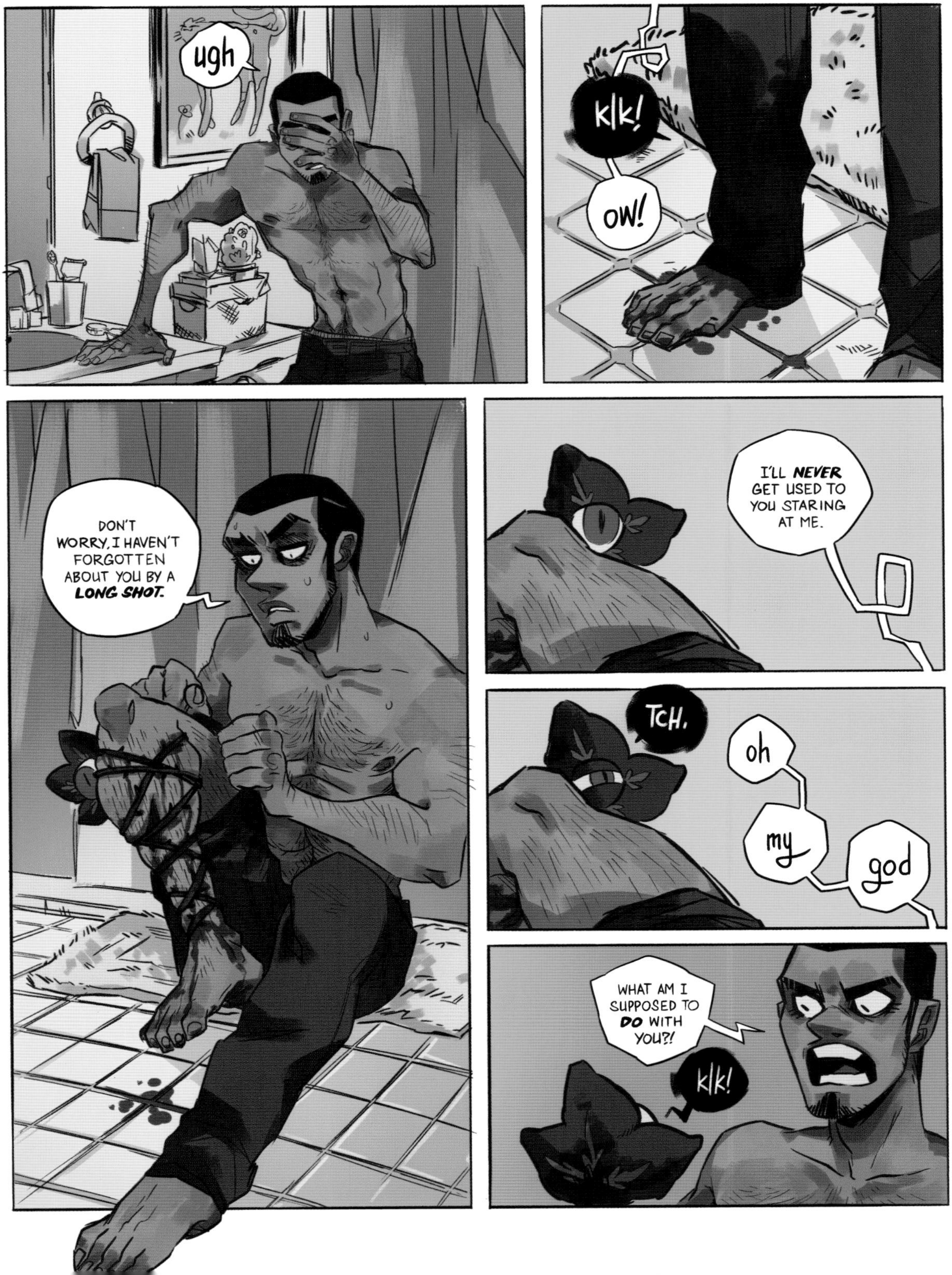
ugh
K|K!
OW!
DON'T WORRY, I HAVEN'T FORGOTTEN ABOUT YOU BY A **LONG SHOT.**
I'LL **NEVER** GET USED TO YOU STARING AT ME.
TCH.
oh
my
god
WHAT AM I SUPPOSED TO **DO** WITH YOU?!
K|K!

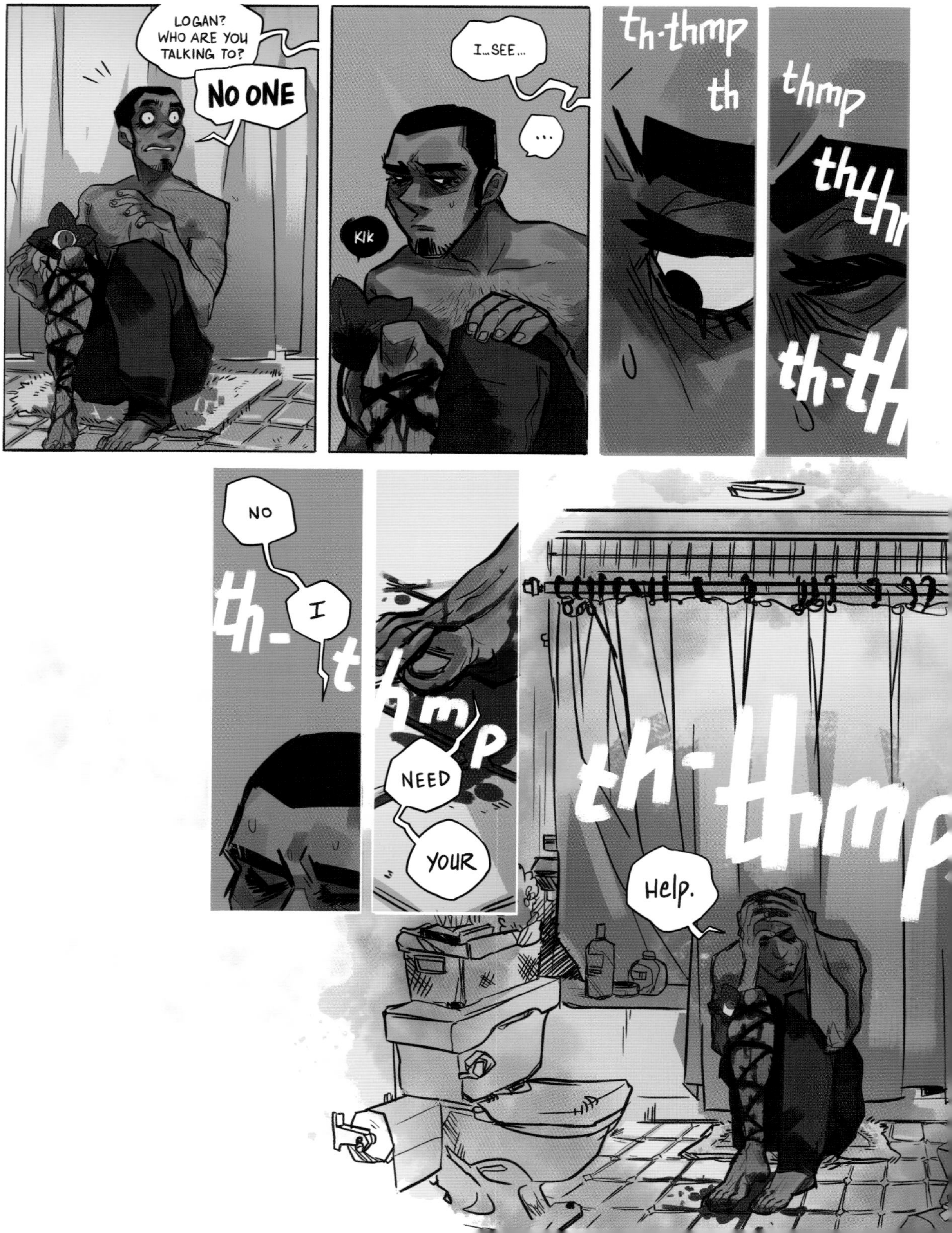
LOGAN? WHO ARE YOU TALKING TO?
NO ONE
I...SEE...
...
KIK
th-thmp
th
thmp
th-thr
th-th
NO
I
th-
NEED
YOUR
th-thmp
Help.

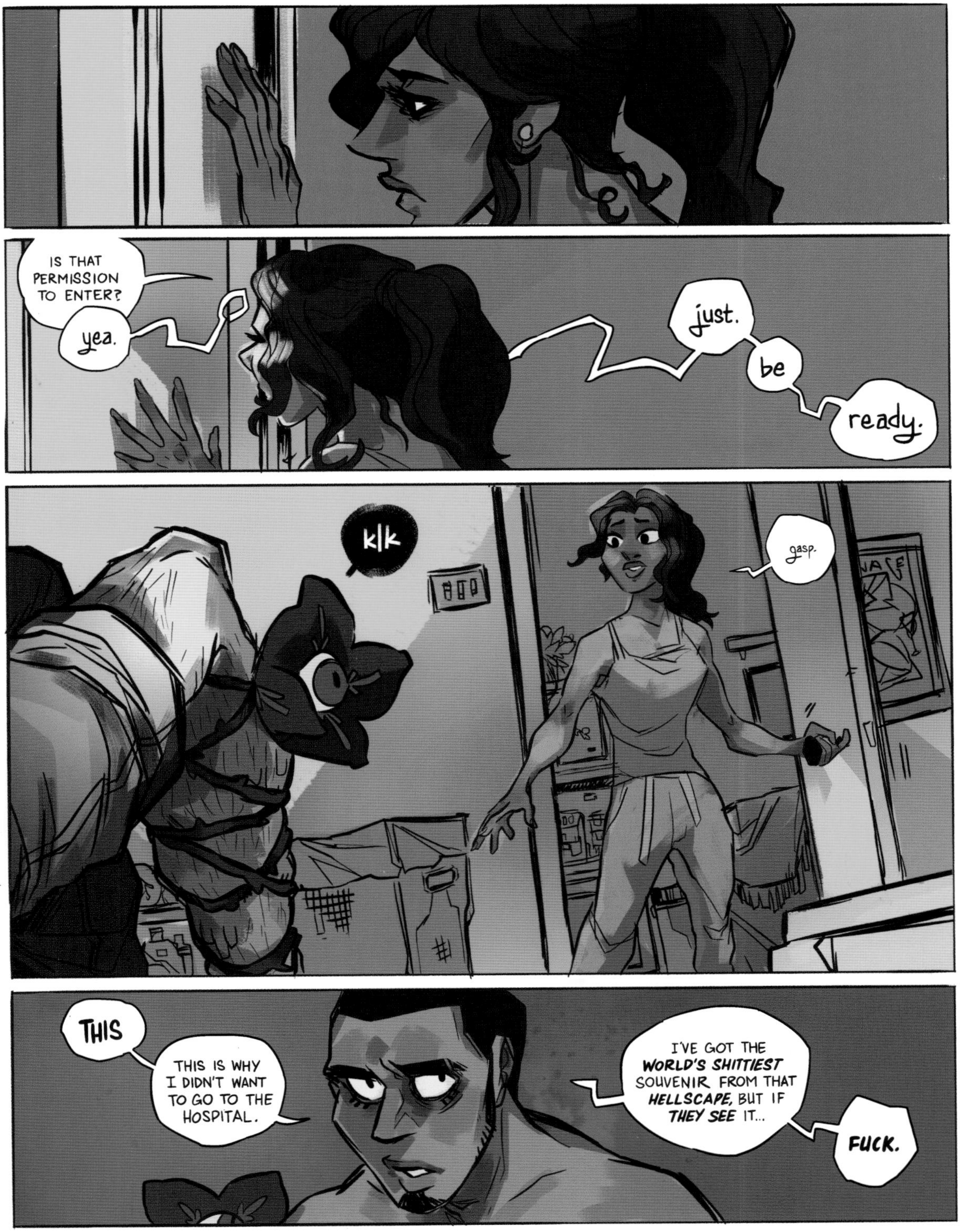
IS THAT PERMISSION TO ENTER?
yea.
just.
be
ready.
k|k
gasp.
THIS
THIS IS WHY I DIDN'T WANT TO GO TO THE HOSPITAL.
I'VE GOT THE WORLD'S SHITTIEST SOUVENIR FROM THAT HELLSCAPE, BUT IF THEY SEE IT...
FUCK.

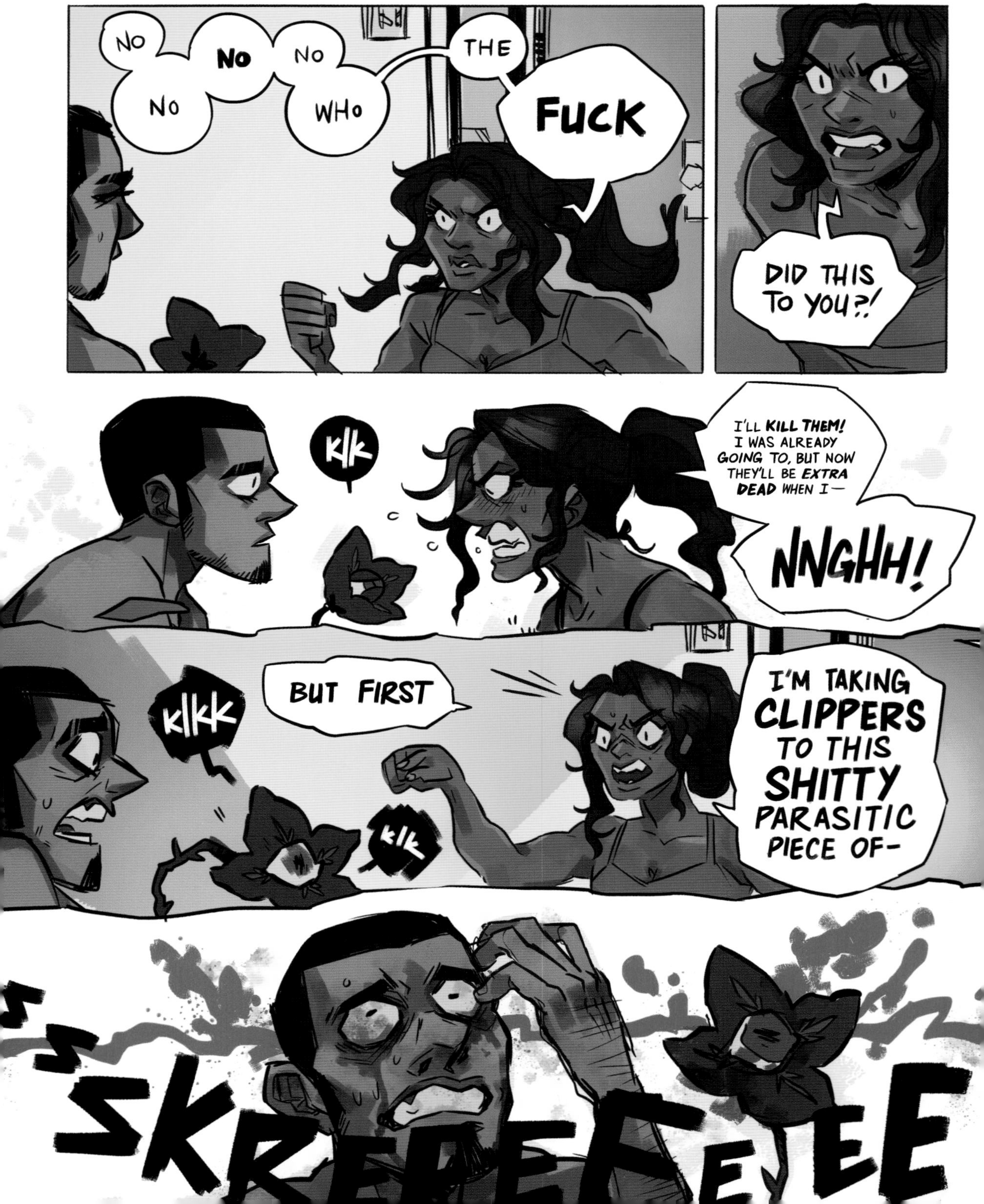
NO
NO
NO
NO
NO
WHO
THE
FUCK
DID THIS TO YOU?!
KLK
I'LL KILL THEM! I WAS ALREADY GOING TO, BUT NOW THEY'LL BE EXTRA DEAD WHEN I—
NNGHH!
KLKK
BUT FIRST
KLK
I'M TAKING CLIPPERS TO THIS SHITTY PARASITIC PIECE OF-
SKREEEEEEE

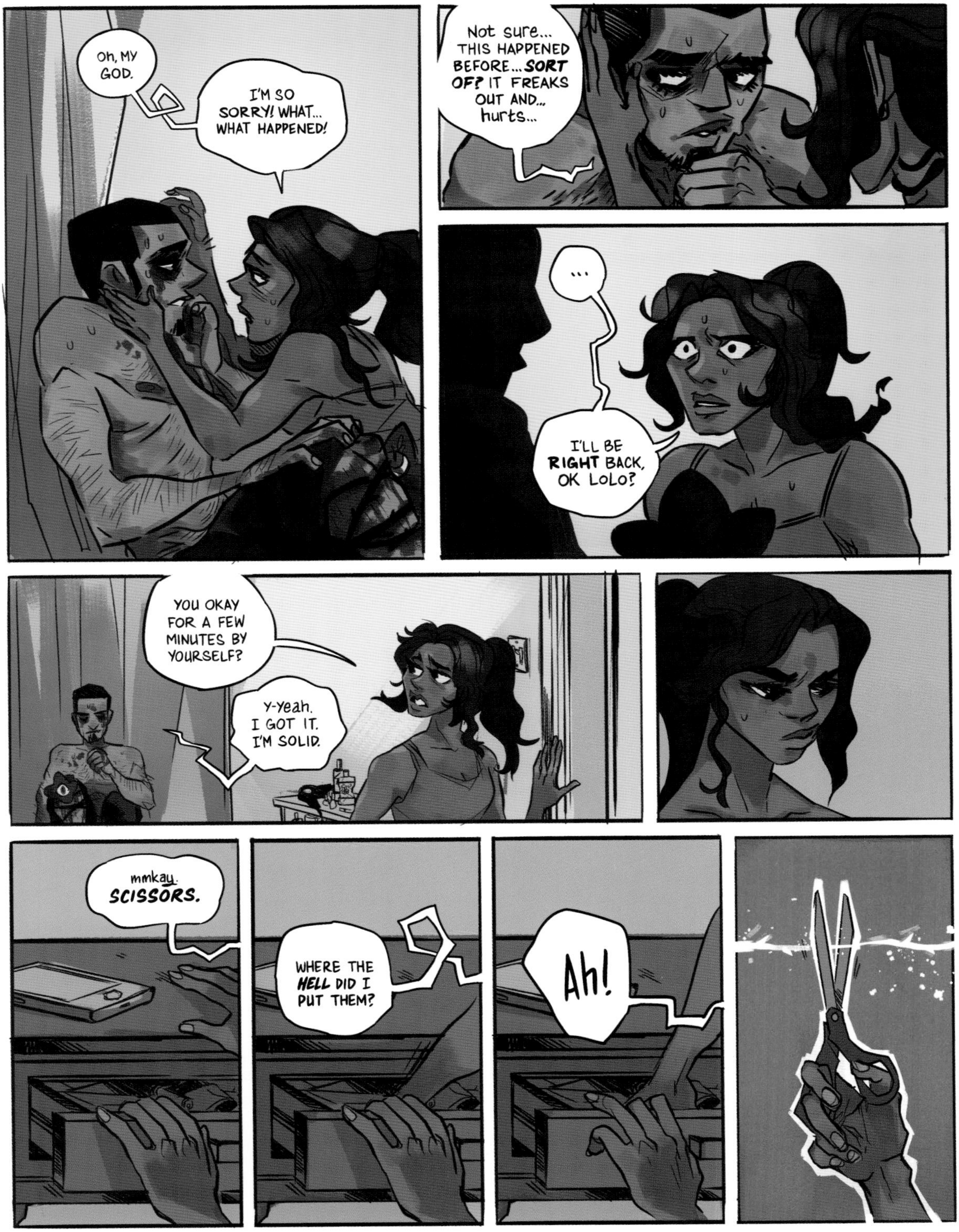
Oh, MY GOD.
I'M SO SORRY! WHAT... WHAT HAPPENED!
Not sure... THIS HAPPENED BEFORE... SORT OF? IT FREAKS OUT AND... hurts...
...
I'LL BE RIGHT BACK, OK LoLo?
YOU OKAY FOR A FEW MINUTES BY YOURSELF?
Y-Yeah. I GOT IT. I'M SOLID.
mmkay. SCISSORS.
WHERE THE HELL DID I PUT THEM?
Ah!

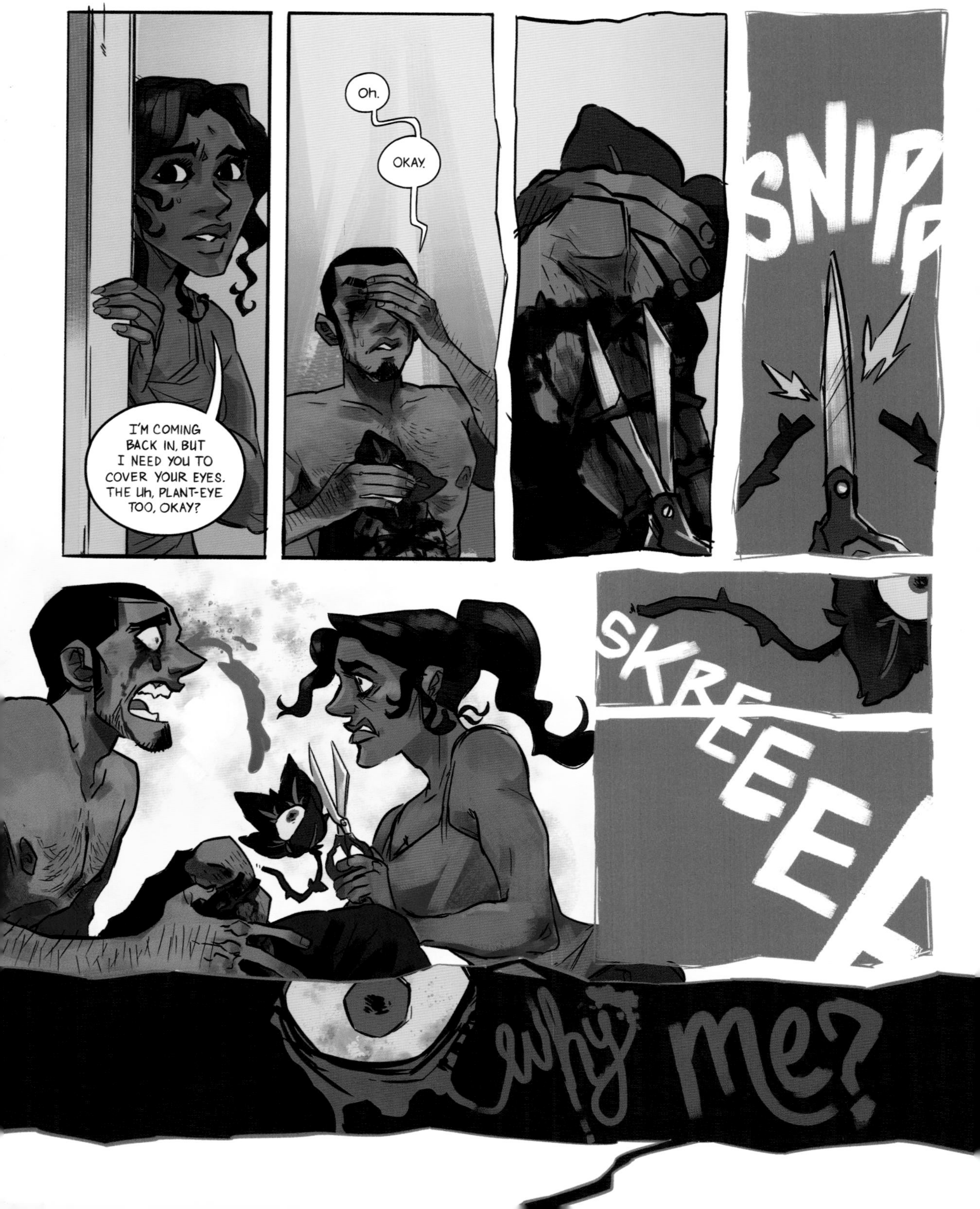
I'M COMING BACK IN, BUT I NEED YOU TO COVER YOUR EYES. THE Uh, PLANT-EYE TOO, OKAY?
Oh.
OKAY.
SNIPP
SKREEEE
why me?

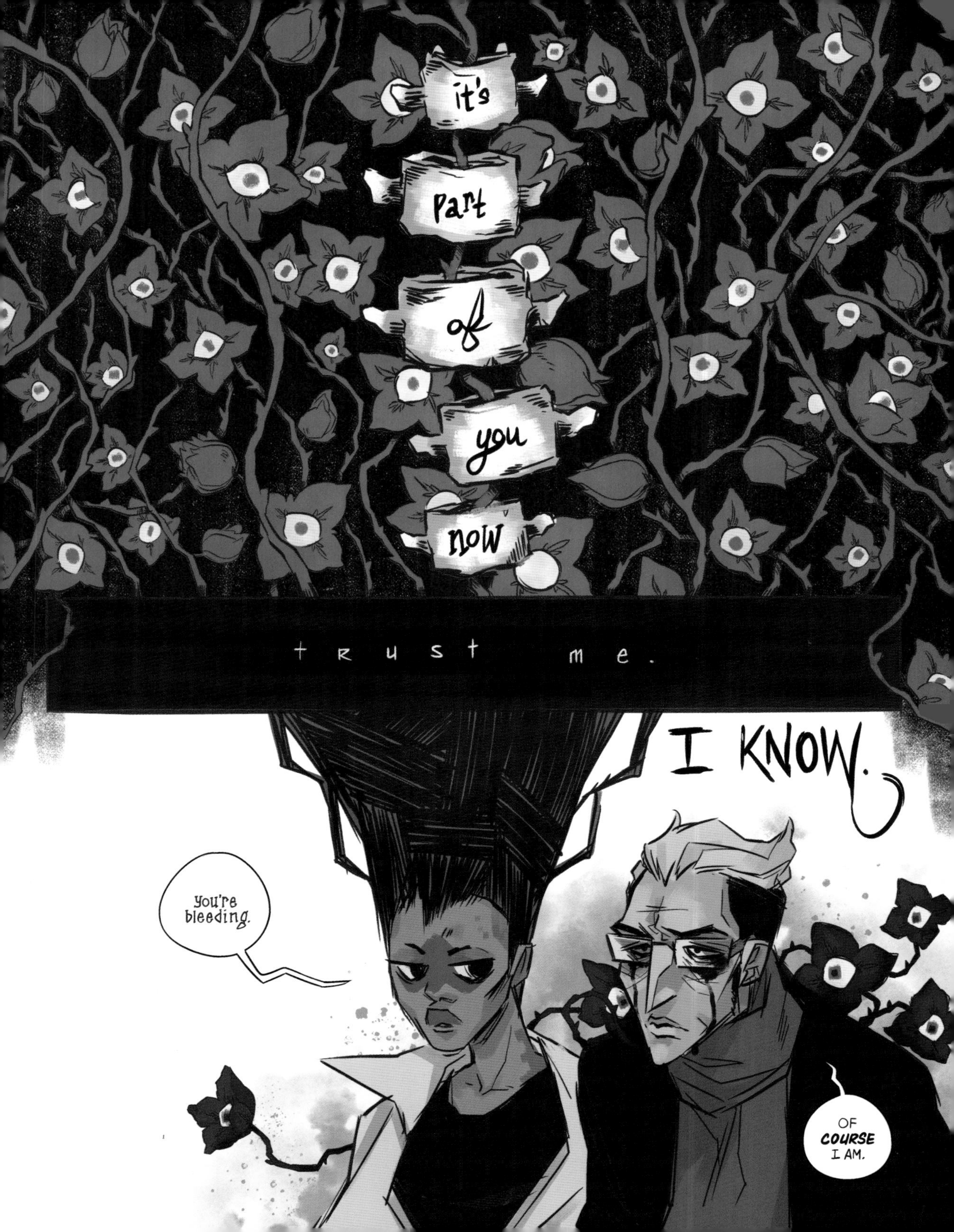
it's
part
of
you
now
trust me.
I KNOW.
you're bleeding.
OF COURSE I AM.

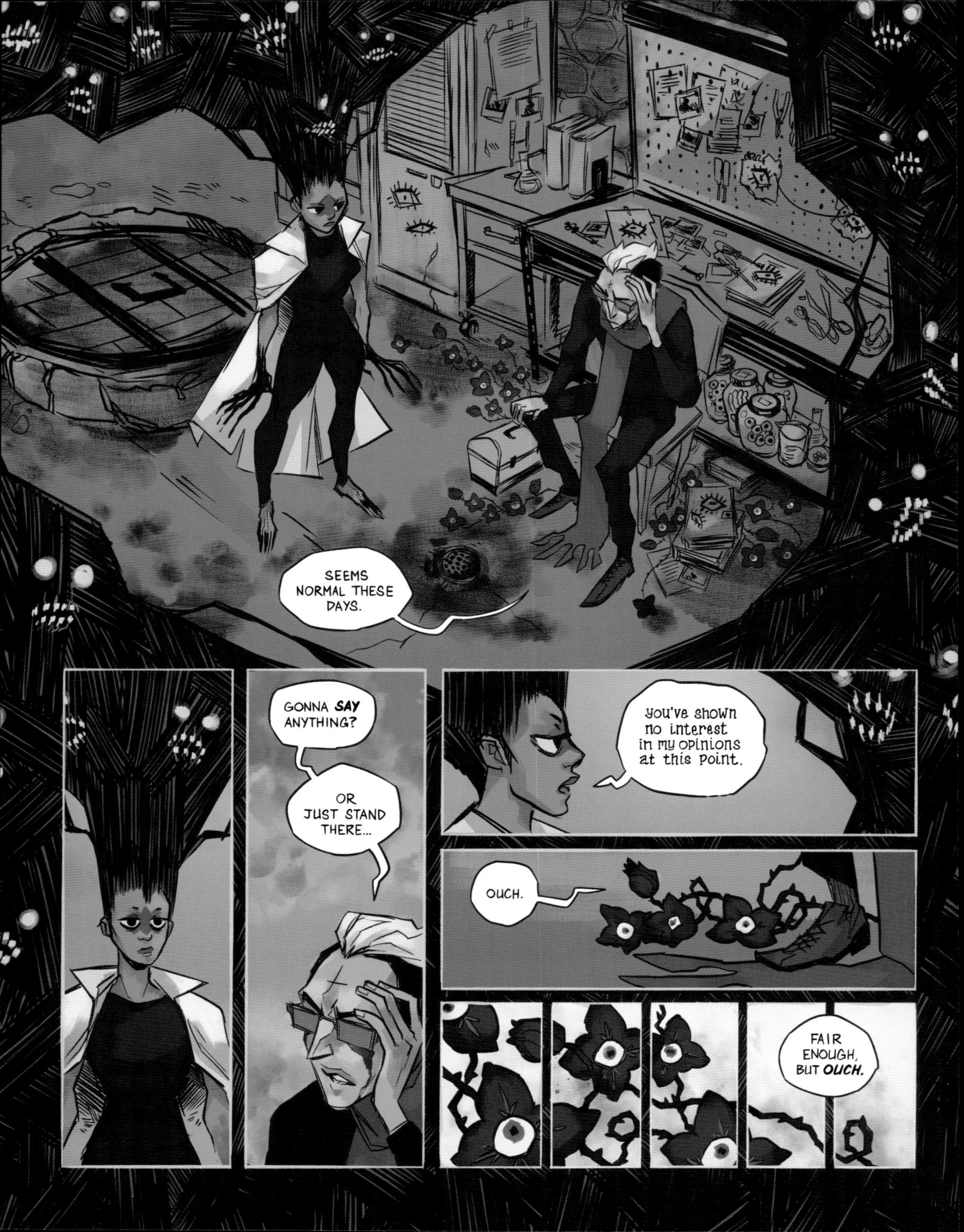
SEEMS NORMAL THESE DAYS.
GONNA **SAY** ANYTHING?
OR JUST STAND THERE...
You've shown no interest in my opinions at this point.
OUCH.
FAIR ENOUGH, BUT **OUCH.**

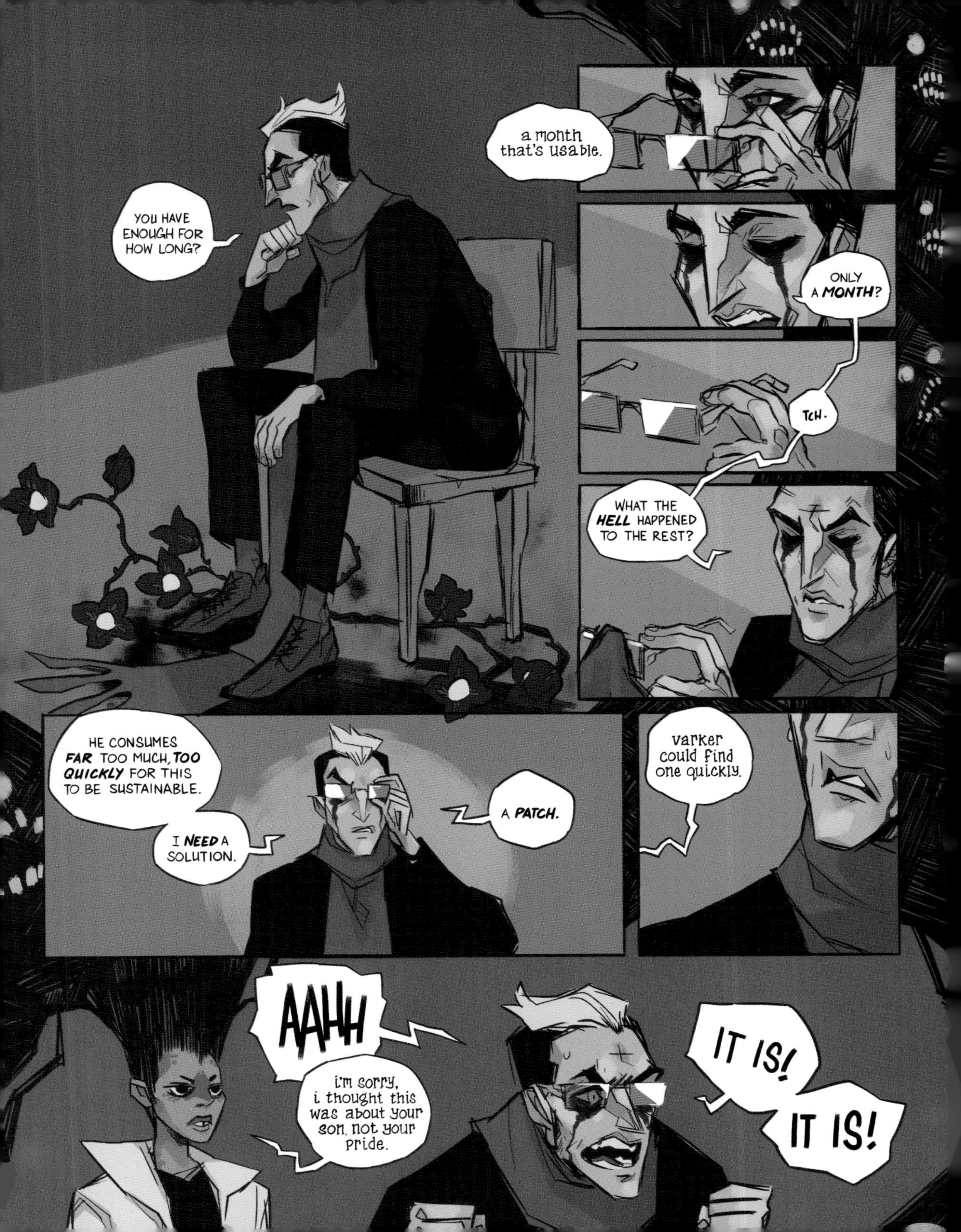
YOU HAVE ENOUGH FOR HOW LONG?
a month that's usable.
ONLY A **MONTH**?
TCH.
WHAT THE **HELL** HAPPENED TO THE REST?
HE CONSUMES **FAR** TOO MUCH, **TOO QUICKLY** FOR THIS TO BE SUSTAINABLE.
I **NEED** A SOLUTION.
A **PATCH.**
varker could find one quickly.
AAHH
i'm sorry, i thought this was about your son, not your pride.
IT IS!
IT IS!

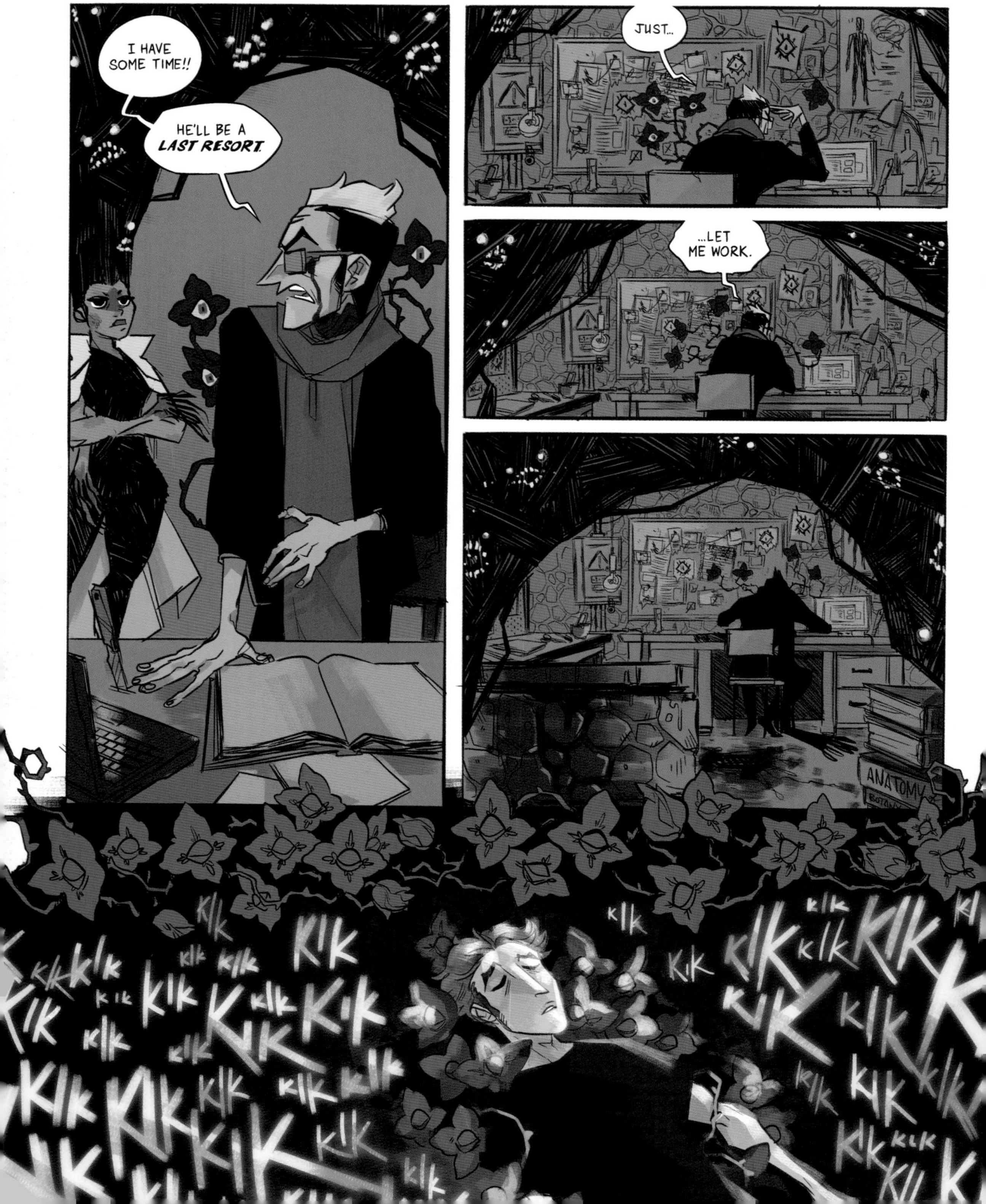
I HAVE SOME TIME!!
HE'LL BE A *LAST RESORT.*
JUST...
...LET ME WORK.
ANATOMY
KIK KIK KIK

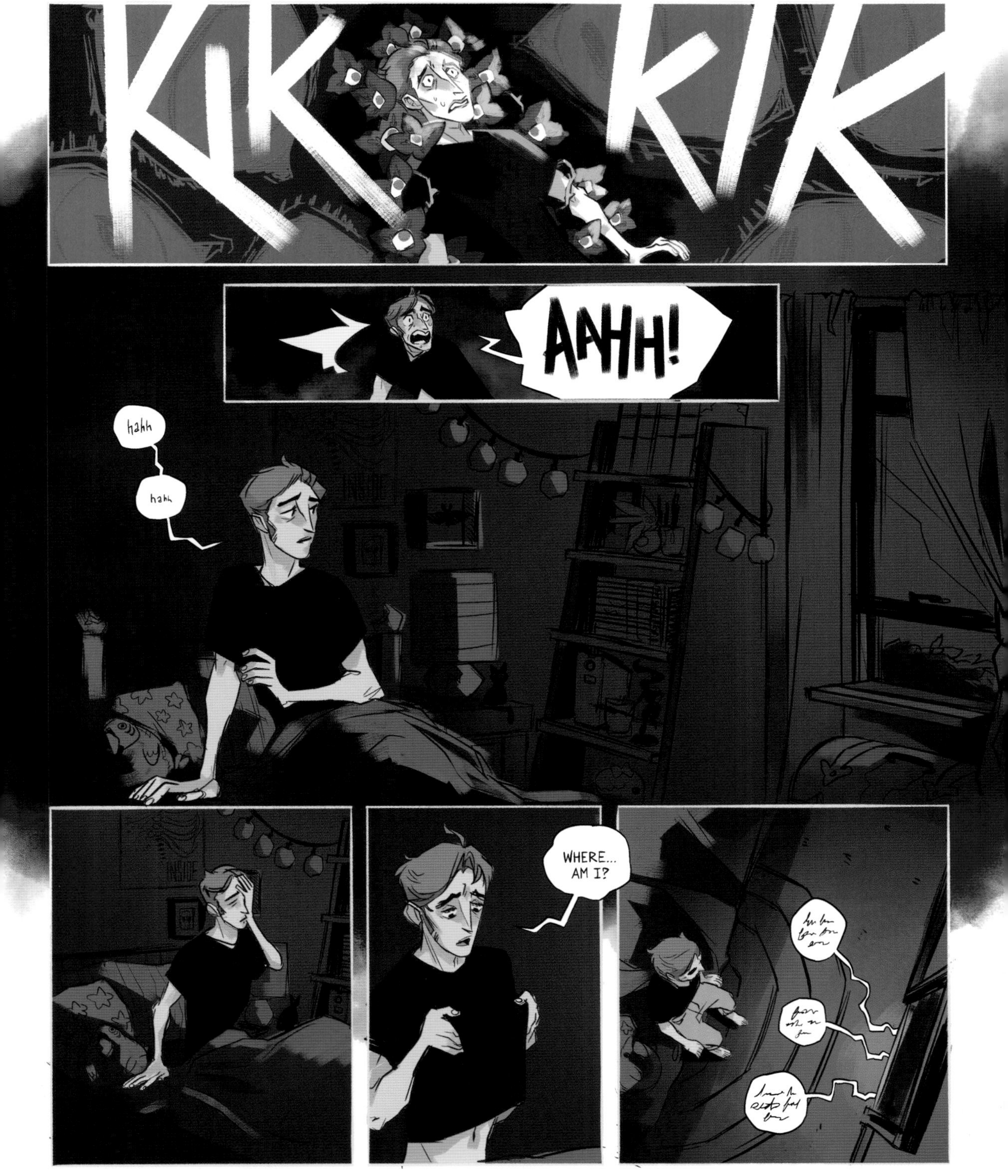
KIK
KIK
AAHH!
hahh
hahh
WHERE... AM I?

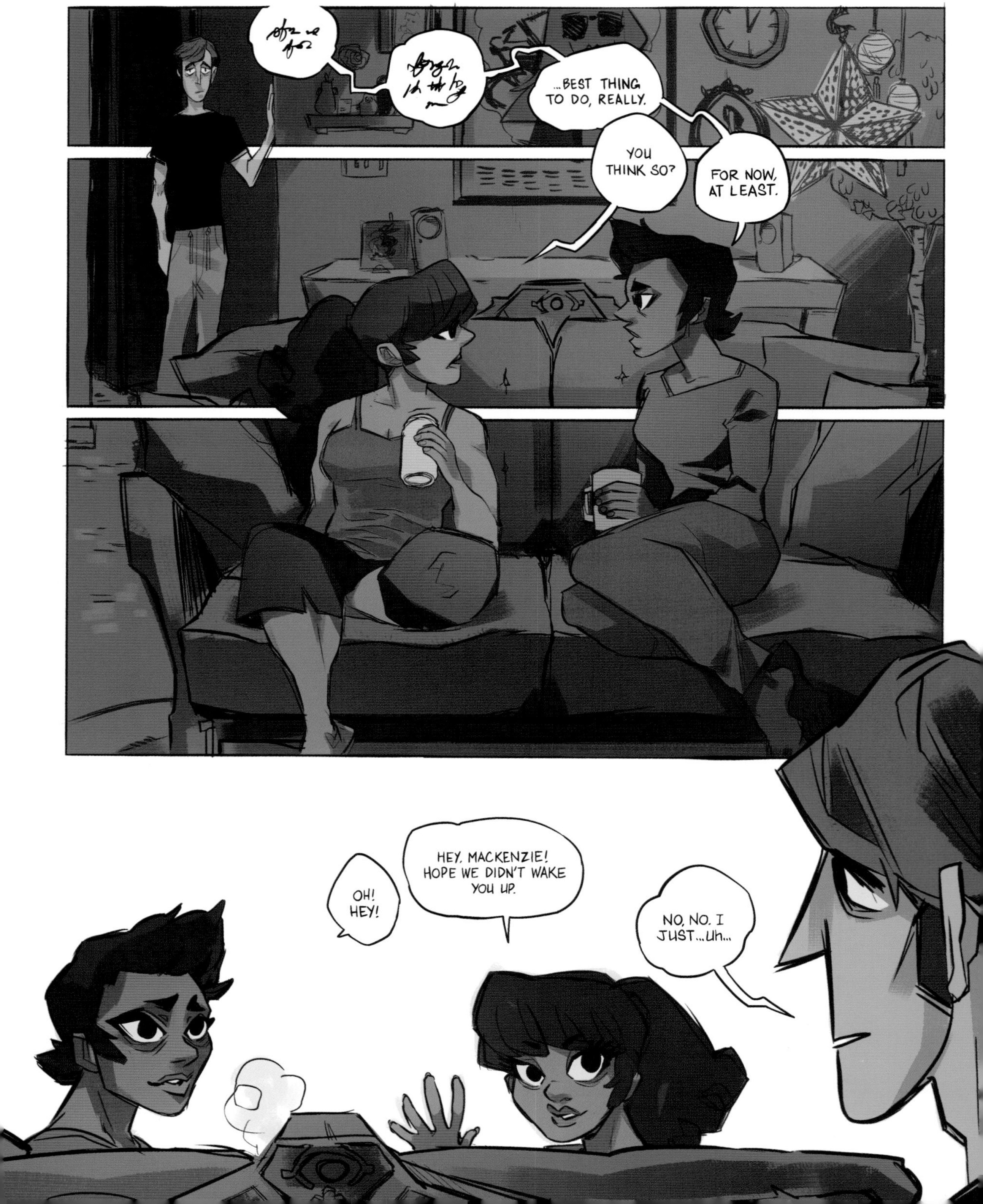
...BEST THING TO DO, REALLY.
YOU THINK SO?
FOR NOW, AT LEAST.
OH! HEY!
HEY, MACKENZIE! HOPE WE DIDN'T WAKE YOU UP.
NO, NO. I JUST...uh...

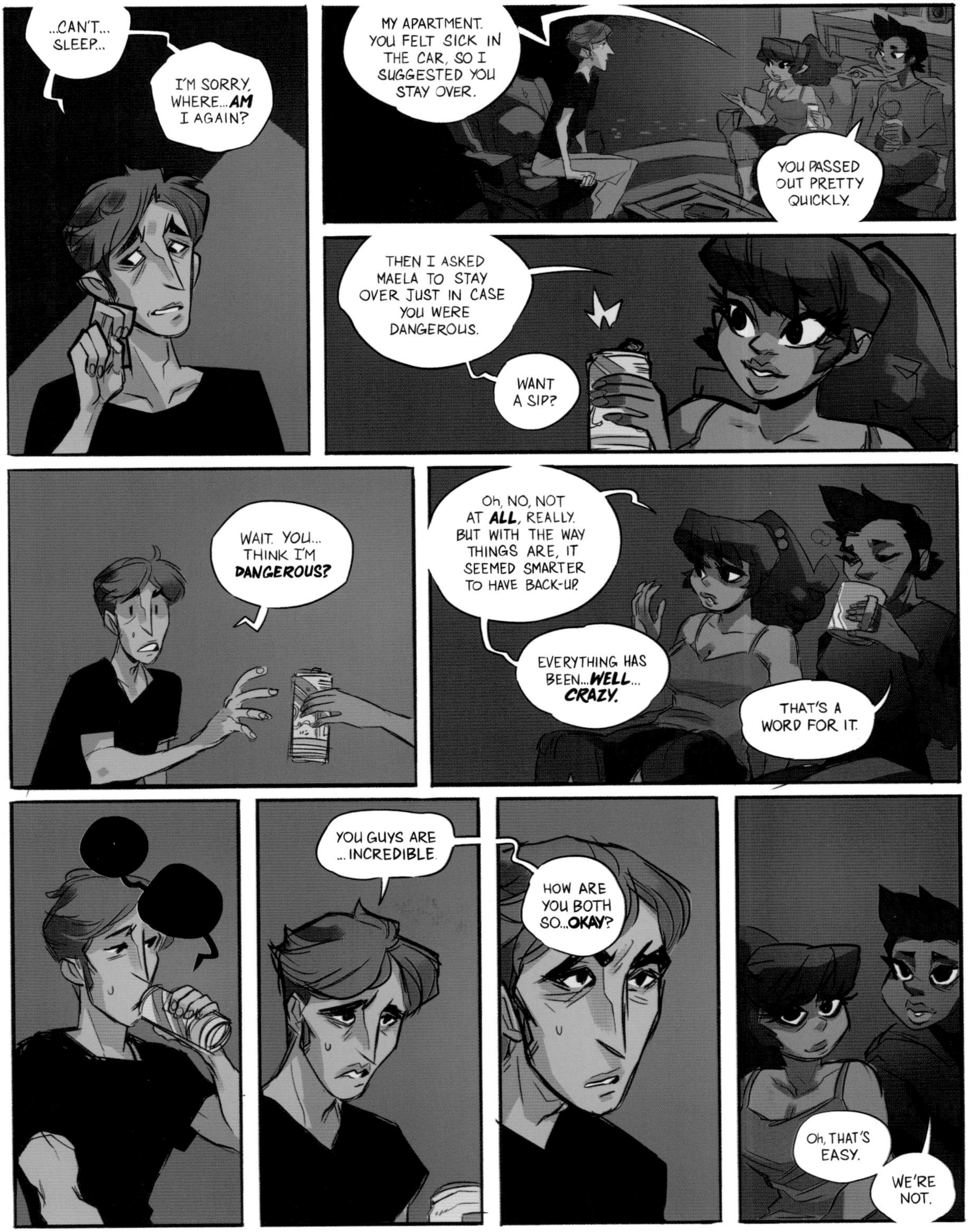

...CAN'T... SLEEP...
I'M SORRY, WHERE...AM I AGAIN?
MY APARTMENT. YOU FELT SICK IN THE CAR, SO I SUGGESTED YOU STAY OVER.
YOU PASSED OUT PRETTY QUICKLY.
THEN I ASKED MAELA TO STAY OVER JUST IN CASE YOU WERE DANGEROUS.
WANT A SIP?
WAIT. YOU... THINK I'M DANGEROUS?
Oh, NO, NOT AT ALL, REALLY. BUT WITH THE WAY THINGS ARE, IT SEEMED SMARTER TO HAVE BACK-UP.
EVERYTHING HAS BEEN...WELL... CRAZY.
THAT'S A WORD FOR IT.
YOU GUYS ARE ...INCREDIBLE.
HOW ARE YOU BOTH SO...OKAY?
Oh, THAT'S EASY.
WE'RE NOT.

I MEAN, WE **WILL BE** OKAY, I THINK.

BUT NOT RIGHT **NOW.** IT'S JUST... GUESS WE'RE...

I **HOPE.**

SHELLSHOCKED? A COPING MECHANISM. IT'S LIKE WHEN YOU'RE RUNNING A MARATHON AND KNOW THAT IF YOU STOP FOR EVEN A **SECOND** TO REALIZE HOW **TIRED** YOU ARE, YOU'LL **NEVER** START RUNNING AGAIN?

IT'S HARD TO BELIEVE THAT IT'S OVER—JUST **LIKE THAT.** IT FEELS LIKE **SOMETHING** NEW IS CREEPING AROUND THE CORNER.

SO IT JUST SEEMS LIKE WE HAVE TO KEEP IT TOGETHER LONG ENOUGH TO BE PROACTIVE.

MY FATHER... HE'S STILL **OUT THERE,** ISN'T HE?

I'M SCARED TO CHECK THE NEWS. TO READ **ANYTHING** ABOUT IT.

I'M...**SO SORRY.** FOR WHAT HE PUT YOU ALL THROUGH.

MACKENZIE...

YOU ARE **NOT** YOUR FATHER, AND THEREFORE DO NOT HAVE TO APOLOGIZE FOR HIM.

WHAT'S... WHAT'S EVEN **LEFT?**

WERE WE THE ONLY SURVIVORS?

IT...APPEARS SO, THOUGH NOT MANY OFFICIAL STATEMENTS HAVE COME FROM THE POLICE THAT AREN'T INCREDIBLY VAGUE. THEY'RE CLEARLY REELING.

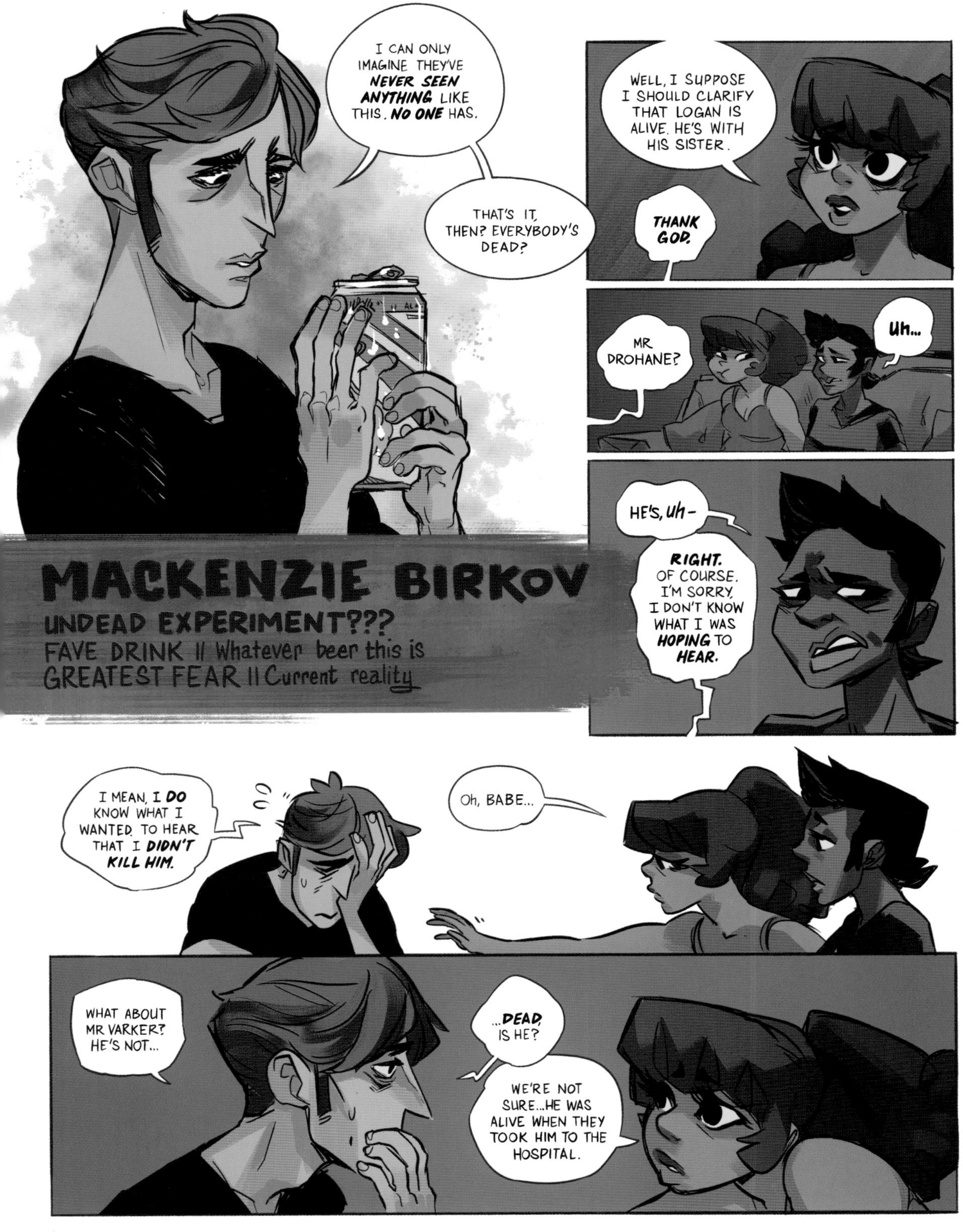
I CAN ONLY IMAGINE THEY'VE **NEVER SEEN ANYTHING** LIKE THIS. **NO ONE** HAS.
THAT'S IT, THEN? EVERYBODY'S DEAD?
MACKENZIE BIRKOV
UNDEAD EXPERIMENT???
FAVE DRINK // Whatever beer this is
GREATEST FEAR // Current reality
WELL, I SUPPOSE I SHOULD CLARIFY THAT LOGAN IS ALIVE. HE'S WITH HIS SISTER.
THANK GOD.
MR DROHANE?
Uh...
HE'S, uh-
RIGHT. OF COURSE. I'M SORRY, I DON'T KNOW WHAT I WAS **HOPING** TO **HEAR.**
I MEAN, I **DO** KNOW WHAT I WANTED TO HEAR THAT I **DIDN'T KILL HIM.**
Oh, BABE...
WHAT ABOUT MR VARKER? HE'S NOT...
...**DEAD,** IS HE?
WE'RE NOT SURE...HE WAS ALIVE WHEN THEY TOOK HIM TO THE HOSPITAL.

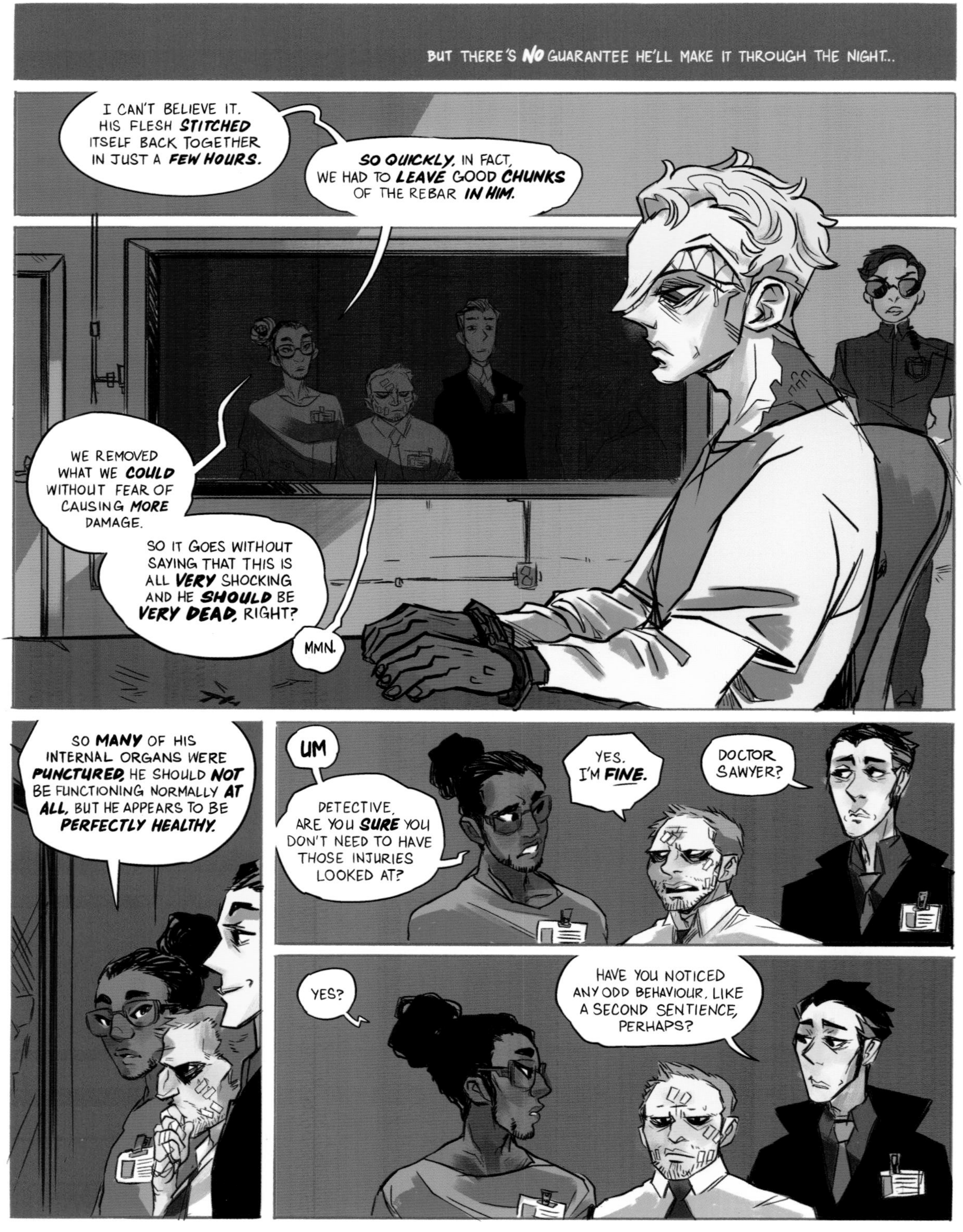
BUT THERE'S NO GUARANTEE HE'LL MAKE IT THROUGH THE NIGHT...
I CAN'T BELIEVE IT. HIS FLESH STITCHED ITSELF BACK TOGETHER IN JUST A FEW HOURS.
SO QUICKLY, IN FACT, WE HAD TO LEAVE GOOD CHUNKS OF THE REBAR IN HIM.
WE REMOVED WHAT WE COULD WITHOUT FEAR OF CAUSING MORE DAMAGE.
SO IT GOES WITHOUT SAYING THAT THIS IS ALL VERY SHOCKING AND HE SHOULD BE VERY DEAD, RIGHT?
MMN.
SO MANY OF HIS INTERNAL ORGANS WERE PUNCTURED, HE SHOULD NOT BE FUNCTIONING NORMALLY AT ALL, BUT HE APPEARS TO BE PERFECTLY HEALTHY.
UM
DETECTIVE, ARE YOU SURE YOU DON'T NEED TO HAVE THOSE INJURIES LOOKED AT?
YES. I'M FINE.
DOCTOR SAWYER?
YES?
HAVE YOU NOTICED ANY ODD BEHAVIOUR, LIKE A SECOND SENTIENCE, PERHAPS?

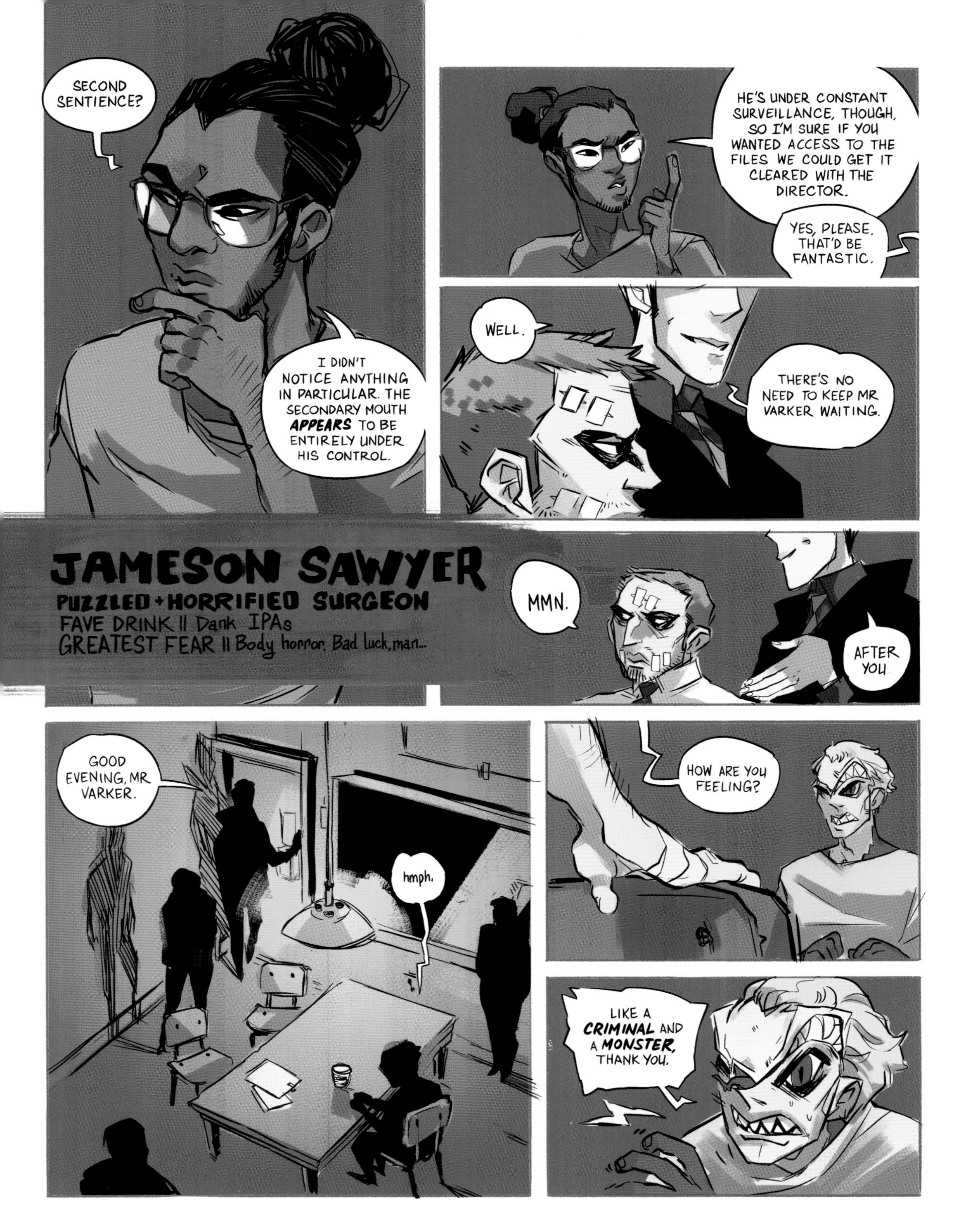
SECOND SENTIENCE?
I DIDN'T NOTICE ANYTHING IN PARTICULAR. THE SECONDARY MOUTH **APPEARS** TO BE ENTIRELY UNDER HIS CONTROL.
HE'S UNDER CONSTANT SURVEILLANCE, THOUGH, SO I'M SURE IF YOU WANTED ACCESS TO THE FILES WE COULD GET IT CLEARED WITH THE DIRECTOR.
YES, PLEASE. THAT'D BE FANTASTIC.
WELL.
THERE'S NO NEED TO KEEP MR VARKER WAITING.
JAMESON SAWYER
PUZZLED + HORRIFIED SURGEON
FAVE DRINK // Dank IPAs
GREATEST FEAR // Body horror. Bad luck, man...
MMN.
AFTER YOU.
GOOD EVENING, MR VARKER.
hmph.
HOW ARE YOU FEELING?
LIKE A **CRIMINAL** AND A **MONSTER**, THANK YOU.

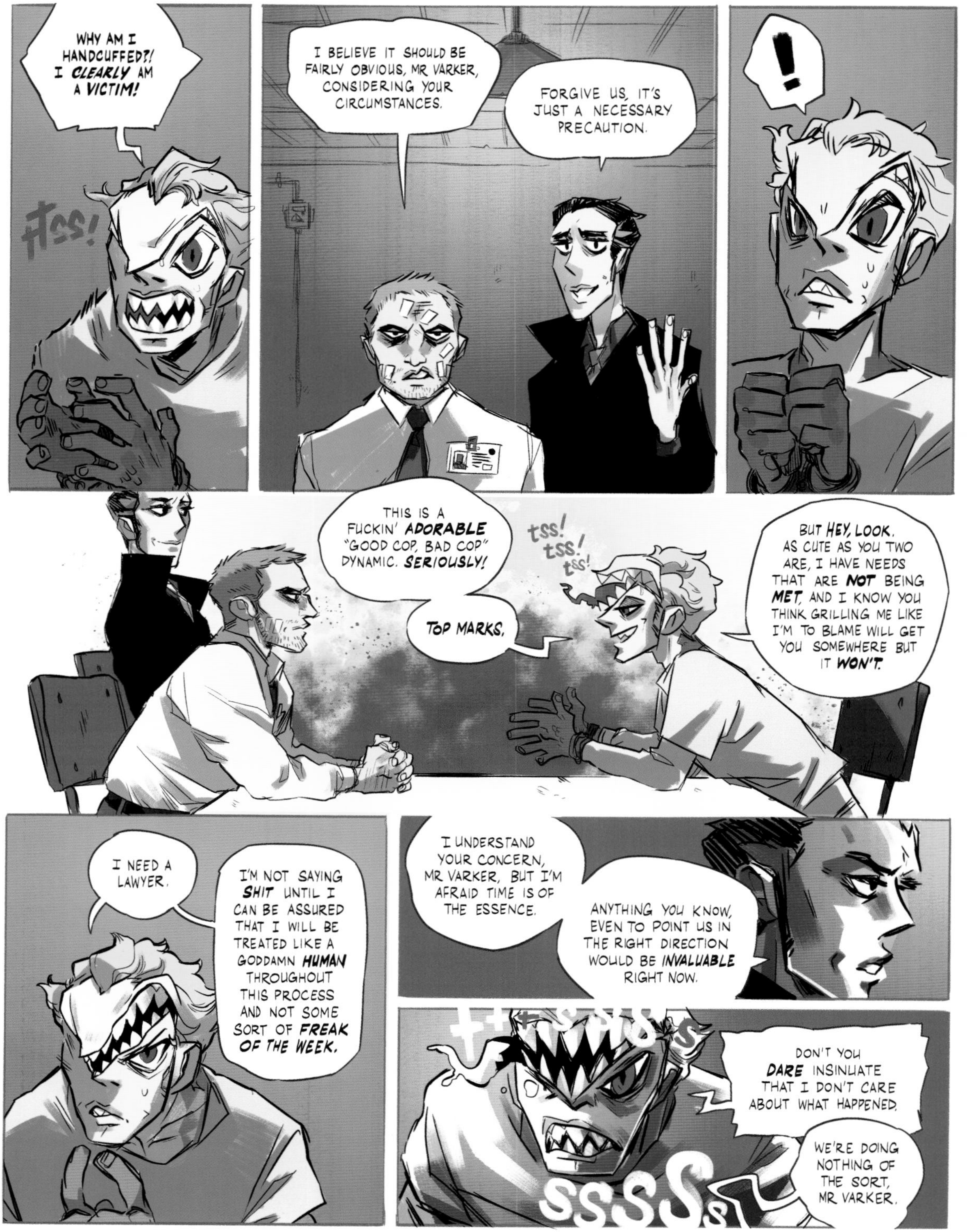
WHY AM I HANDCUFFED?! I CLEARLY AM A VICTIM!
ftss!
I BELIEVE IT SHOULD BE FAIRLY OBVIOUS, MR VARKER, CONSIDERING YOUR CIRCUMSTANCES.
FORGIVE US, IT'S JUST A NECESSARY PRECAUTION.
!
THIS IS A FUCKIN' ADORABLE "GOOD COP, BAD COP" DYNAMIC. SERIOUSLY!
TOP MARKS.
tss! tss! tss!
BUT HEY, LOOK. AS CUTE AS YOU TWO ARE, I HAVE NEEDS THAT ARE NOT BEING MET, AND I KNOW YOU THINK GRILLING ME LIKE I'M TO BLAME WILL GET YOU SOMEWHERE BUT IT WON'T.
I NEED A LAWYER.
I'M NOT SAYING SHIT UNTIL I CAN BE ASSURED THAT I WILL BE TREATED LIKE A GODDAMN HUMAN THROUGHOUT THIS PROCESS AND NOT SOME SORT OF FREAK OF THE WEEK.
I UNDERSTAND YOUR CONCERN, MR VARKER, BUT I'M AFRAID TIME IS OF THE ESSENCE.
ANYTHING YOU KNOW, EVEN TO POINT US IN THE RIGHT DIRECTION WOULD BE INVALUABLE RIGHT NOW.
DON'T YOU DARE INSINUATE THAT I DON'T CARE ABOUT WHAT HAPPENED.
WE'RE DOING NOTHING OF THE SORT, MR VARKER.
SSSSs

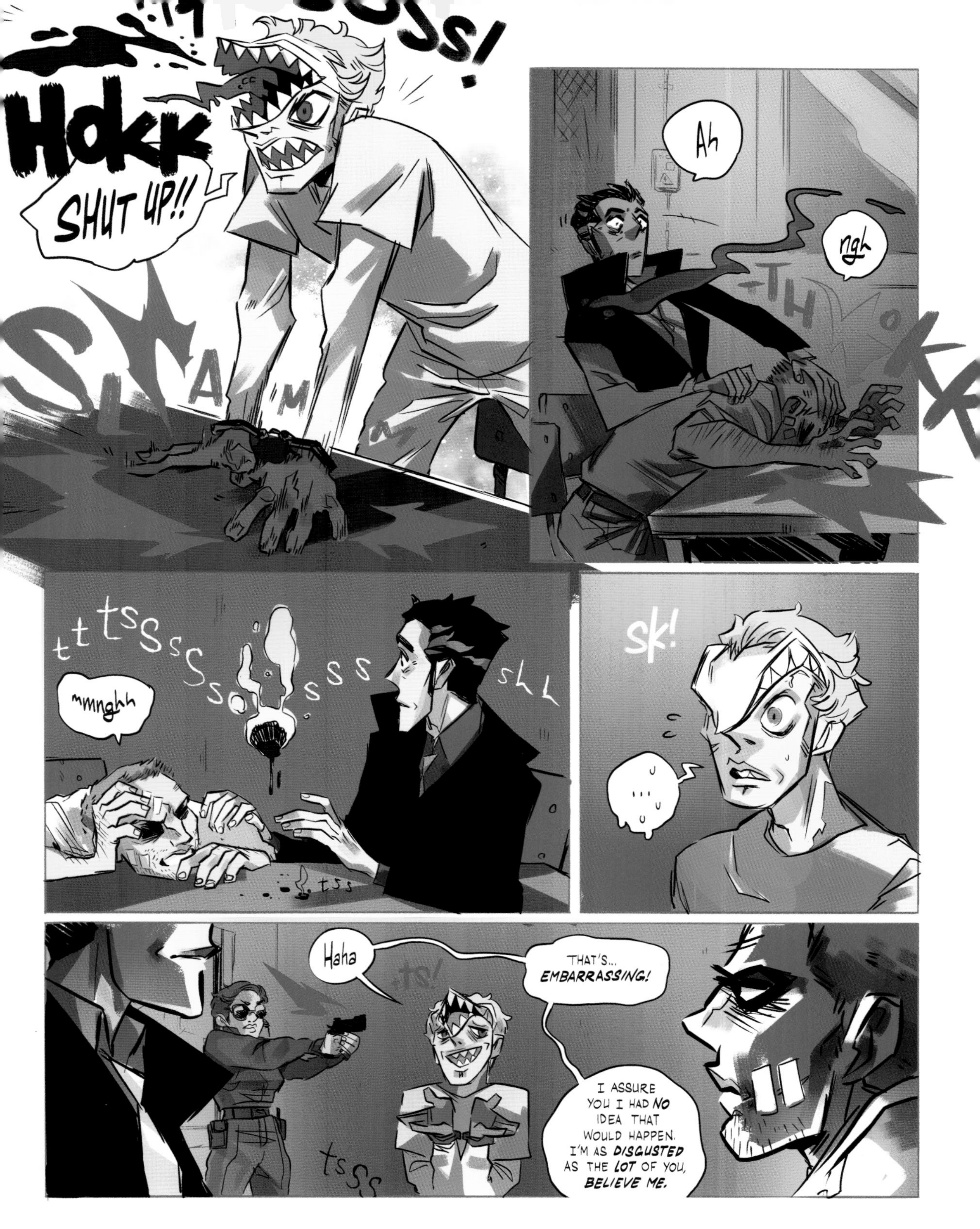

HOKK
SHUT UP!!
SLAM
Ah
ngh
THOKK
ttts SSSsss
mmnghh
shh
tss
sk!
. . .
Haha
tts!
THAT'S... **EMBARRASSING!**
I ASSURE YOU I HAD **NO** IDEA THAT WOULD HAPPEN. I'M AS **DISGUSTED** AS THE **LOT** OF YOU, **BELIEVE ME.**
tsss

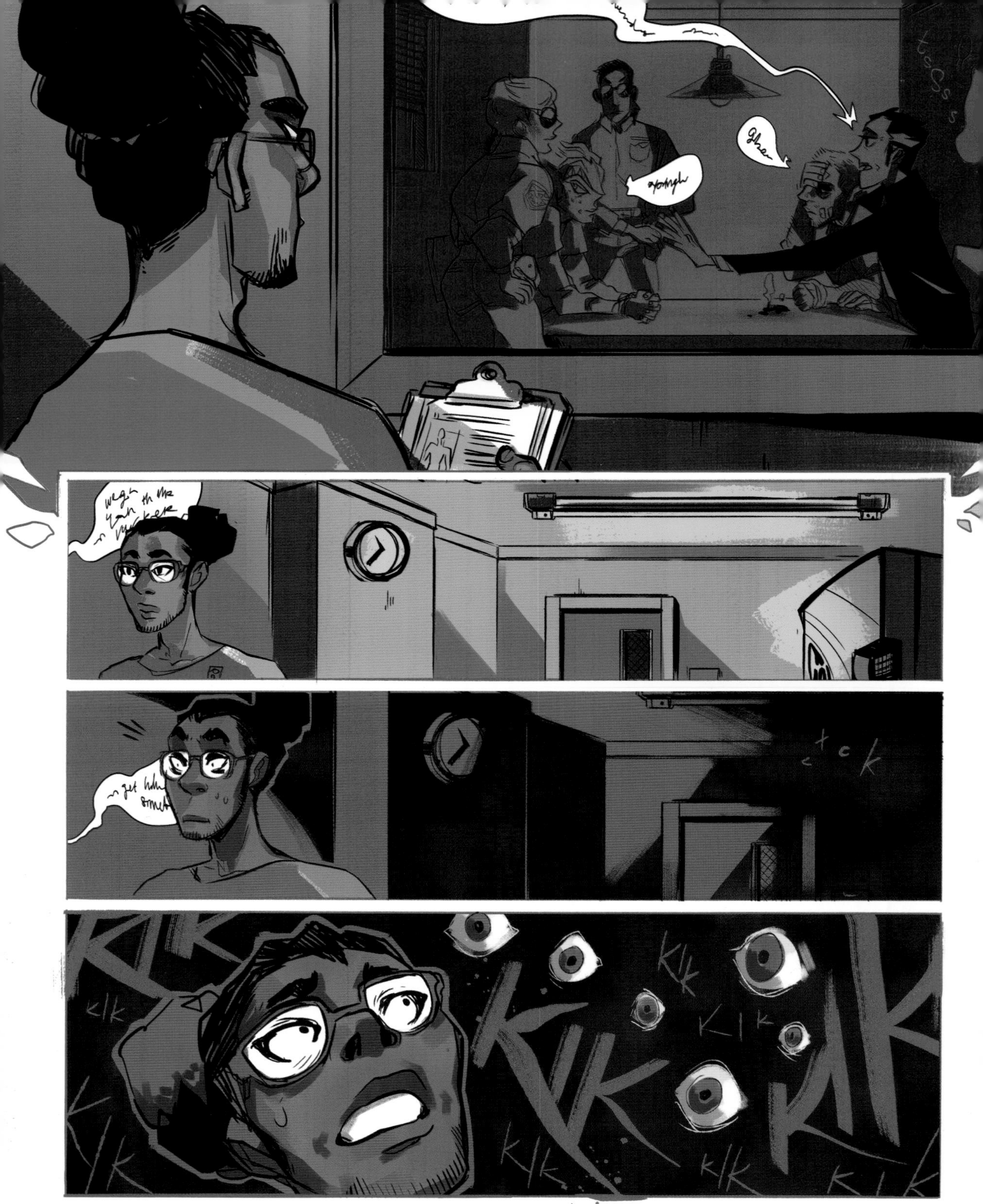

tsSss
tck
KIK
klk

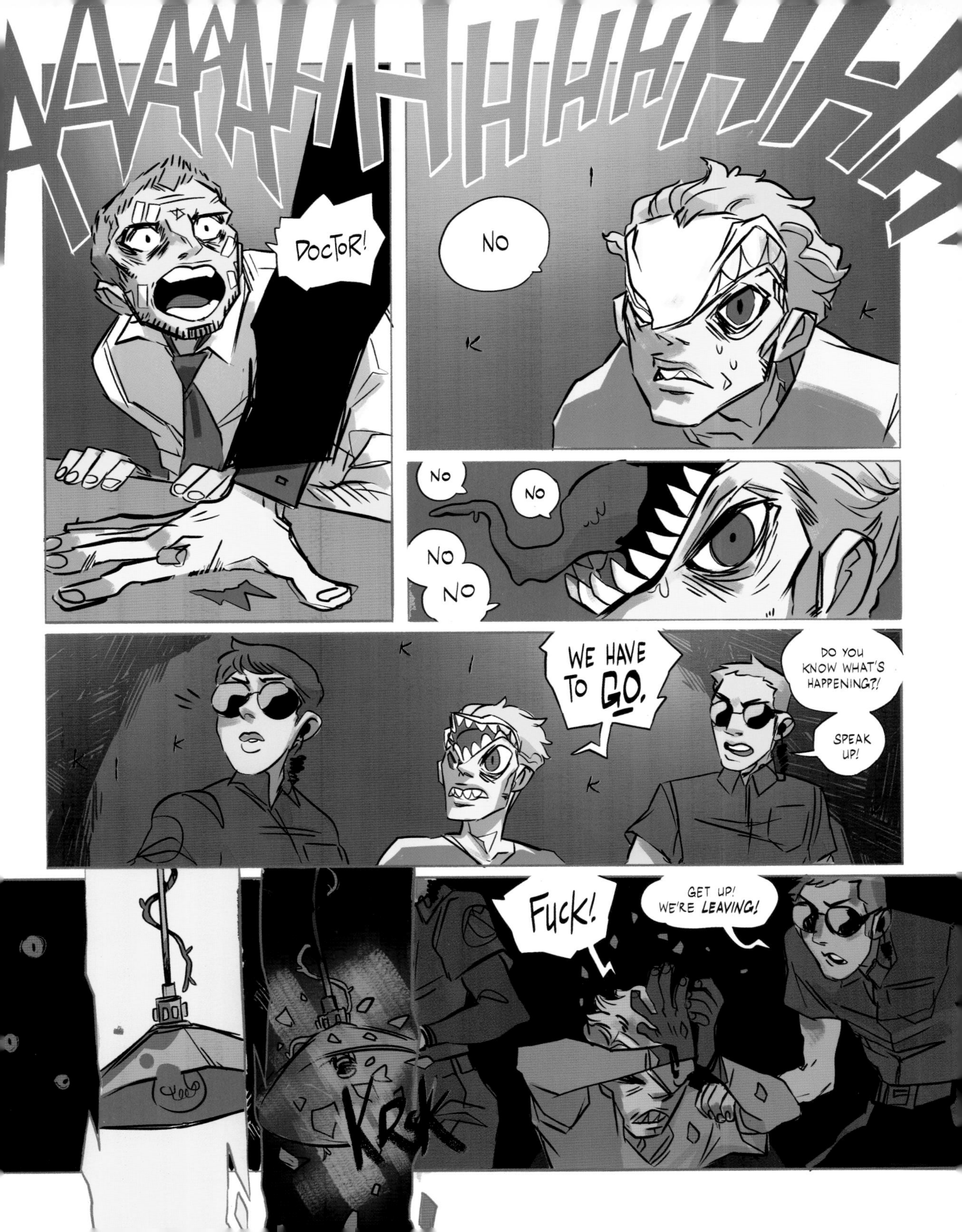
AAAAAHHHHHHHH
DOCTOR!
NO
NO
NO
NO
NO
WE HAVE TO GO.
DO YOU KNOW WHAT'S HAPPENING?!
SPEAK UP!
KRAK
FUCK!
GET UP! WE'RE LEAVING!

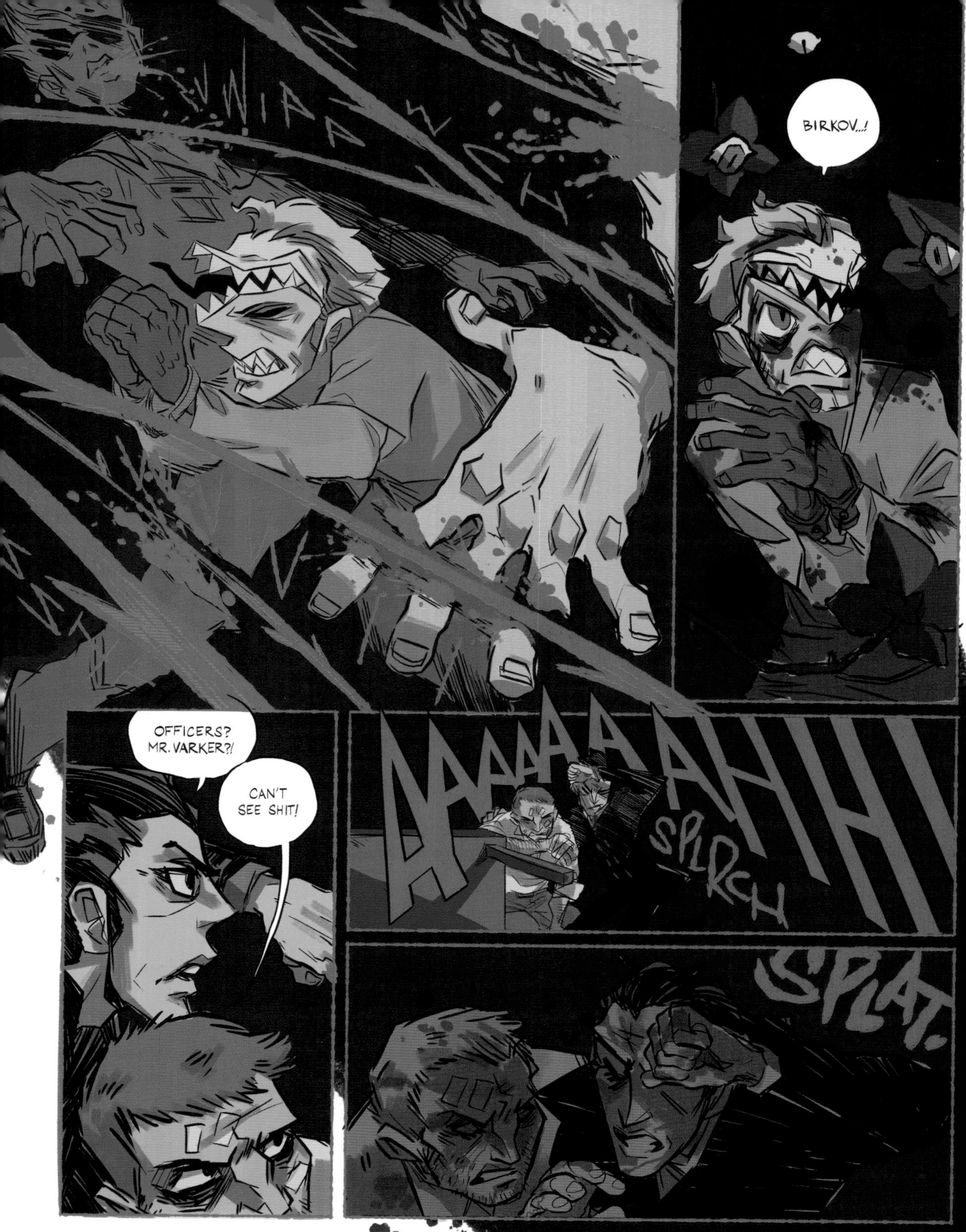
BIRKOV...!
OFFICERS? MR. VARKER?!
CAN'T SEE SHIT!
SPLRCH
SPLAT!

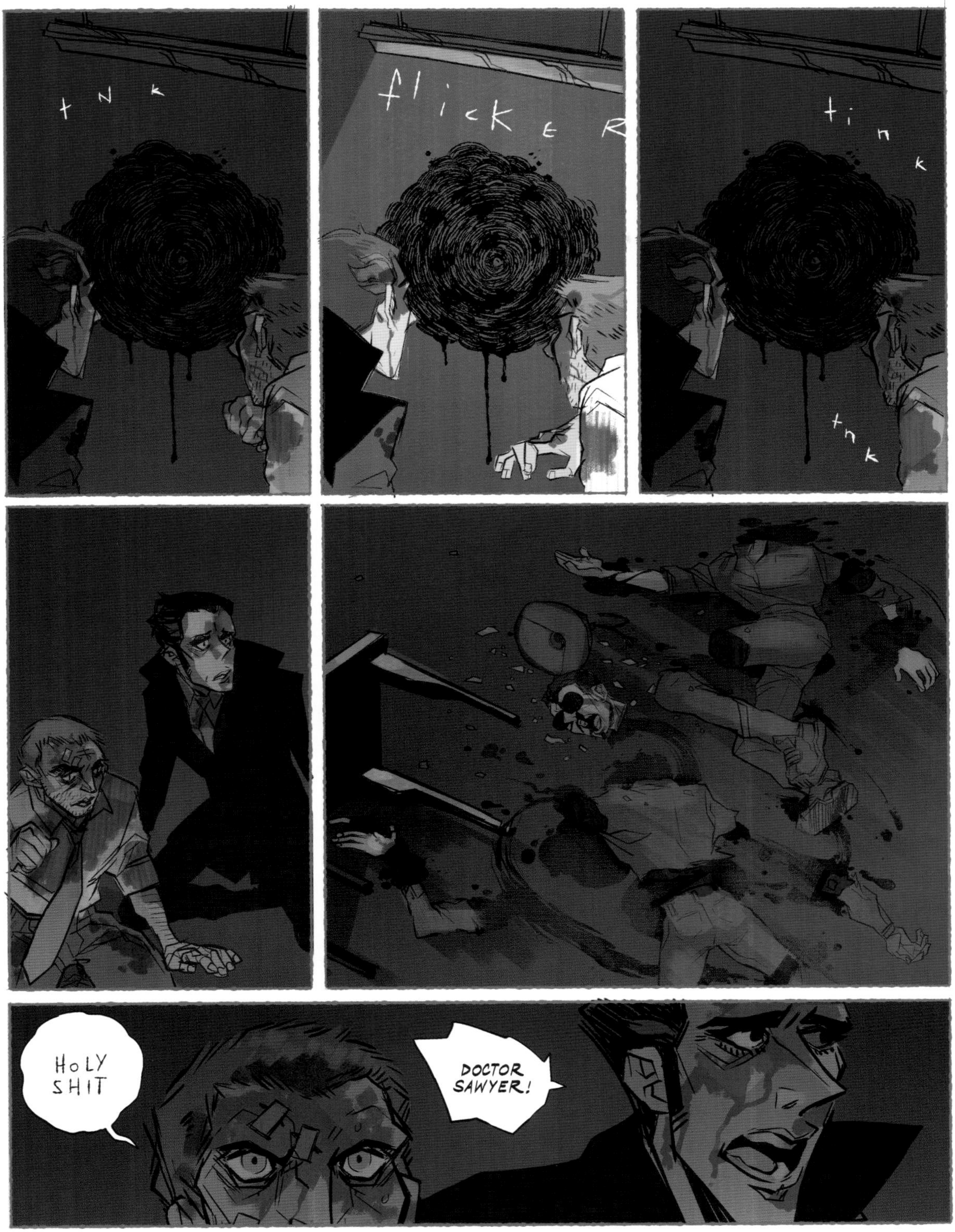
tnk
flicker
tink
tnk
HOLY SHIT
DOCTOR SAWYER!

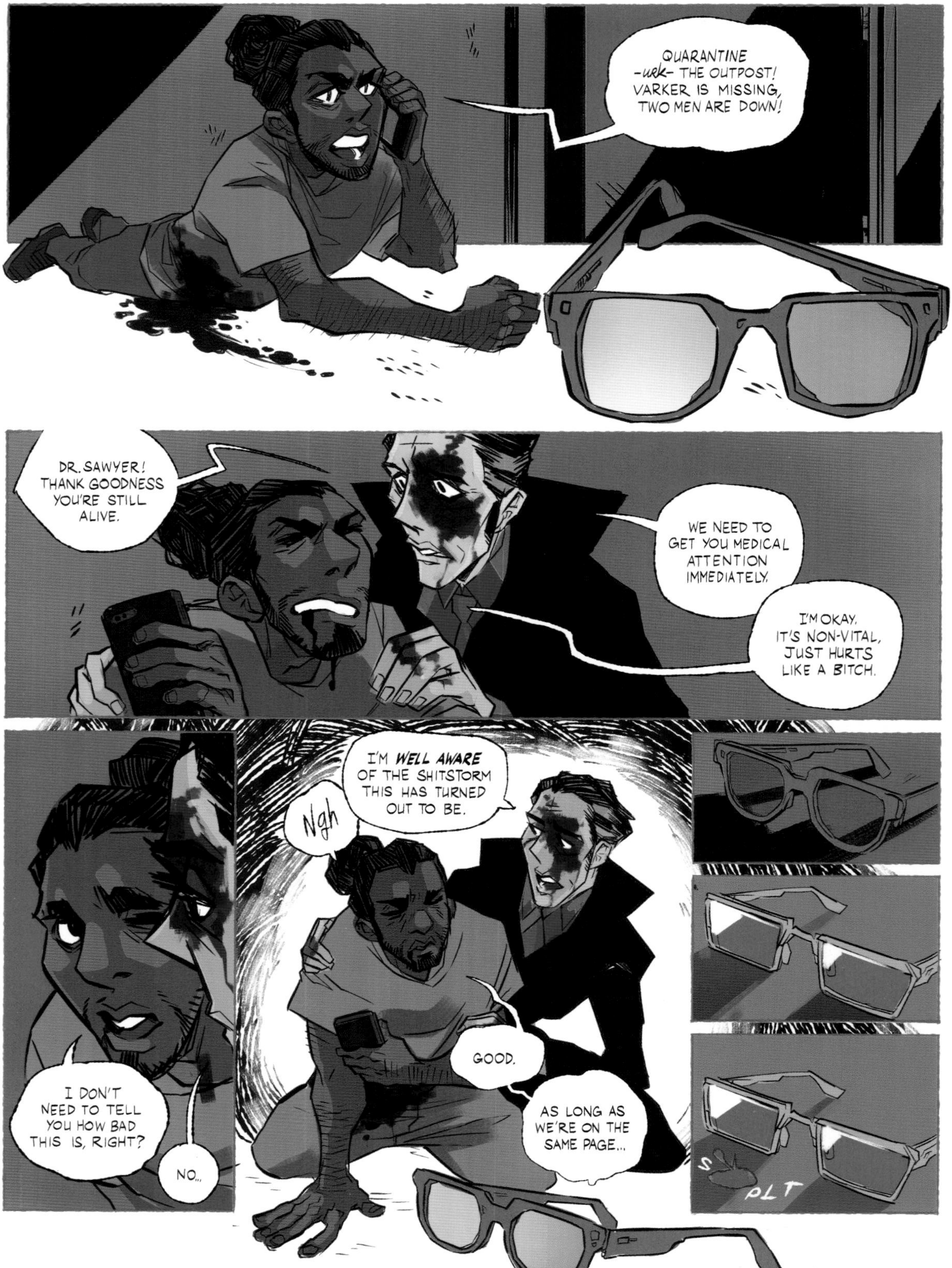
QUARANTINE -urk- THE OUTPOST! VARKER IS MISSING, TWO MEN ARE DOWN!
DR. SAWYER! THANK GOODNESS YOU'RE STILL ALIVE.
WE NEED TO GET YOU MEDICAL ATTENTION IMMEDIATELY.
I'M OKAY. IT'S NON-VITAL, JUST HURTS LIKE A BITCH.
I DON'T NEED TO TELL YOU HOW BAD THIS IS, RIGHT?
NO...
Ngh
I'M **WELL AWARE** OF THE SHITSTORM THIS HAS TURNED OUT TO BE.
GOOD.
AS LONG AS WE'RE ON THE SAME PAGE...
S PLT

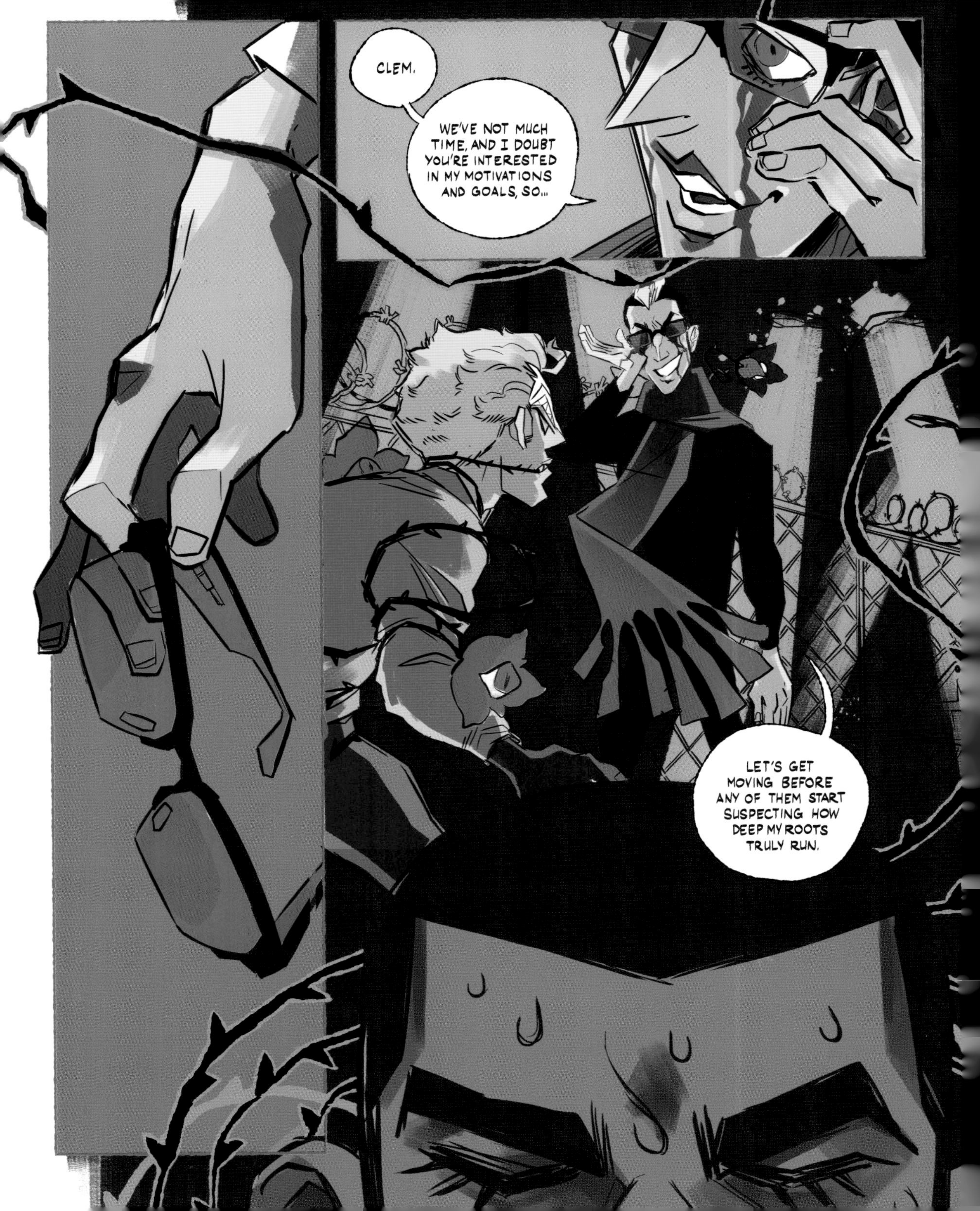
CLEM.
WE'VE NOT MUCH TIME, AND I DOUBT YOU'RE INTERESTED IN MY MOTIVATIONS AND GOALS, SO...
LET'S GET MOVING BEFORE ANY OF THEM START SUSPECTING HOW DEEP MY ROOTS TRULY RUN.

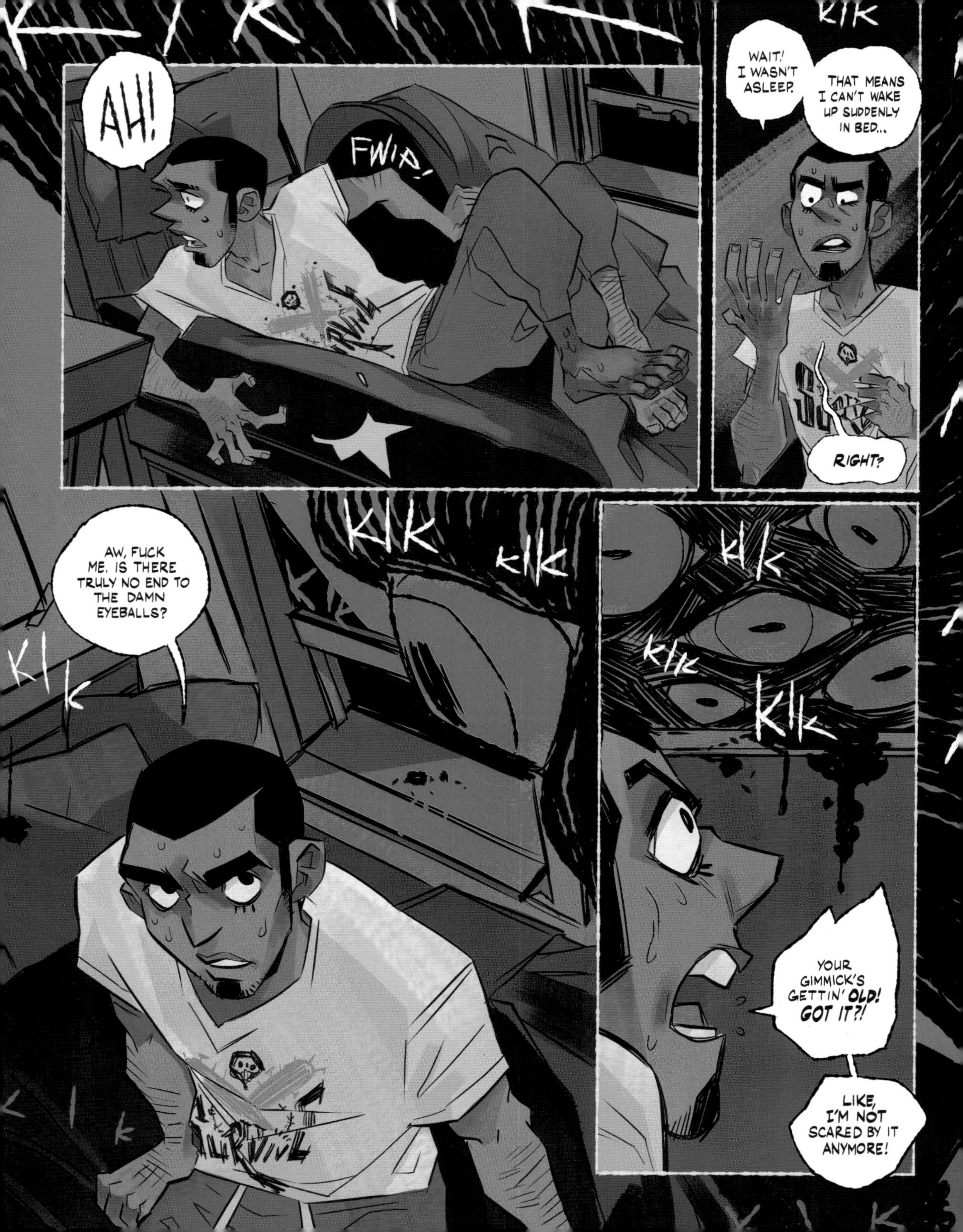
KIK
AH!
FWIP!
WAIT! I WASN'T ASLEEP.
THAT MEANS I CAN'T WAKE UP SUDDENLY IN BED...
RIGHT?
KIK
KIK
AW, FUCK ME. IS THERE TRULY NO END TO THE DAMN EYEBALLS?
KIK
KIK
KIK
KIK
KIK
YOUR GIMMICK'S GETTIN' **OLD! GOT IT?!**
LIKE, I'M NOT SCARED BY IT ANYMORE!

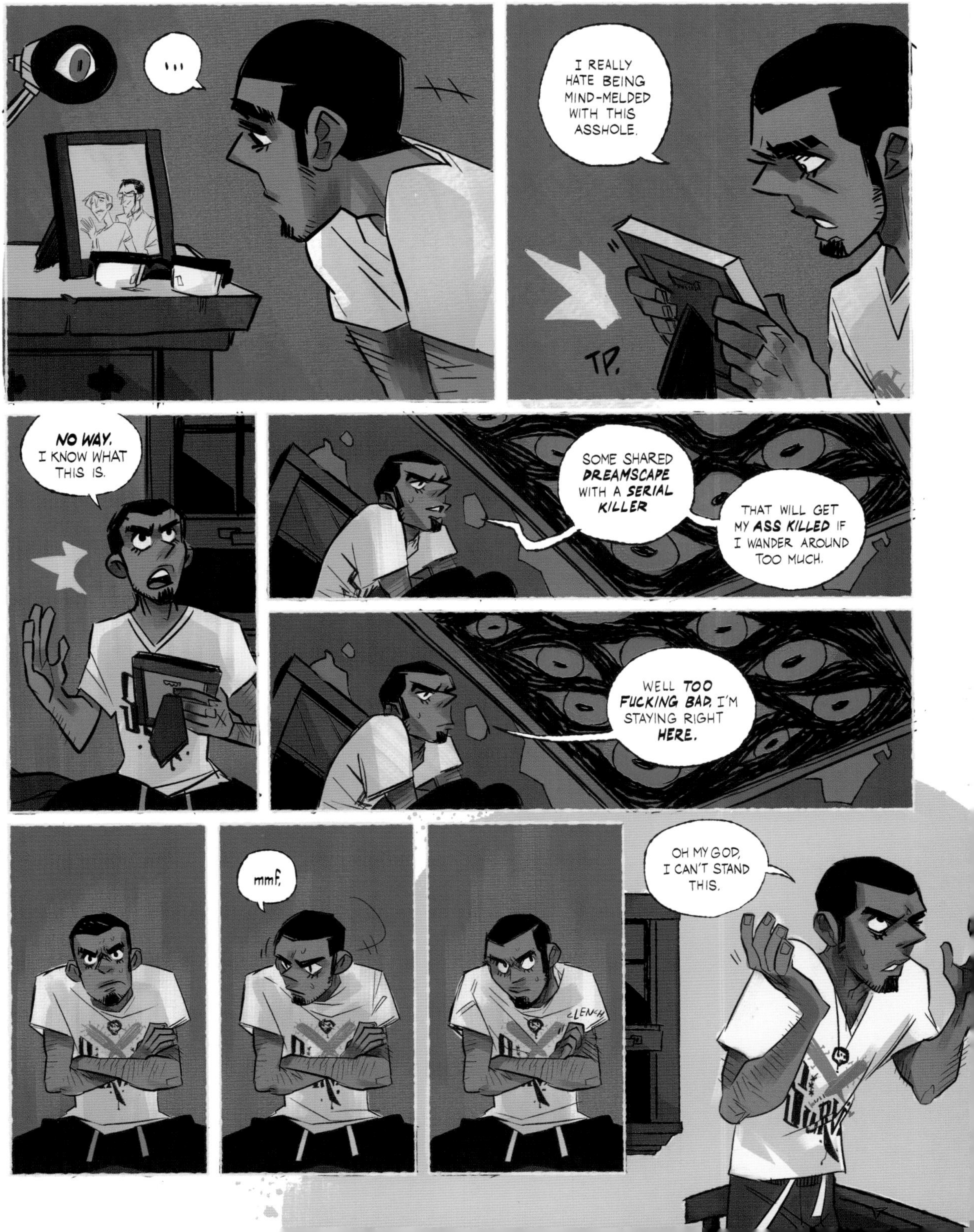
...
I REALLY HATE BEING MIND-MELDED WITH THIS ASSHOLE.
TP.
NO WAY. I KNOW WHAT THIS IS.
SOME SHARED DREAMSCAPE WITH A SERIAL KILLER
THAT WILL GET MY ASS KILLED IF I WANDER AROUND TOO MUCH.
WELL TOO FUCKING BAD, I'M STAYING RIGHT HERE.
mmf.
CLENCH
OH MY GOD, I CAN'T STAND THIS.

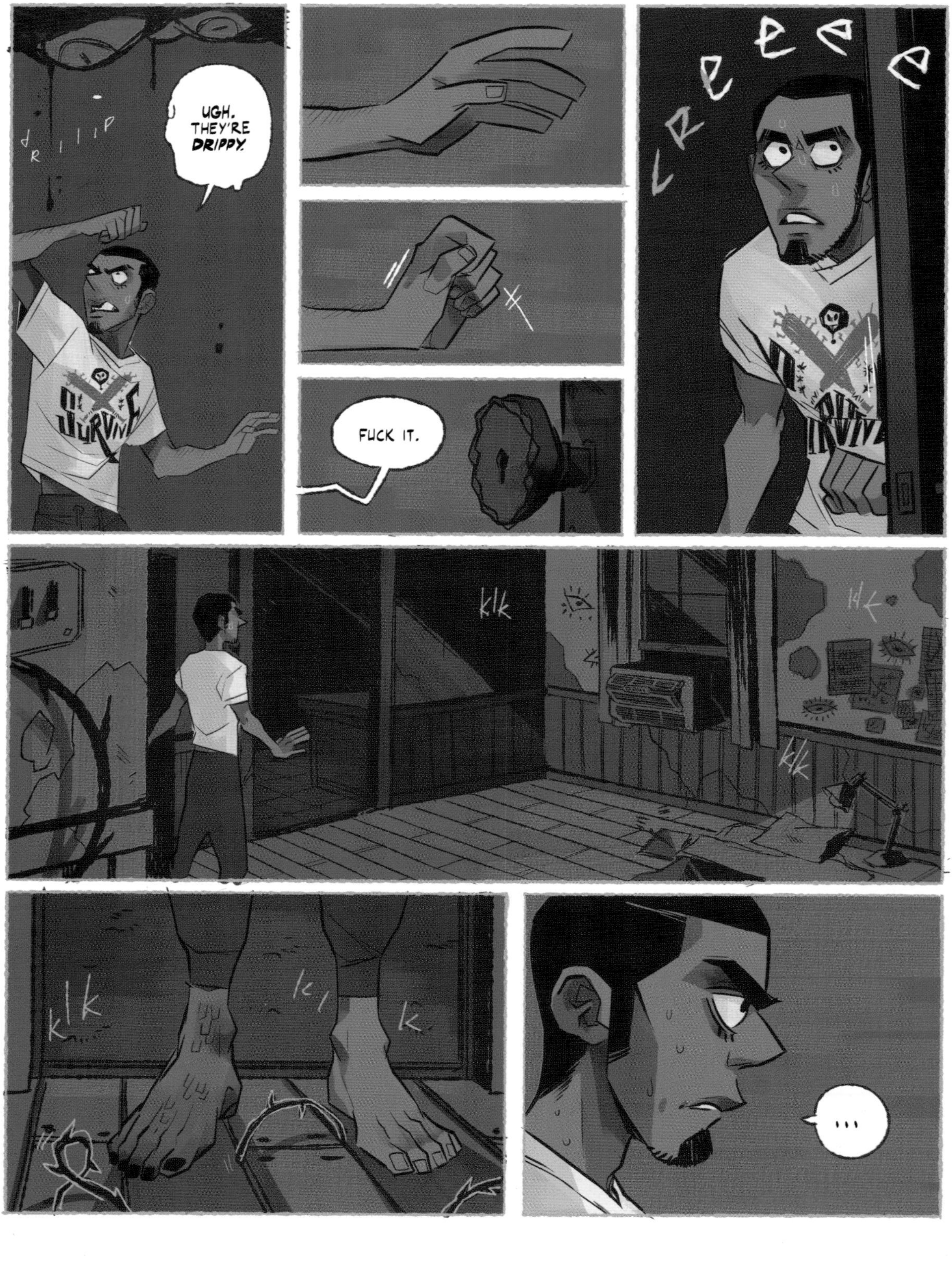
drIIIP
UGH. THEY'RE DRIPPY.
FUCK IT.
CREEEE
KLK
KLK
KLK
KLK
K
...

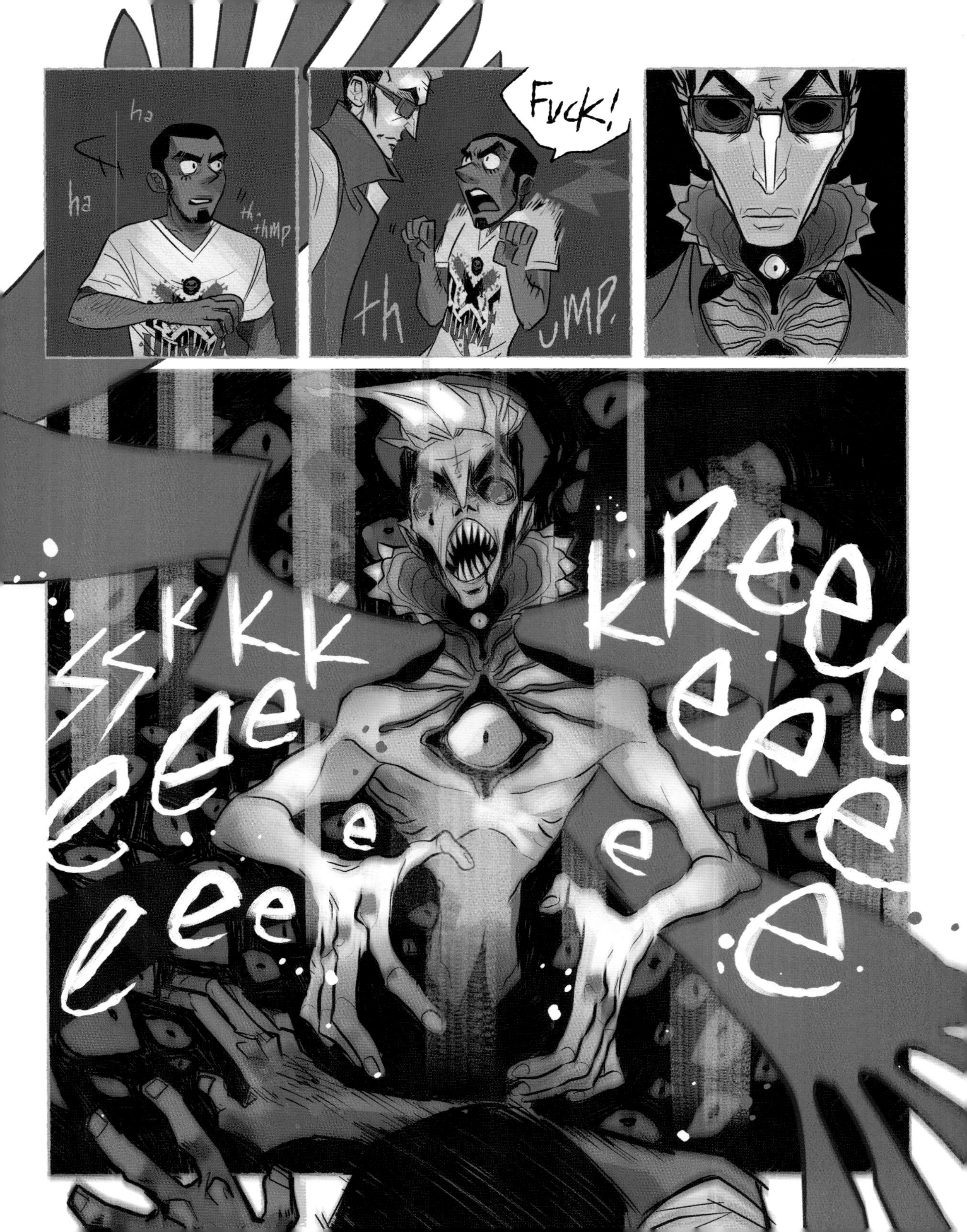

ha
ha
th-thmp
Fuck!
th
uMP.
SSKKK
eeee
e
e
eee
kReeeeeeee

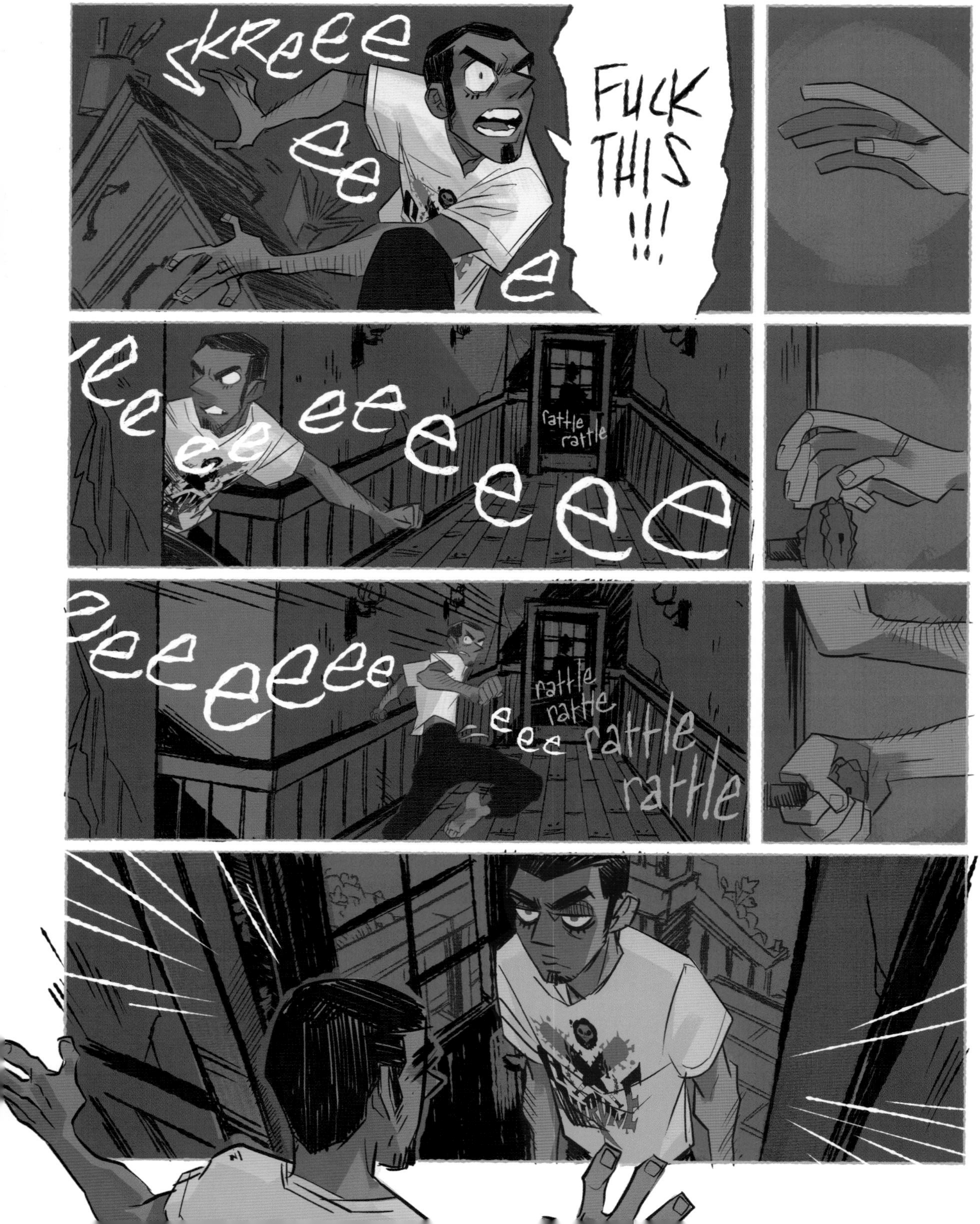

skreeeeeee
FUCK THIS !!!
eeeeeeeeeee
rattle rattle
eeeeeeeee
rattle rattle
eee rattle rattle

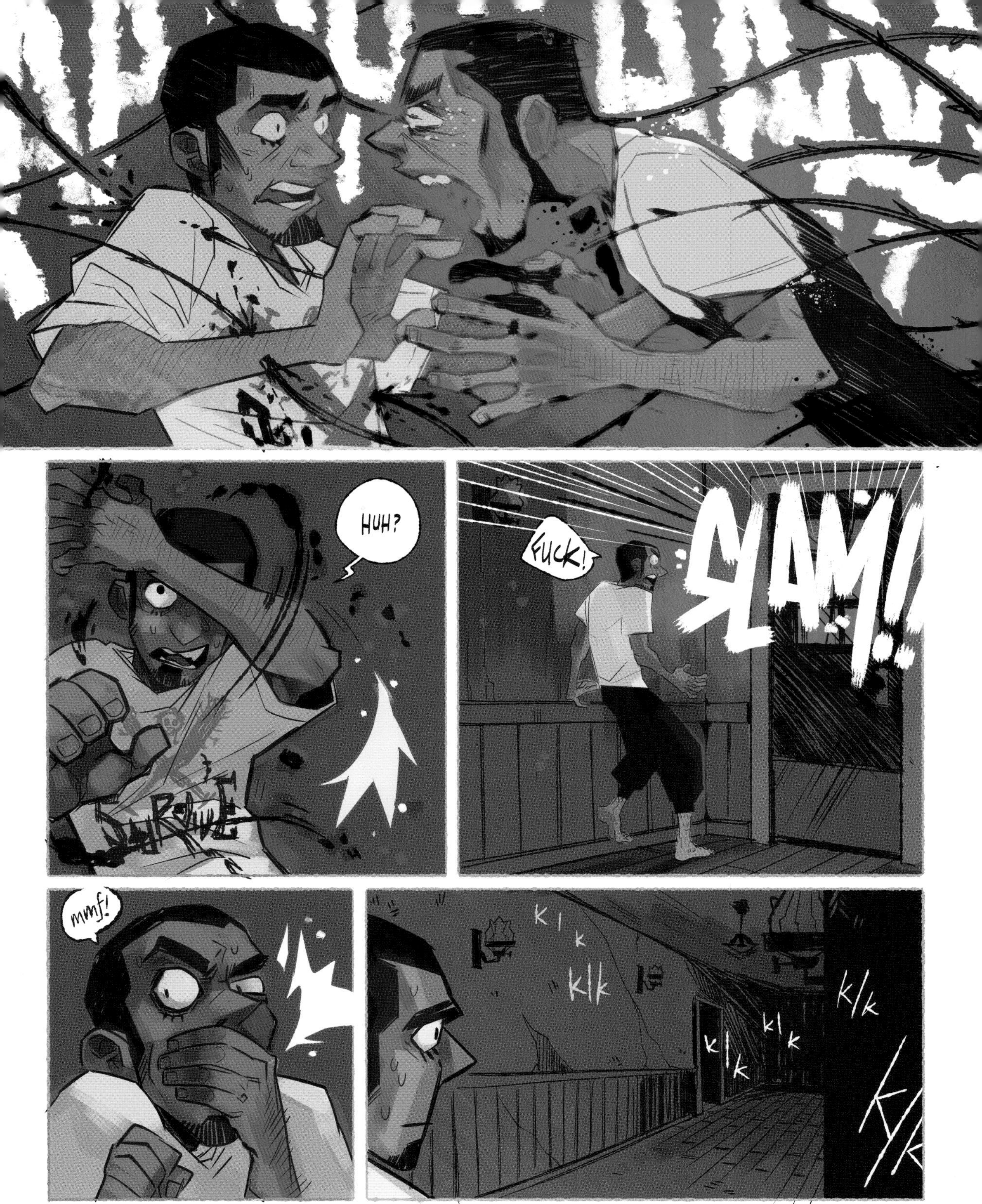
HUH?
FUCK!
SLAM!!
mmf!
KlK
KlK
KlK
KlK
KlK
KlK

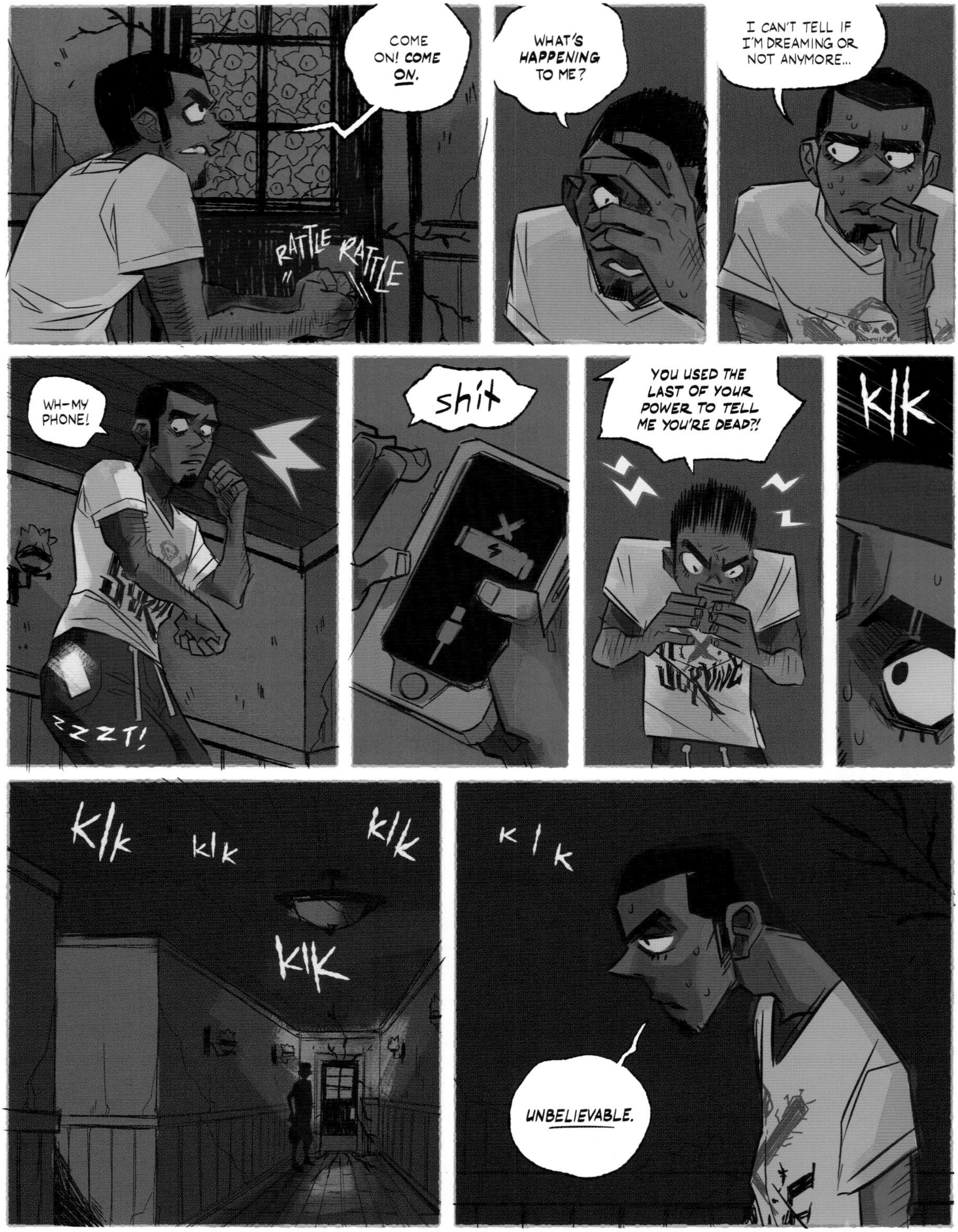
COME ON! COME ON.
RATTLE RATTLE
WHAT'S HAPPENING TO ME?
I CAN'T TELL IF I'M DREAMING OR NOT ANYMORE...
WH-MY PHONE!
ZZZT!
shit
YOU USED THE LAST OF YOUR POWER TO TELL ME YOU'RE DEAD?!
KLK
KLK KLK KLK
KLK
KLK
UNBELIEVABLE.

Chapter [SIX]

for him to eat.

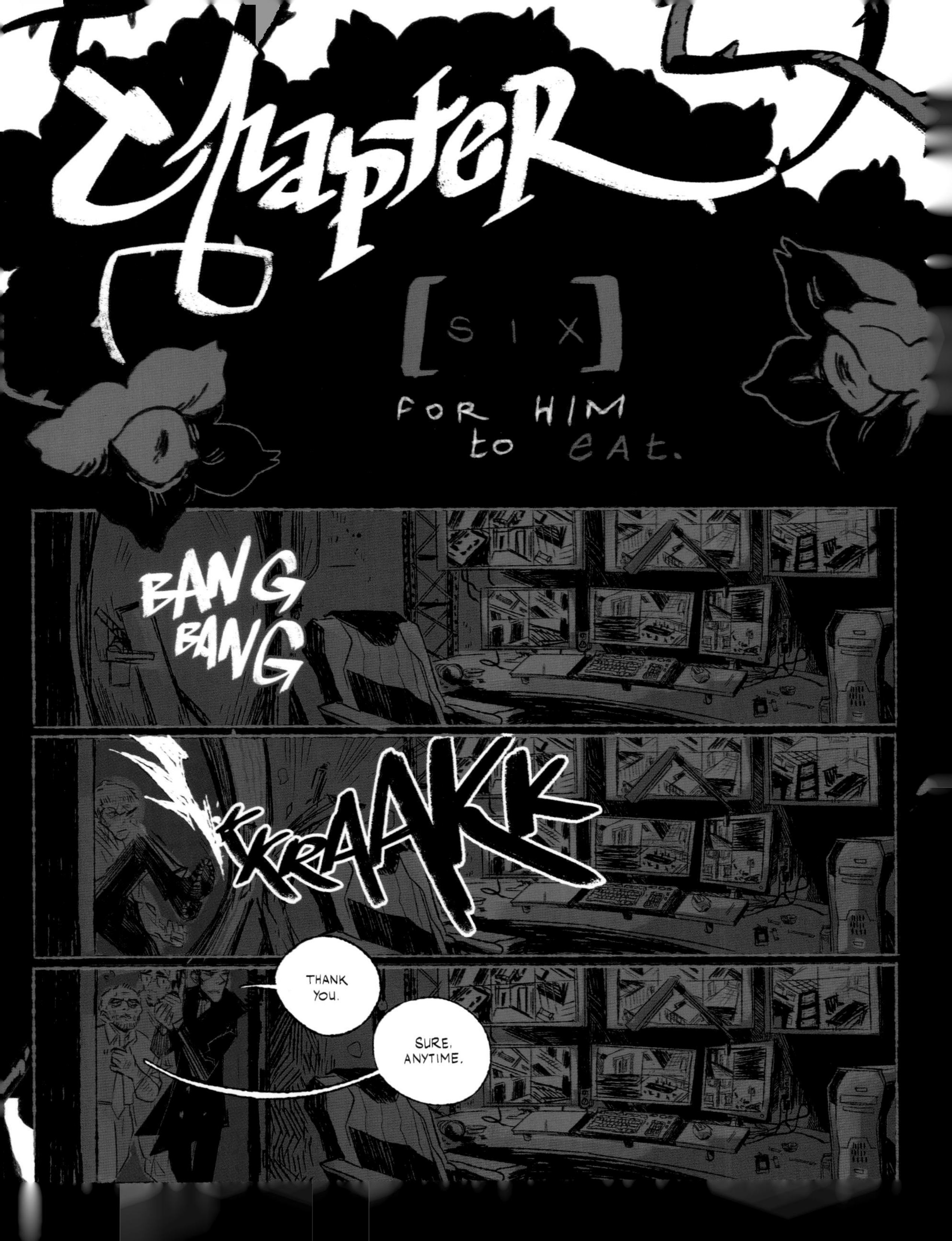
BANG
BANG
KKRAAKK
THANK YOU.
SURE. ANYTIME.

IT'S CLEAR, BUT MIND THE VISCERA.

URK

OH, GOD, IS THIS ALL THAT'S LEFT OF THE BODIES!

SO MANY HAVE DIED ALREADY. WE MUST HAVE LOST CONTAINMENT.

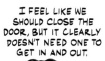

I FEEL LIKE WE SHOULD CLOSE THE DOOR, BUT IT CLEARLY DOESN'T NEED ONE TO GET IN AND OUT.

YOU'RE RIGHT.

COME LOOK.

YOU OKAY, OFFICER?

MRRREFF. *yes.

SEE! HERE.

▶PLAY

▶PLAY

▶PLAY

❚❚ PAUSED

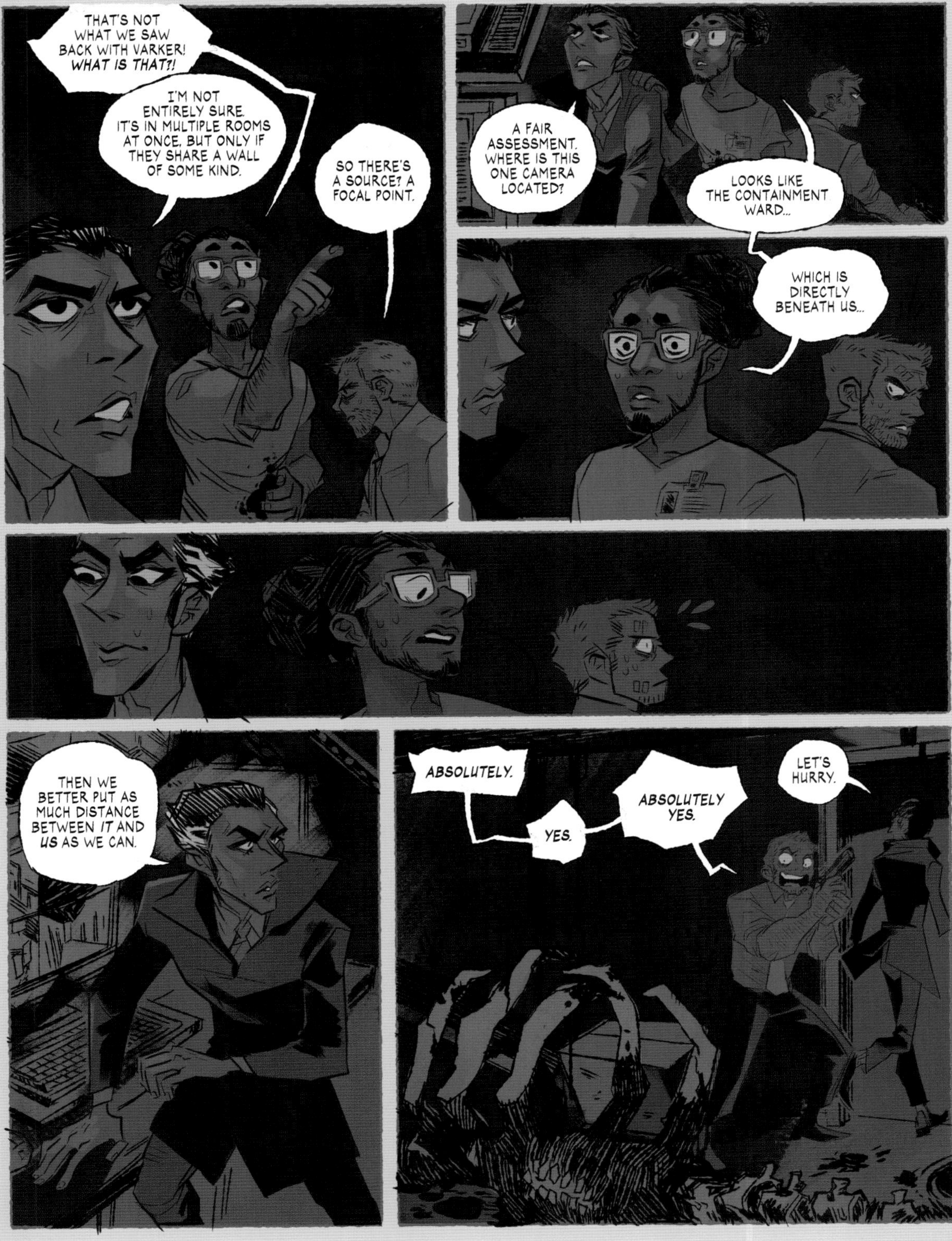
THAT'S NOT WHAT WE SAW BACK WITH VARKER! *WHAT IS THAT?!*
I'M NOT ENTIRELY SURE. IT'S IN MULTIPLE ROOMS AT ONCE, BUT ONLY IF THEY SHARE A WALL OF SOME KIND.
SO THERE'S A SOURCE? A FOCAL POINT.
A FAIR ASSESSMENT. WHERE IS THIS ONE CAMERA LOCATED?
LOOKS LIKE THE CONTAINMENT WARD...
WHICH IS DIRECTLY BENEATH US...
THEN WE BETTER PUT AS MUCH DISTANCE BETWEEN *IT* AND *US* AS WE CAN.
ABSOLUTELY.
YES.
ABSOLUTELY YES.
LET'S HURRY.

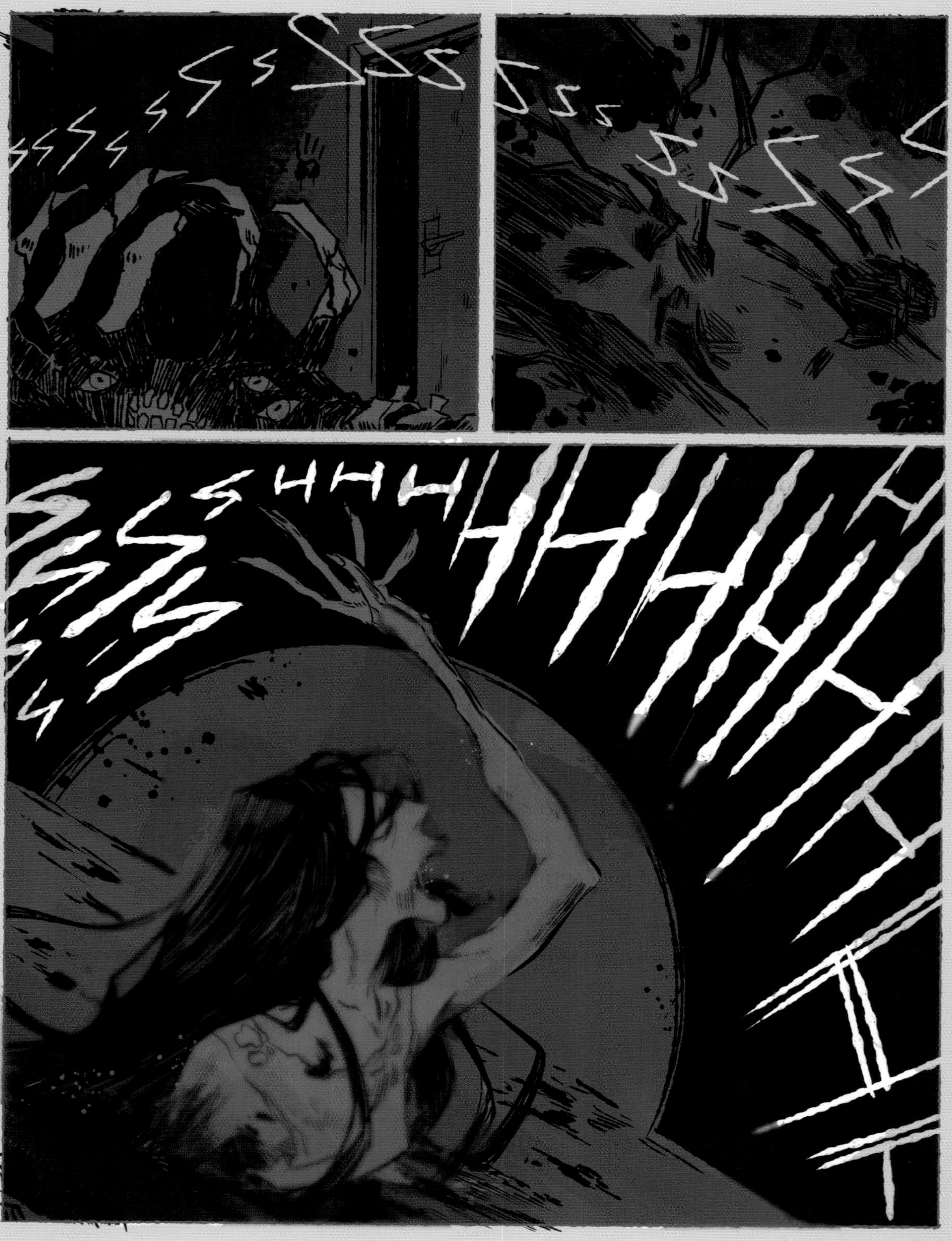
SSSSSSSSSSZZZ
SSSSSZZZ
SSSSHHHHHHHHHHHHH

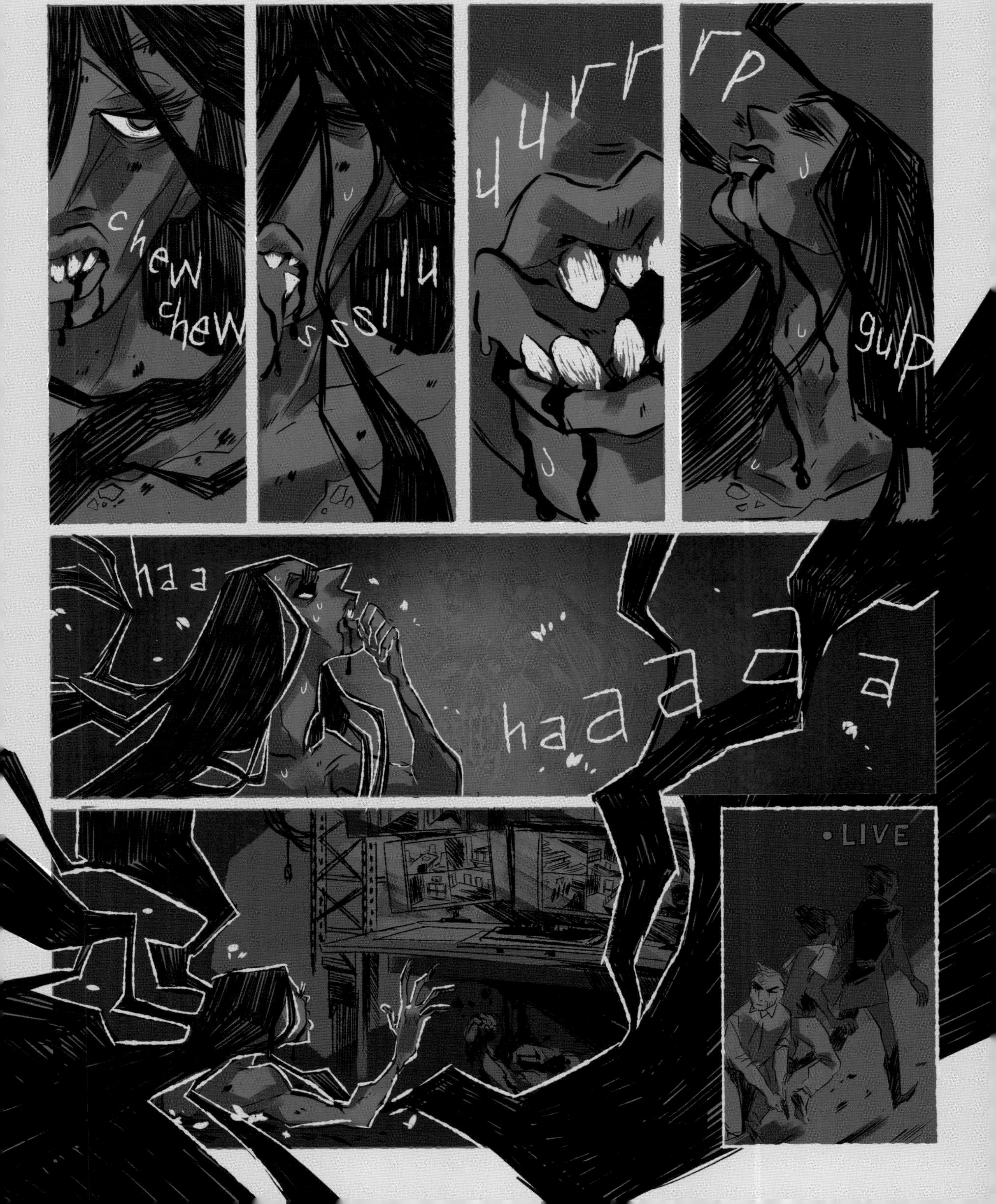

chew chew
sslu
uurrrp
gulp
haa
haaaaa
•LIVE

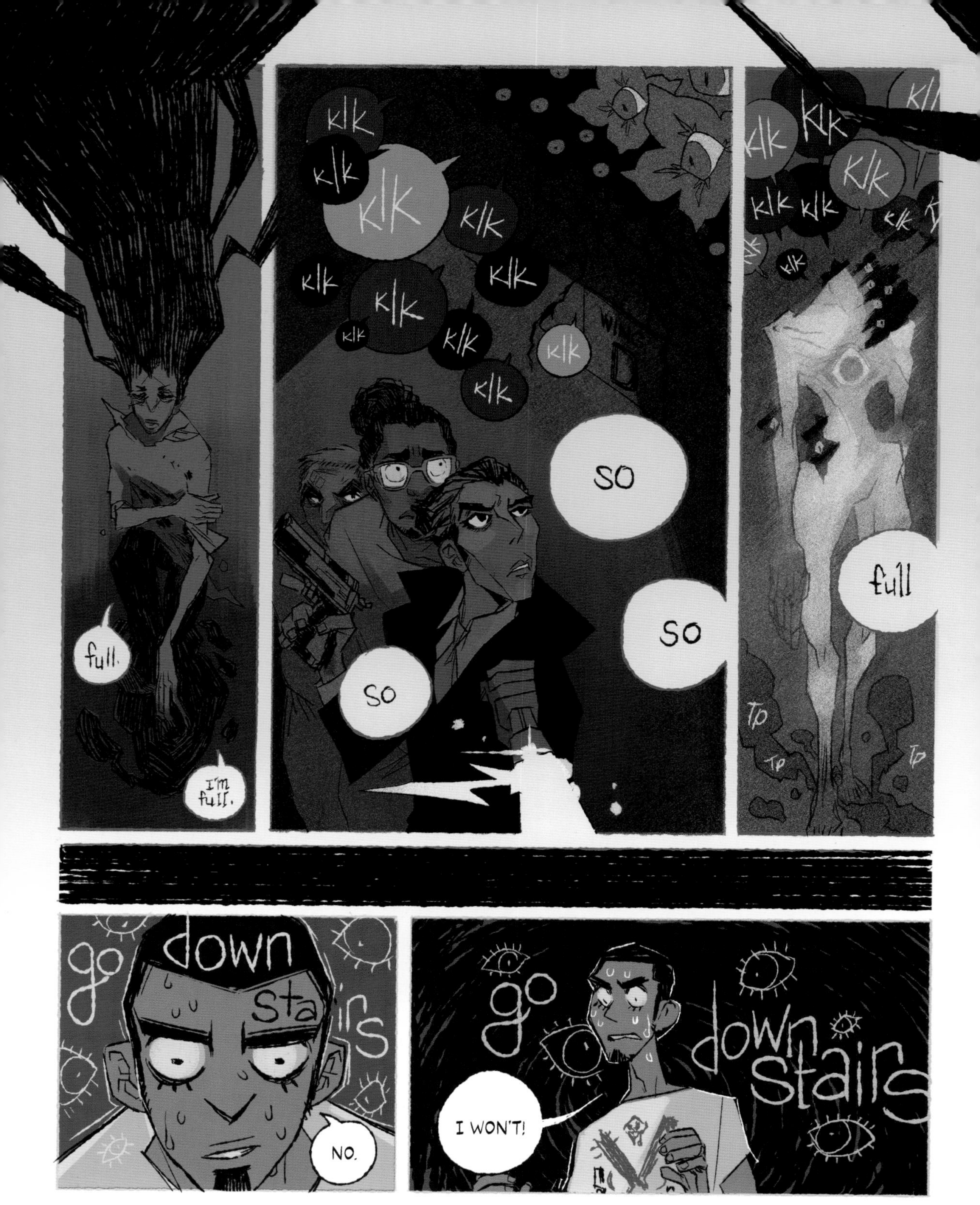
full.
I'm full.
K|K
K|K
K|K
K|K
K|K
K|K
K|K
K|K
K|K
K|K
K|K
SO
SO
SO
K|K
K|K
K|K
K|K
K|K
K|K
K|K
K|K
full
TP
TP
TP
go down stairs
NO.
go down stairs
I WON'T!

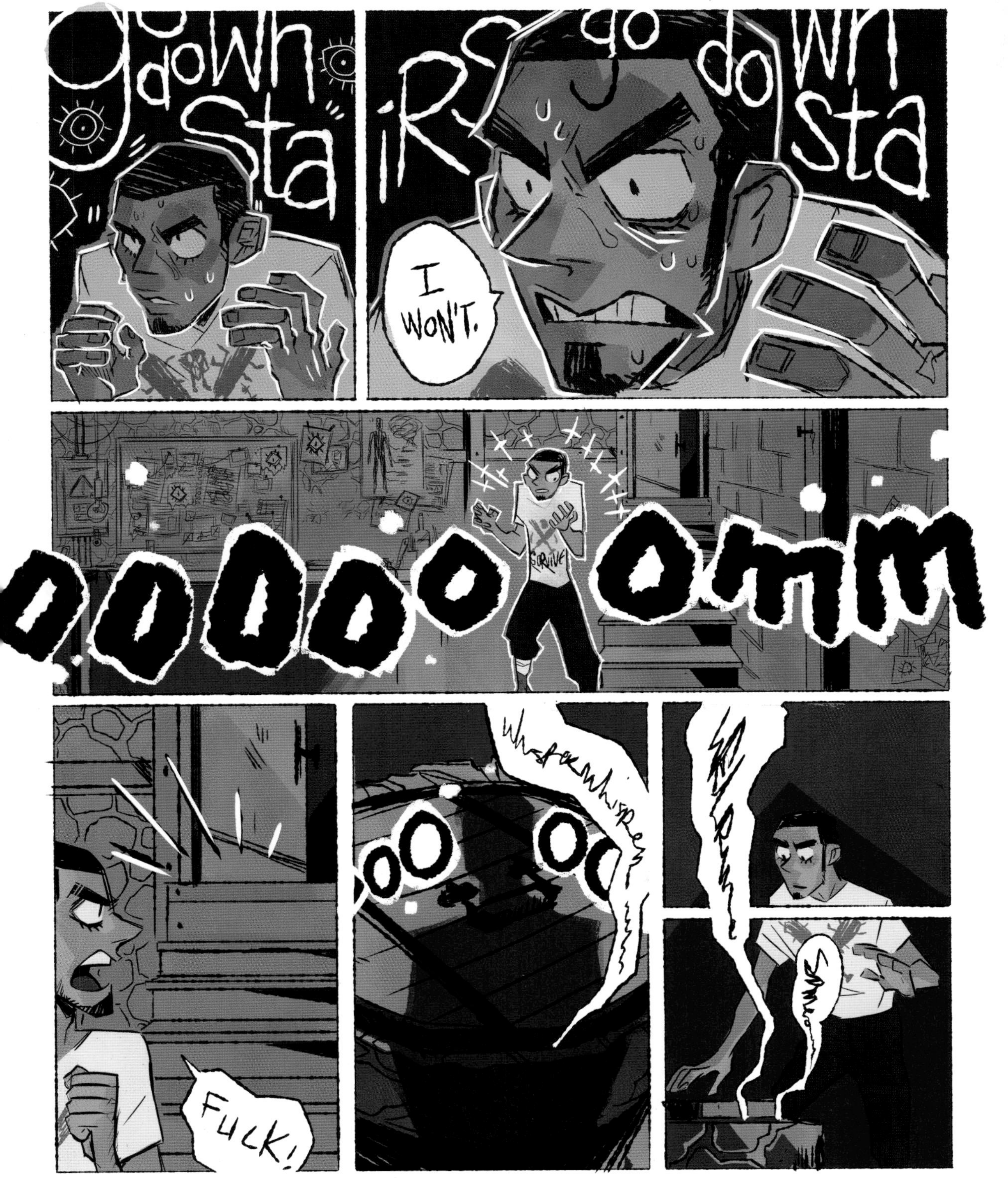
go down sta
iRS go down sta
I WON'T.
OOOOOOMM
FUCK!
OOOO
whisperwhisper

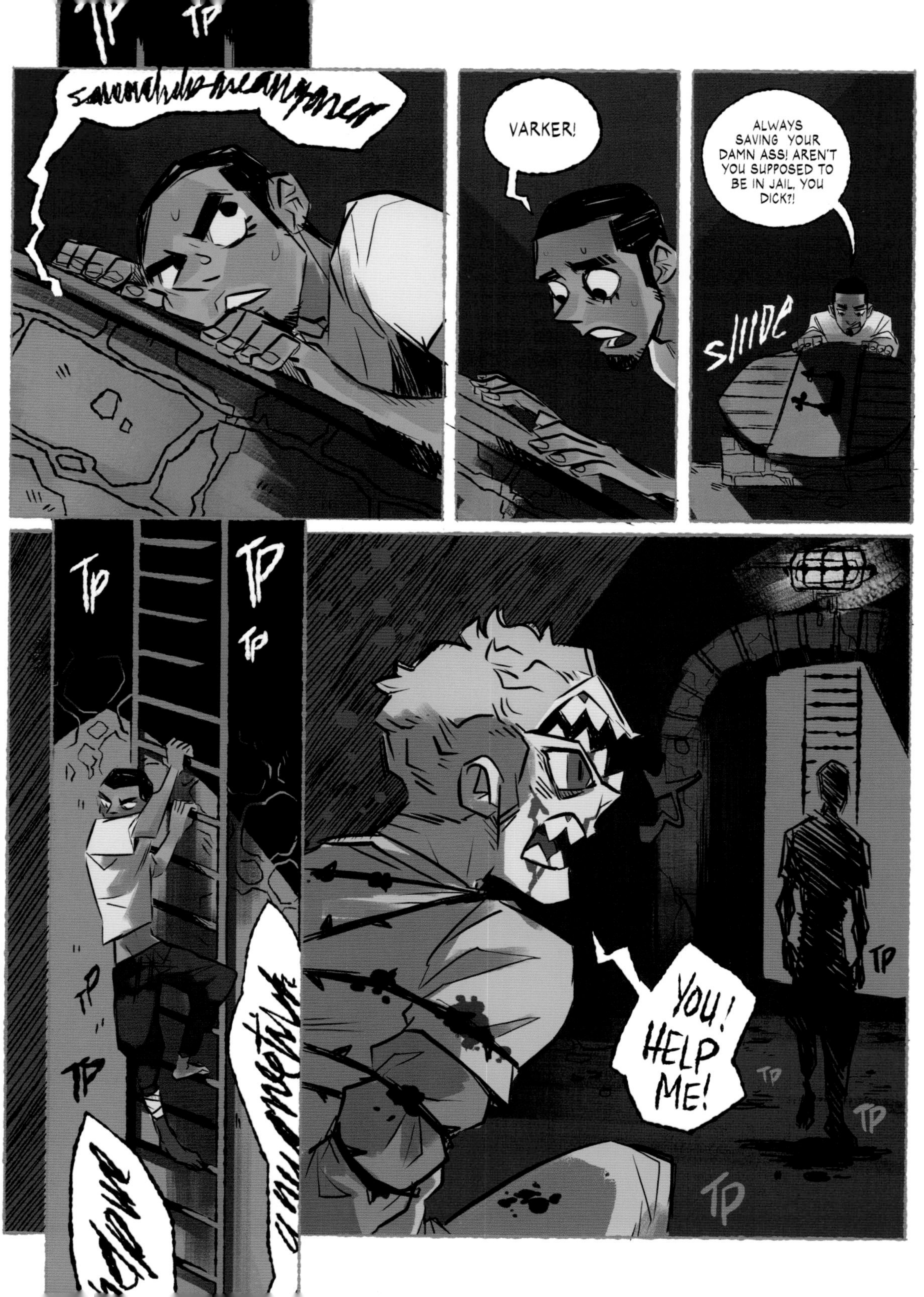
TP TP
VARKER!
ALWAYS SAVING YOUR DAMN ASS! AREN'T YOU SUPPOSED TO BE IN JAIL, YOU DICK?!
SLIIDE
TP
TP
TP
TP
TP
YOU! HELP ME!
TP
TP
TP
TP

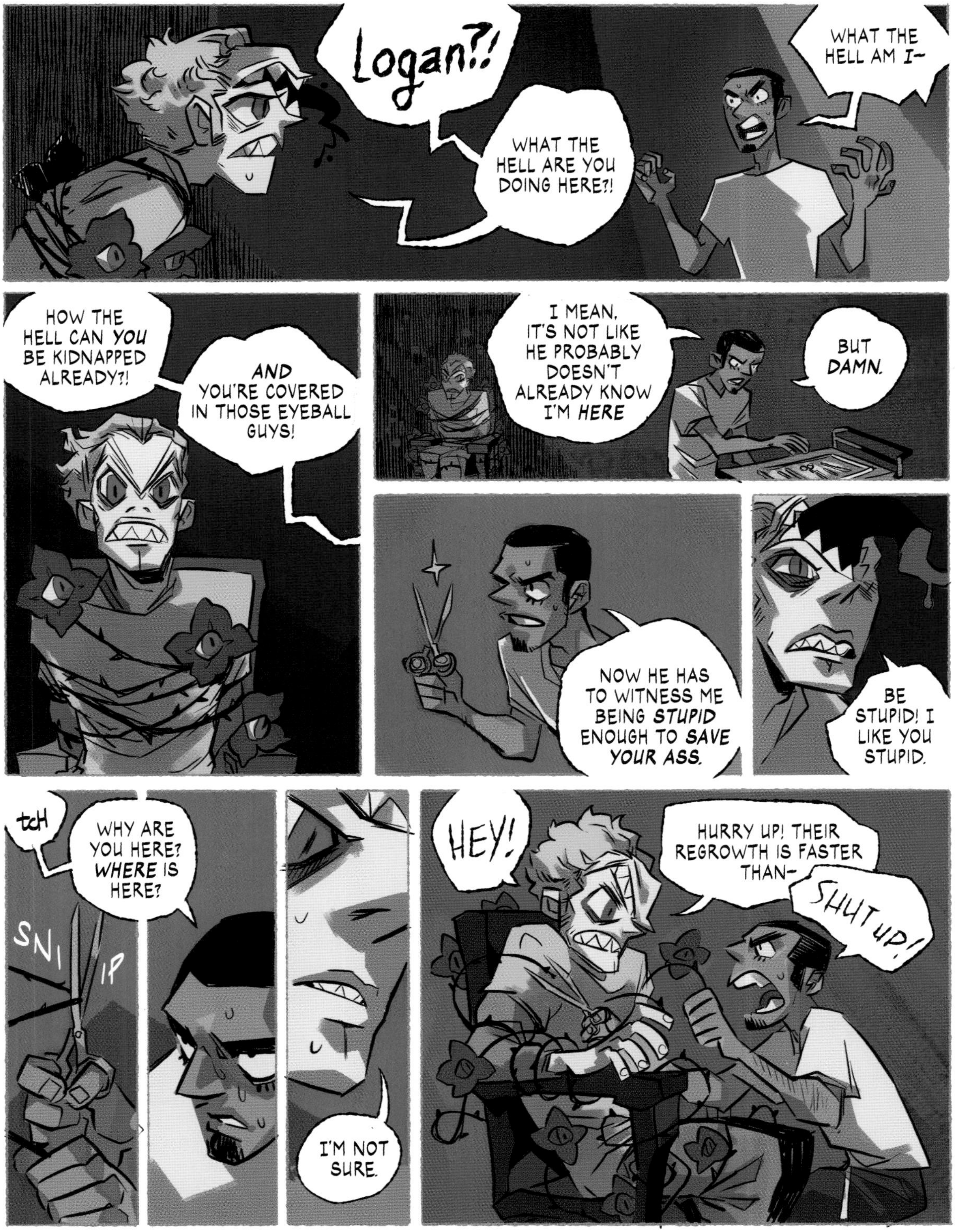
Logan?!
WHAT THE HELL ARE YOU DOING HERE?!
WHAT THE HELL AM I–
HOW THE HELL CAN YOU BE KIDNAPPED ALREADY?!
AND YOU'RE COVERED IN THOSE EYEBALL GUYS!
I MEAN, IT'S NOT LIKE HE PROBABLY DOESN'T ALREADY KNOW I'M HERE
BUT DAMN.
NOW HE HAS TO WITNESS ME BEING STUPID ENOUGH TO SAVE YOUR ASS.
BE STUPID! I LIKE YOU STUPID.
tcH
WHY ARE YOU HERE? WHERE IS HERE?
SNIIP
I'M NOT SURE.
HEY!
HURRY UP! THEIR REGROWTH IS FASTER THAN–
SHUT UP!

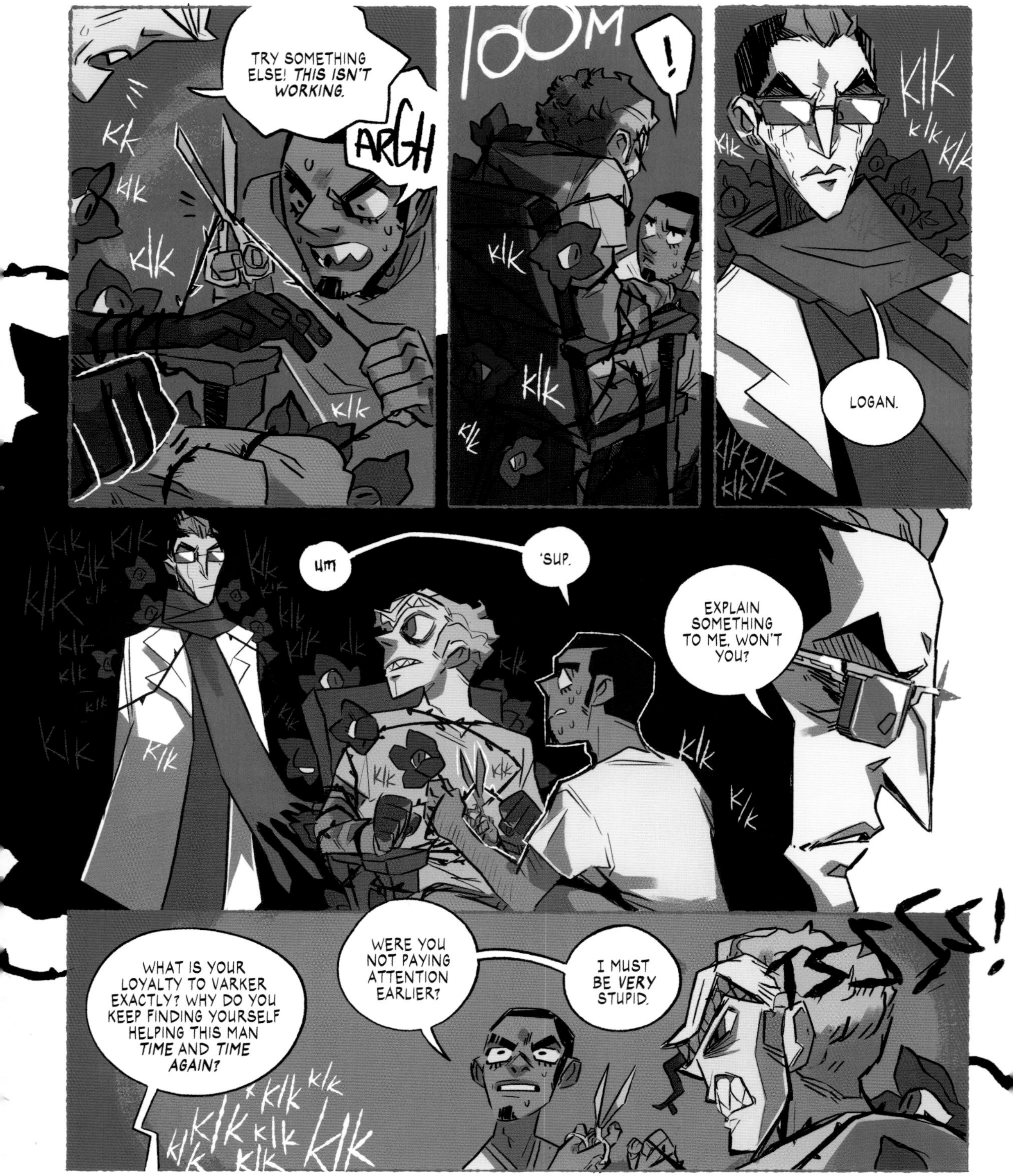
TRY SOMETHING ELSE! *THIS ISN'T WORKING.*
ARGH
KIK
KIK
KIK
KIK
OOOM
!
KIK
KIK
KIK
KIK
KIK
KIK
LOGAN.
KIKKIK
um
'SUP.
EXPLAIN SOMETHING TO ME, WON'T YOU?
KIK
KIK
KIK
WHAT IS YOUR LOYALTY TO VARKER EXACTLY? WHY DO YOU KEEP FINDING YOURSELF HELPING THIS MAN *TIME* AND *TIME* AGAIN?
WERE YOU NOT PAYING ATTENTION EARLIER?
I MUST BE *VERY* STUPID.
TSSSS!
KIK KIK KIK KIK KIK KIK

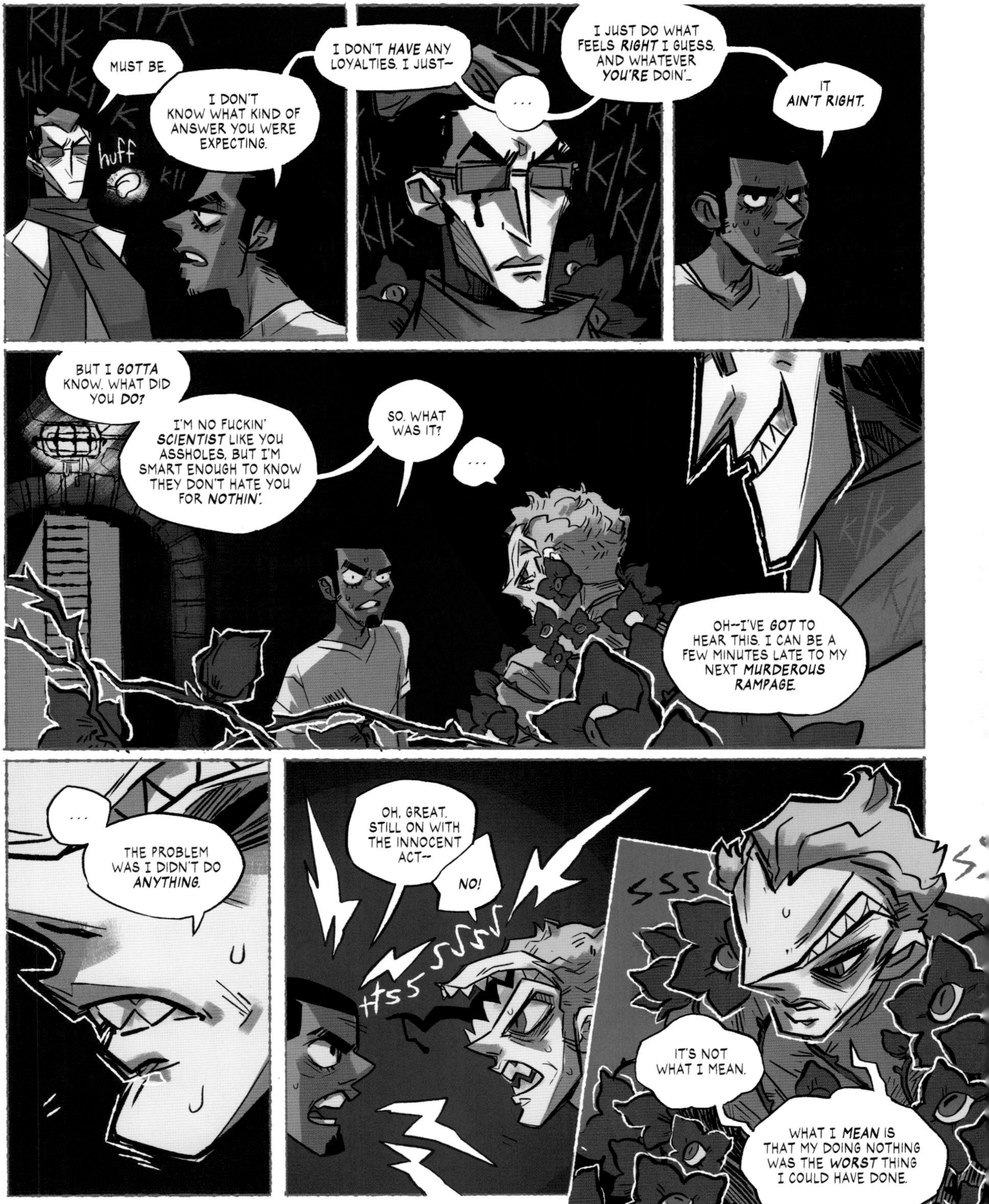
MUST BE.
I DON'T KNOW WHAT KIND OF ANSWER YOU WERE EXPECTING.
I DON'T *HAVE* ANY LOYALTIES. I JUST--
...
I JUST DO WHAT FEELS *RIGHT* I GUESS. AND WHATEVER *YOU'RE* DOIN'...
IT *AIN'T RIGHT.*
BUT I *GOTTA* KNOW. WHAT DID YOU *DO?*
I'M NO FUCKIN' *SCIENTIST* LIKE YOU ASSHOLES, BUT I'M SMART ENOUGH TO KNOW THEY DON'T HATE YOU FOR *NOTHIN'.*
SO. WHAT WAS IT?
...
OH--I'VE *GOT* TO HEAR THIS. I CAN BE A FEW MINUTES LATE TO MY NEXT *MURDEROUS RAMPAGE.*
...
THE PROBLEM WAS I DIDN'T DO *ANYTHING.*
OH, GREAT. STILL ON WITH THE INNOCENT ACT--
NO!
IT'S NOT WHAT I MEAN.
WHAT I *MEAN* IS THAT MY DOING NOTHING WAS THE *WORST* THING I COULD HAVE DONE.

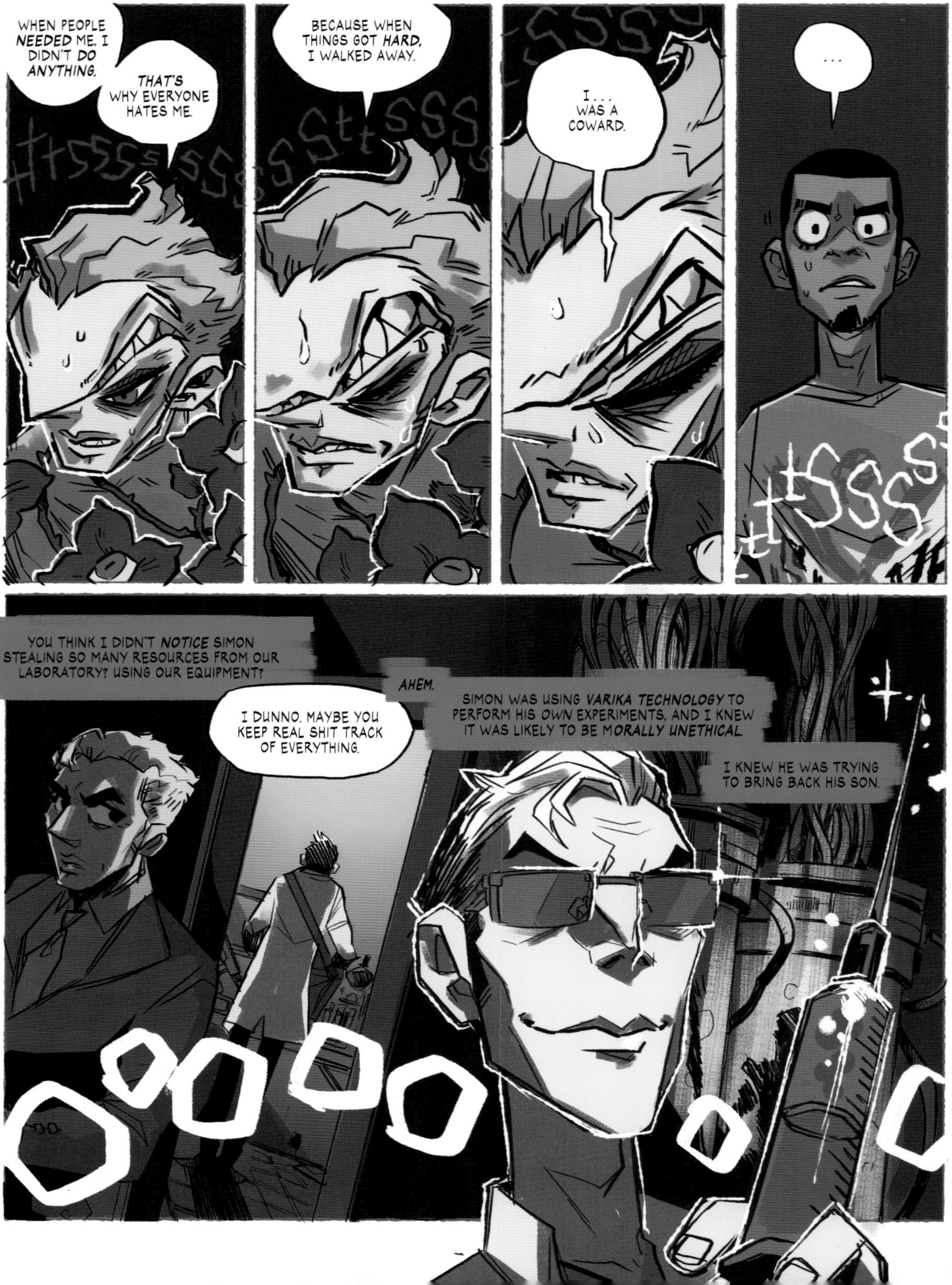

WHEN PEOPLE NEEDED ME, I DIDN'T DO ANYTHING.
THAT'S WHY EVERYONE HATES ME.
HTSSSSSSS
BECAUSE WHEN THINGS GOT HARD, I WALKED AWAY.
SSSTTSSSS
I . . . WAS A COWARD.
. . .
TTSSSSS
YOU THINK I DIDN'T NOTICE SIMON STEALING SO MANY RESOURCES FROM OUR LABORATORY? USING OUR EQUIPMENT?
I DUNNO. MAYBE YOU KEEP REAL SHIT TRACK OF EVERYTHING.
AHEM.
SIMON WAS USING VARIKA TECHNOLOGY TO PERFORM HIS OWN EXPERIMENTS, AND I KNEW IT WAS LIKELY TO BE MORALLY UNETHICAL.
I KNEW HE WAS TRYING TO BRING BACK HIS SON.

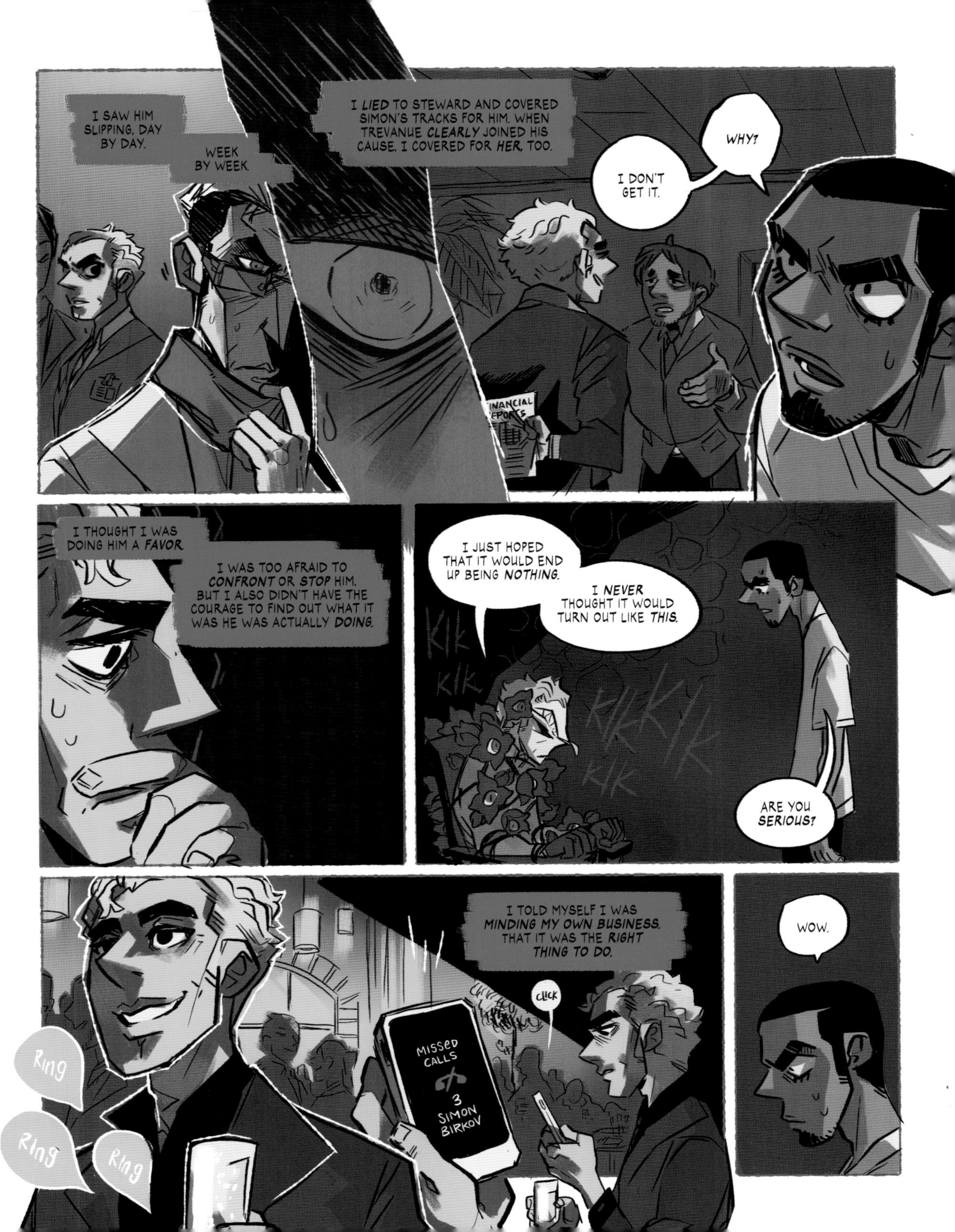
I SAW HIM SLIPPING, DAY BY DAY.
WEEK BY WEEK.
I *LIED* TO STEWARD AND COVERED SIMON'S TRACKS FOR HIM. WHEN TREVANUE *CLEARLY* JOINED HIS CAUSE, I COVERED FOR *HER*, TOO.
FINANCIAL REPORTS
I DON'T GET IT.
WHY?
I THOUGHT I WAS DOING HIM A *FAVOR*.
I WAS TOO AFRAID TO *CONFRONT* OR *STOP* HIM, BUT I ALSO DIDN'T HAVE THE COURAGE TO FIND OUT WHAT IT WAS HE WAS ACTUALLY *DOING*.
I JUST HOPED THAT IT WOULD END UP BEING *NOTHING*.
I *NEVER* THOUGHT IT WOULD TURN OUT LIKE *THIS*.
KIK KIK
KIK KIK KIK KIK
ARE YOU *SERIOUS?*
Ring
Ring
Ring
MISSED CALLS
3 SIMON BIRKOV
CLICK
I TOLD MYSELF I WAS *MINDING MY OWN BUSINESS*, THAT IT WAS THE *RIGHT THING TO DO*.
WOW.

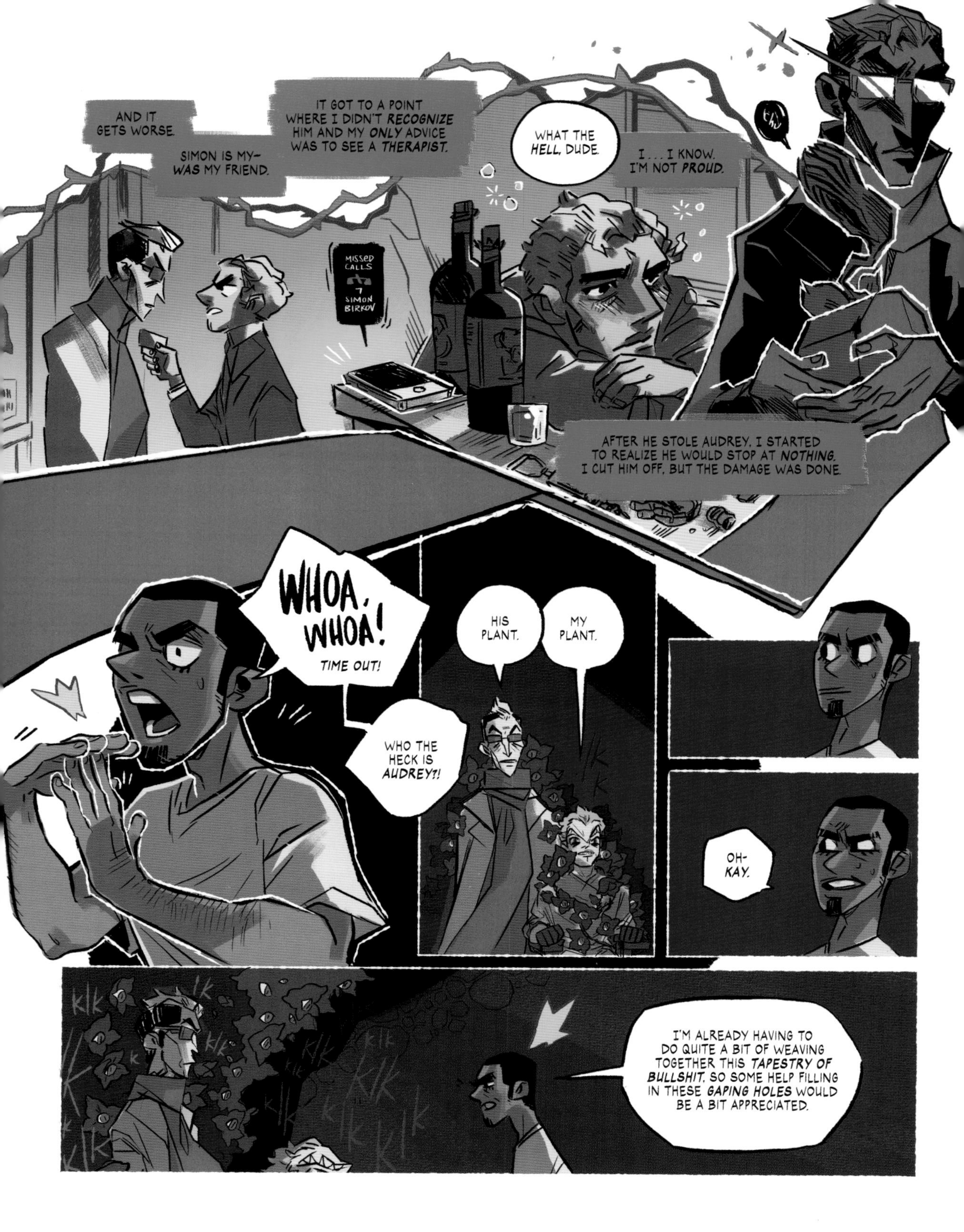

AND IT GETS WORSE.
SIMON IS MY— WAS MY FRIEND.
IT GOT TO A POINT WHERE I DIDN'T RECOGNIZE HIM AND MY ONLY ADVICE WAS TO SEE A THERAPIST.
MISSED CALLS 7 SIMON BIRKOV
WHAT THE HELL, DUDE.
I... I KNOW. I'M NOT PROUD.
AFTER HE STOLE AUDREY, I STARTED TO REALIZE HE WOULD STOP AT NOTHING. I CUT HIM OFF, BUT THE DAMAGE WAS DONE.
WHOA, WHOA! TIME OUT!
WHO THE HECK IS AUDREY?!
HIS PLANT.
MY PLANT.
OH-KAY.
I'M ALREADY HAVING TO DO QUITE A BIT OF WEAVING TOGETHER THIS TAPESTRY OF BULLSHIT, SO SOME HELP FILLING IN THESE GAPING HOLES WOULD BE A BIT APPRECIATED.

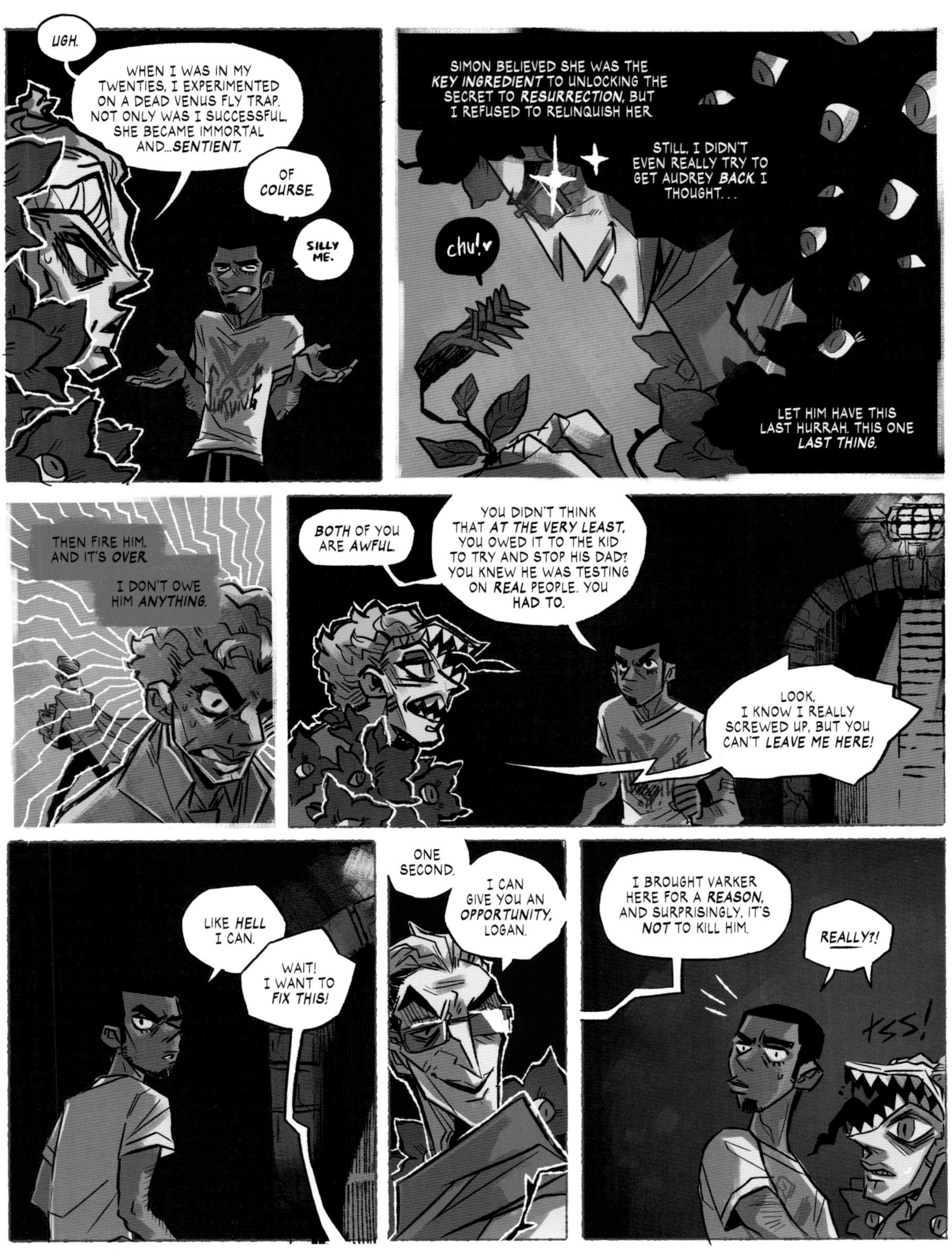
UGH.
WHEN I WAS IN MY TWENTIES, I EXPERIMENTED ON A DEAD VENUS FLY TRAP. NOT ONLY WAS I SUCCESSFUL, SHE BECAME IMMORTAL AND...SENTIENT.
OF COURSE.
SILLY ME.
SIMON BELIEVED SHE WAS THE KEY INGREDIENT TO UNLOCKING THE SECRET TO RESURRECTION, BUT I REFUSED TO RELINQUISH HER.
STILL, I DIDN'T EVEN REALLY TRY TO GET AUDREY BACK. I THOUGHT. . .
chu!♥
LET HIM HAVE THIS LAST HURRAH. THIS ONE LAST THING.
THEN FIRE HIM, AND IT'S OVER.
I DON'T OWE HIM ANYTHING.
BOTH OF YOU ARE AWFUL.
YOU DIDN'T THINK THAT AT THE VERY LEAST, YOU OWED IT TO THE KID TO TRY AND STOP HIS DAD? YOU KNEW HE WAS TESTING ON REAL PEOPLE. YOU HAD TO.
LOOK, I KNOW I REALLY SCREWED UP, BUT YOU CAN'T LEAVE ME HERE!
LIKE HELL I CAN.
WAIT! I WANT TO FIX THIS!
ONE SECOND.
I CAN GIVE YOU AN OPPORTUNITY, LOGAN.
I BROUGHT VARKER HERE FOR A REASON, AND SURPRISINGLY, IT'S NOT TO KILL HIM.
REALLY?!
HSS!

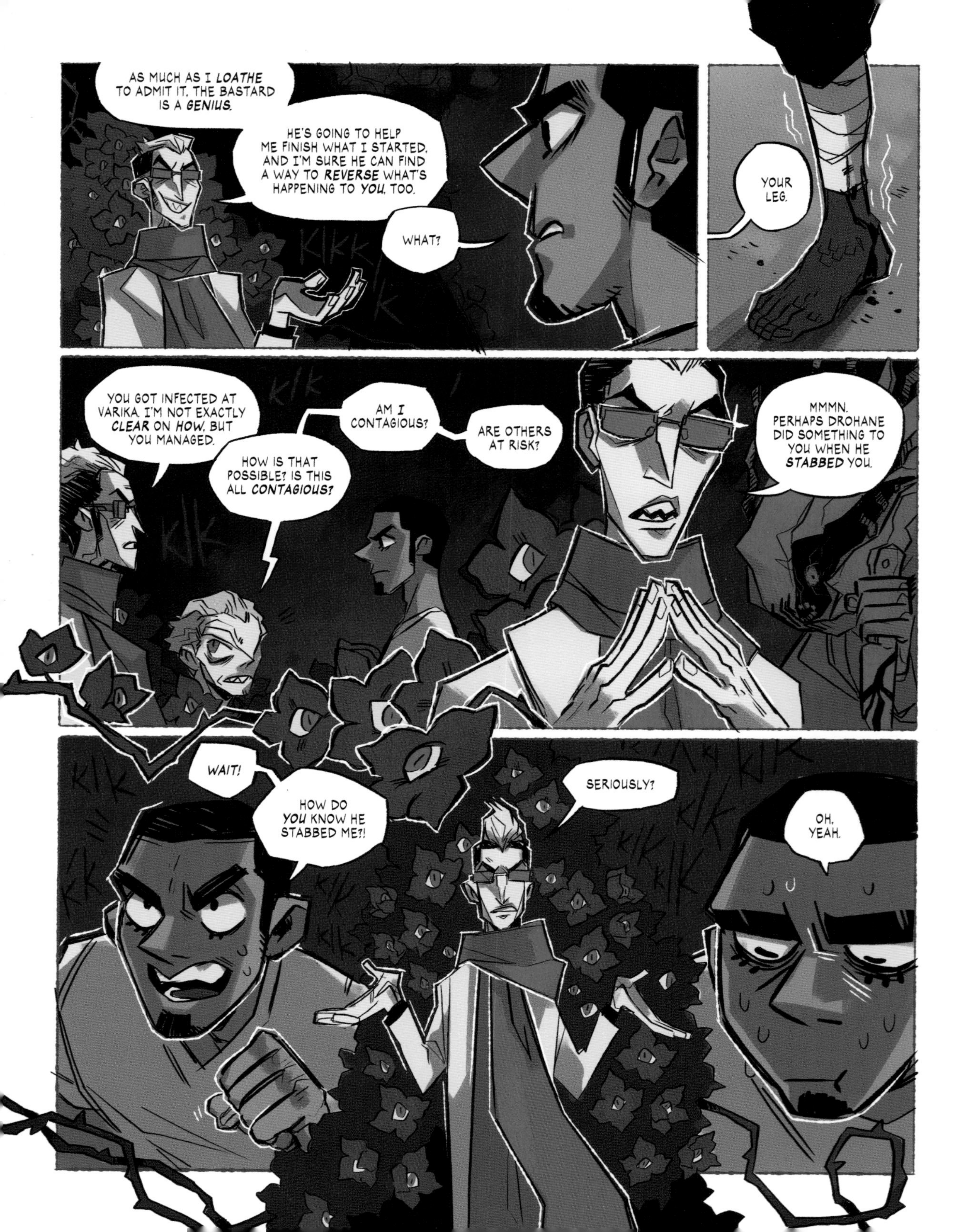
AS MUCH AS I *LOATHE* TO ADMIT IT, THE BASTARD IS A *GENIUS.*
HE'S GOING TO HELP ME FINISH WHAT I STARTED, AND I'M SURE HE CAN FIND A WAY TO *REVERSE* WHAT'S HAPPENING TO *YOU*, TOO.
KIKK
WHAT?
YOUR LEG.
YOU GOT INFECTED AT VARIKA. I'M NOT EXACTLY *CLEAR* ON *HOW*, BUT YOU MANAGED.
HOW IS THAT POSSIBLE? IS THIS ALL *CONTAGIOUS?*
AM *I* CONTAGIOUS?
ARE OTHERS AT RISK?
MMMN. PERHAPS DROHANE DID SOMETHING TO YOU WHEN HE *STABBED* YOU.
WAIT!
HOW DO *YOU* KNOW HE STABBED ME?!
SERIOUSLY?
OH, YEAH.

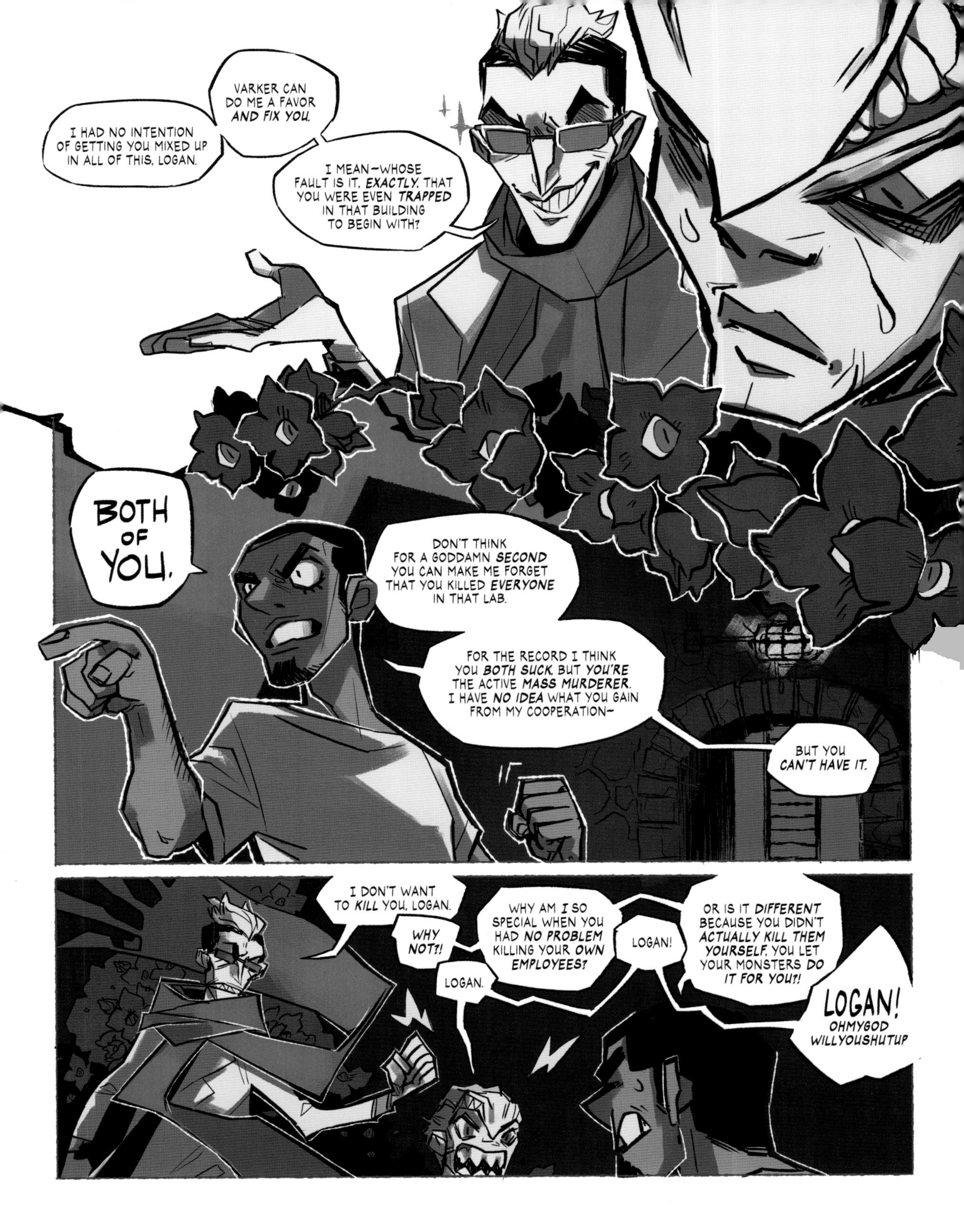
I HAD NO INTENTION OF GETTING YOU MIXED UP IN ALL OF THIS, LOGAN.
VARKER CAN DO ME A FAVOR *AND FIX YOU.*
I MEAN—WHOSE FAULT IS IT, *EXACTLY,* THAT YOU WERE EVEN *TRAPPED* IN THAT BUILDING TO BEGIN WITH?
BOTH OF YOU.
DON'T THINK FOR A GODDAMN *SECOND* YOU CAN MAKE ME FORGET THAT YOU KILLED *EVERYONE* IN THAT LAB.
FOR THE RECORD I THINK YOU *BOTH SUCK,* BUT *YOU'RE* THE ACTIVE *MASS MURDERER.* I HAVE *NO IDEA* WHAT YOU GAIN FROM MY COOPERATION—
BUT YOU *CAN'T HAVE IT.*
I DON'T WANT TO *KILL* YOU, LOGAN.
WHY NOT?!
LOGAN.
WHY AM *I* SO SPECIAL WHEN YOU HAD *NO PROBLEM* KILLING YOUR *OWN EMPLOYEES?*
LOGAN!
OR IS IT *DIFFERENT* BECAUSE YOU DIDN'T *ACTUALLY KILL THEM YOURSELF,* YOU LET YOUR MONSTERS *DO IT FOR YOU?!*
LOGAN! OHMYGOD WILLYOUSHUTUP

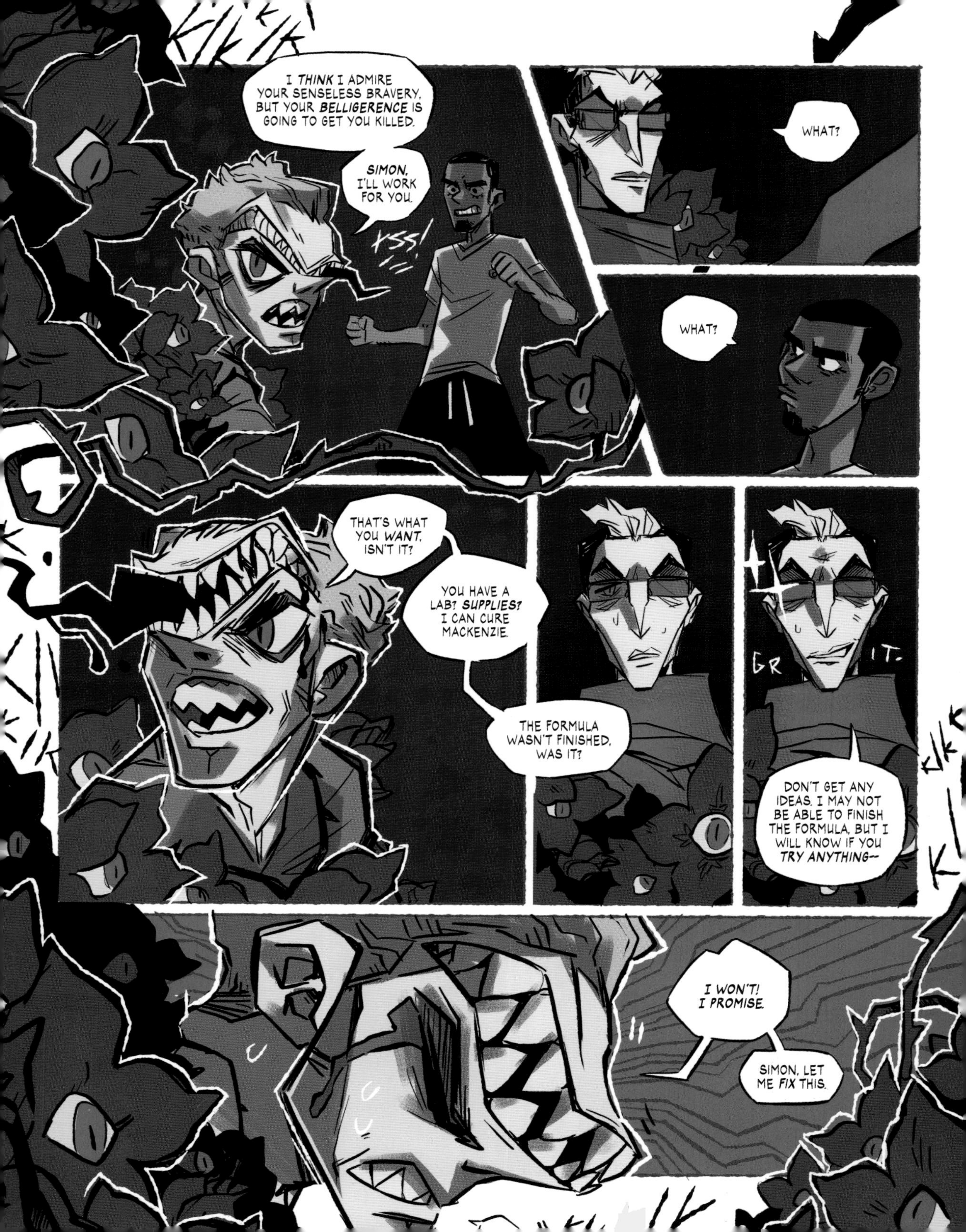
KIKIKI
I THINK I ADMIRE YOUR SENSELESS BRAVERY, BUT YOUR BELLIGERENCE IS GOING TO GET YOU KILLED.
SIMON, I'LL WORK FOR YOU.
YSS!
WHAT?
WHAT?
THAT'S WHAT YOU WANT, ISN'T IT?
YOU HAVE A LAB? SUPPLIES? I CAN CURE MACKENZIE.
THE FORMULA WASN'T FINISHED, WAS IT?
GR IT.
DON'T GET ANY IDEAS. I MAY NOT BE ABLE TO FINISH THE FORMULA, BUT I WILL KNOW IF YOU TRY ANYTHING--
KIKK
I WON'T! I PROMISE.
SIMON, LET ME FIX THIS.

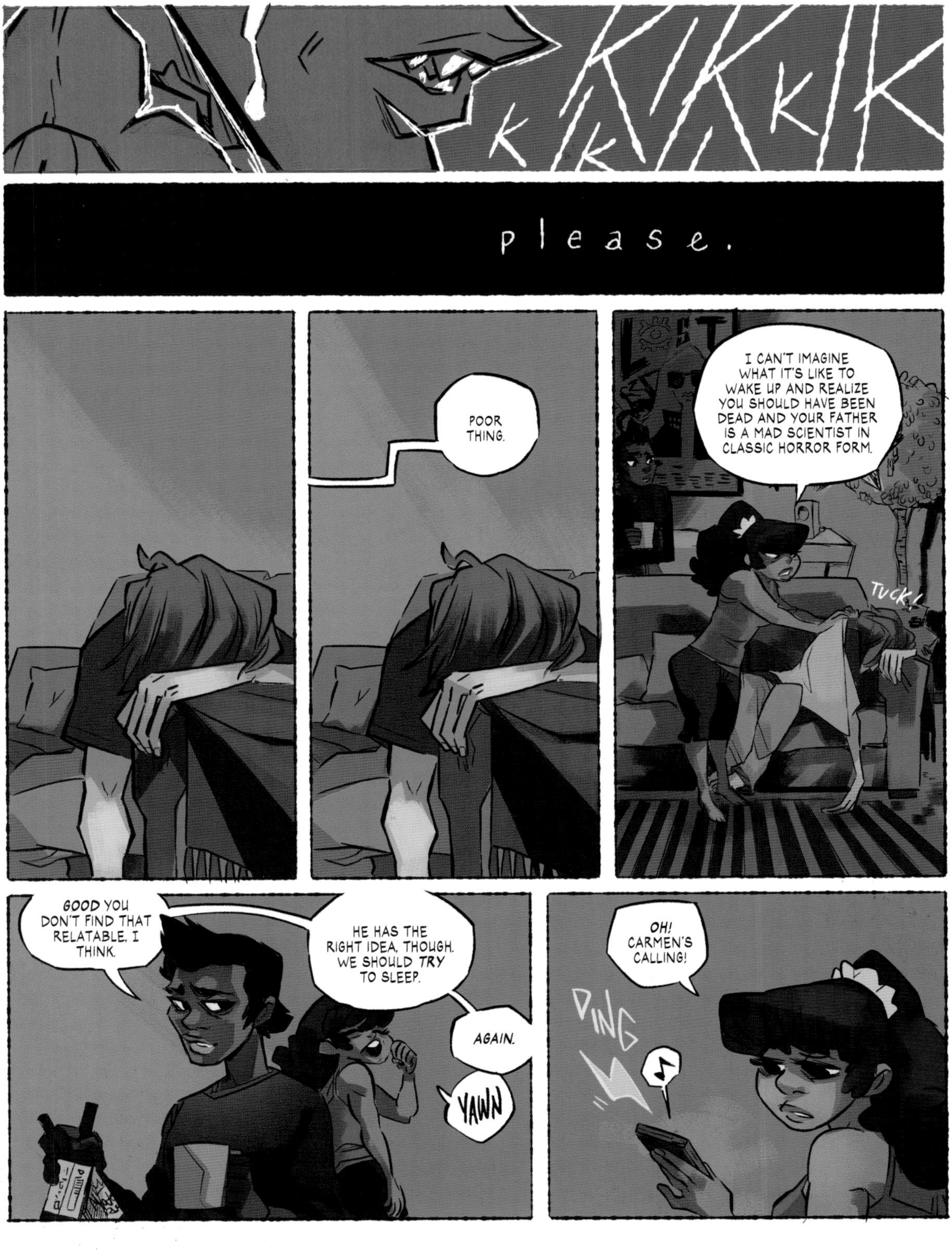
KKKKKKK
please.
POOR THING.
I CAN'T IMAGINE WHAT IT'S LIKE TO WAKE UP AND REALIZE YOU SHOULD HAVE BEEN DEAD AND YOUR FATHER IS A MAD SCIENTIST IN CLASSIC HORROR FORM.
TUCK!
GOOD YOU DON'T FIND THAT RELATABLE. I THINK.
HE HAS THE RIGHT IDEA, THOUGH. WE SHOULD TRY TO SLEEP.
AGAIN.
YAWN
OH! CARMEN'S CALLING!
DING

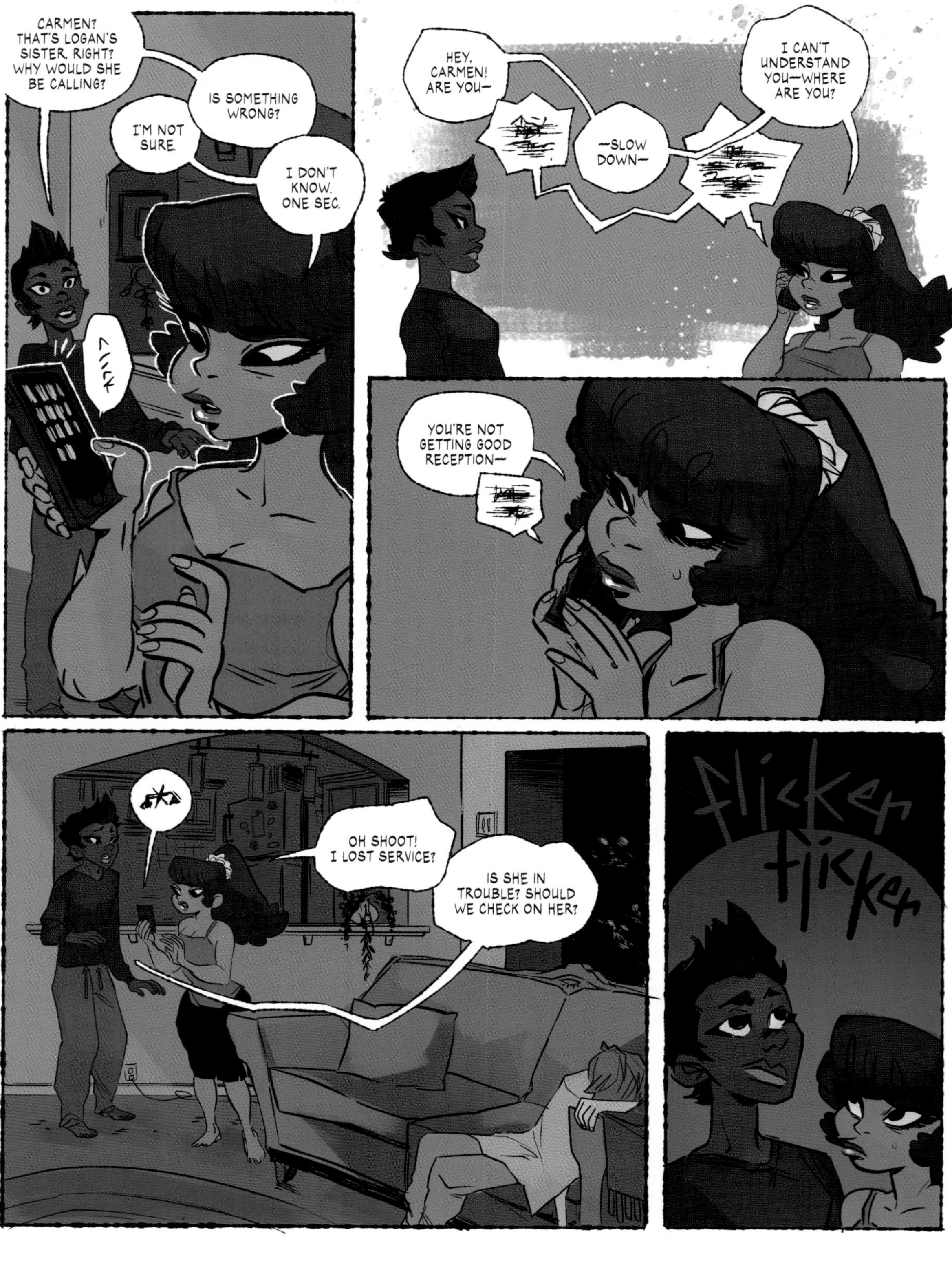
CARMEN? THAT'S LOGAN'S SISTER, RIGHT? WHY WOULD SHE BE CALLING?
IS SOMETHING WRONG?
I'M NOT SURE.
I DON'T KNOW. ONE SEC.
CLICK
HEY, CARMEN! ARE YOU—
—SLOW DOWN—
I CAN'T UNDERSTAND YOU—WHERE ARE YOU?
YOU'RE NOT GETTING GOOD RECEPTION—
OH SHOOT! I LOST SERVICE?
IS SHE IN TROUBLE? SHOULD WE CHECK ON HER?
flicker
flicker

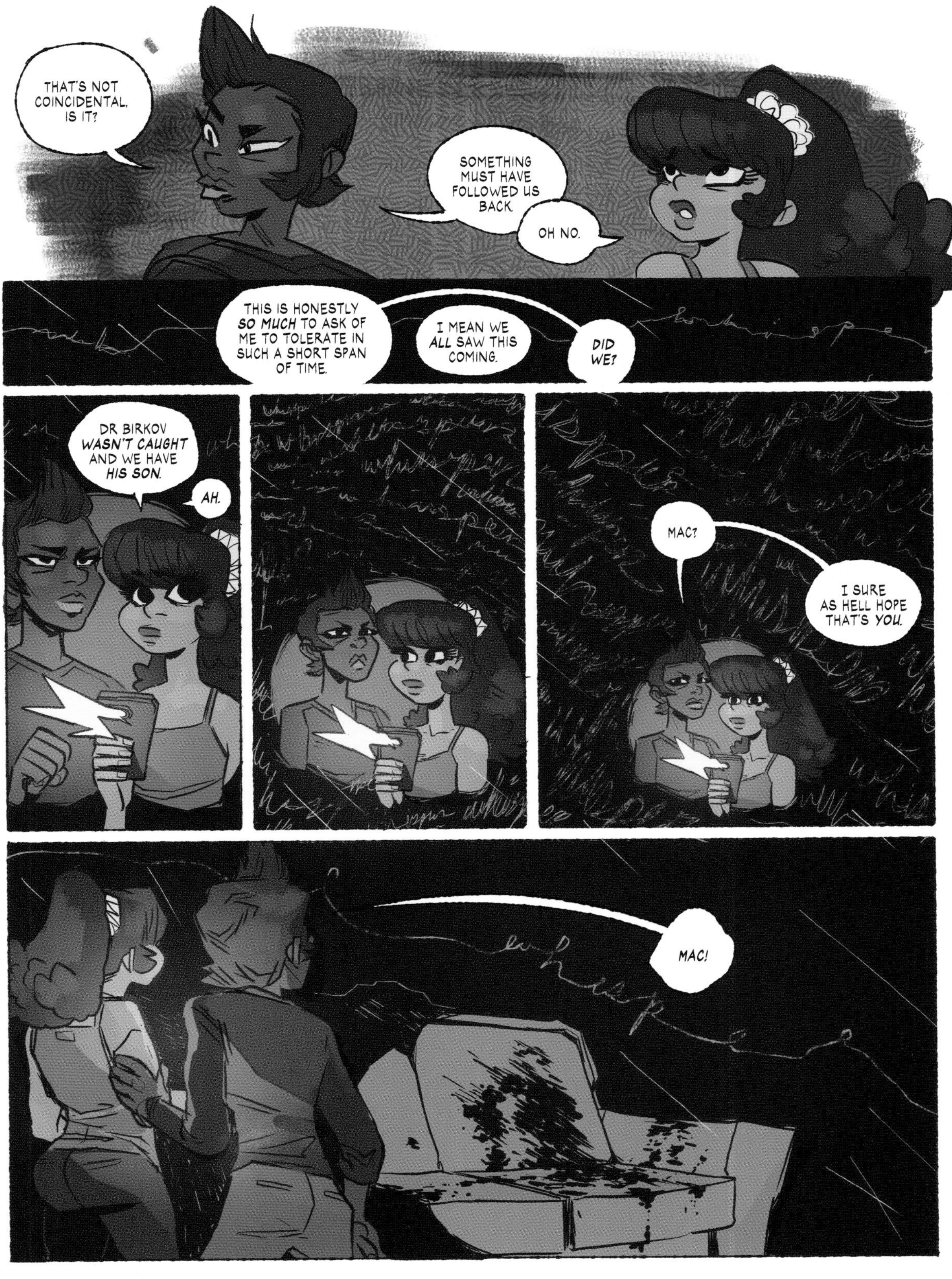
THAT'S NOT COINCIDENTAL, IS IT?
SOMETHING MUST HAVE FOLLOWED US BACK.
OH NO.
THIS IS HONESTLY *SO MUCH* TO ASK OF ME TO TOLERATE IN SUCH A SHORT SPAN OF TIME.
I MEAN WE *ALL* SAW THIS COMING.
DID WE?
DR BIRKOV *WASN'T CAUGHT* AND WE HAVE *HIS SON.*
AH.
MAC?
I SURE AS HELL HOPE THAT'S *YOU.*
MAC!

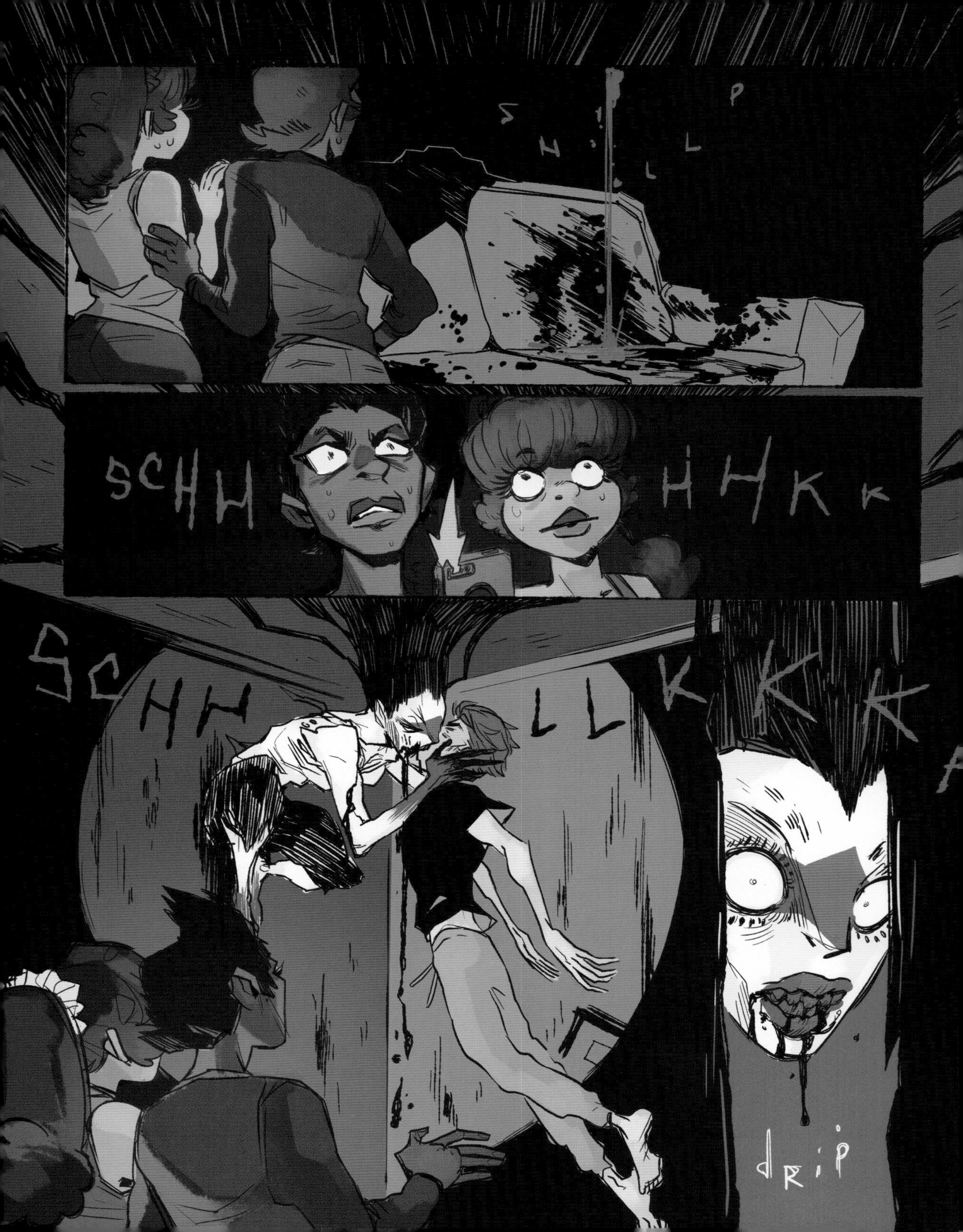
SHLLP
SCHH
HHKK
SCHH
LL
KKKA
drip

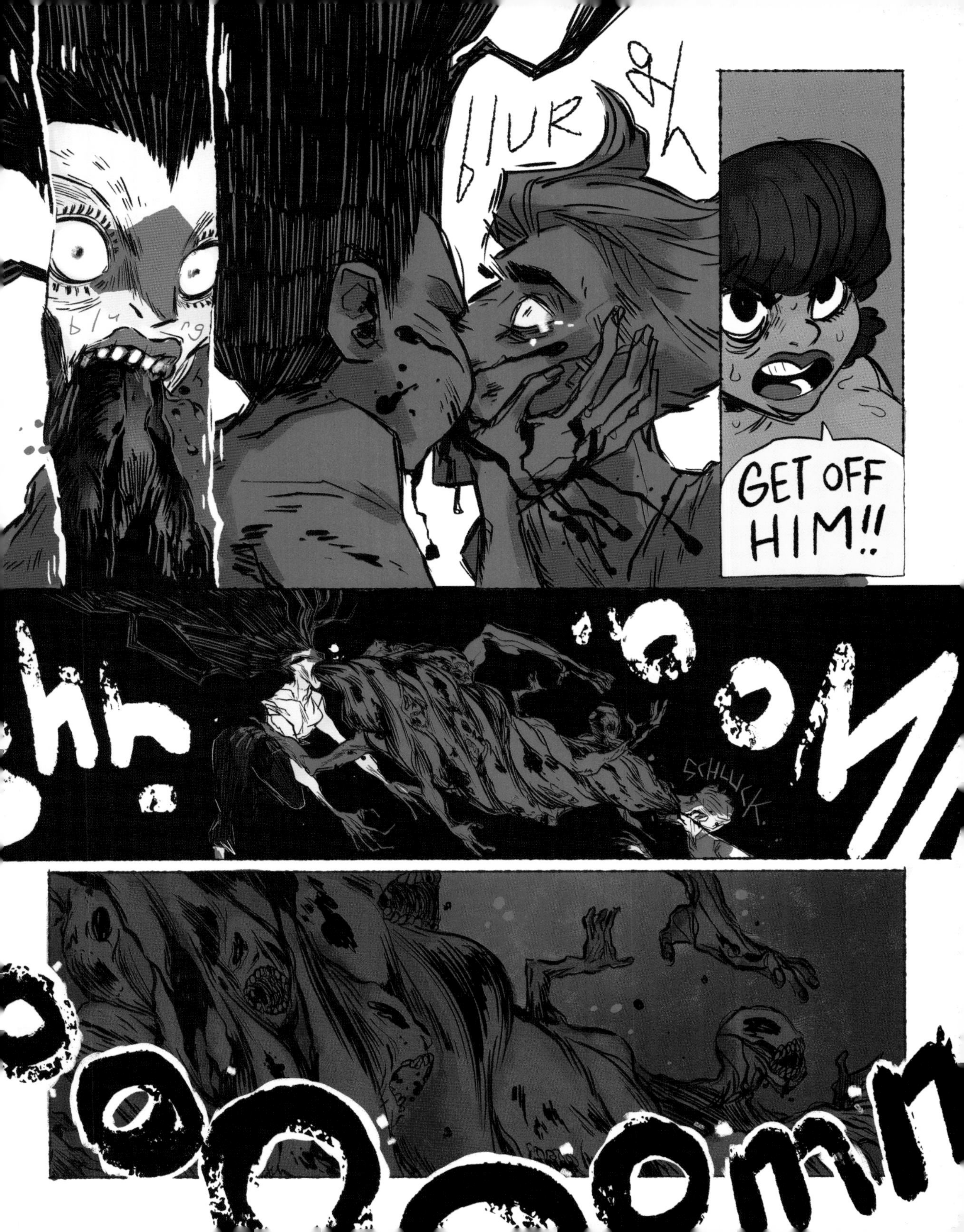
blurg
HURgh
GET OFF HIM!!
SCHLUCK.

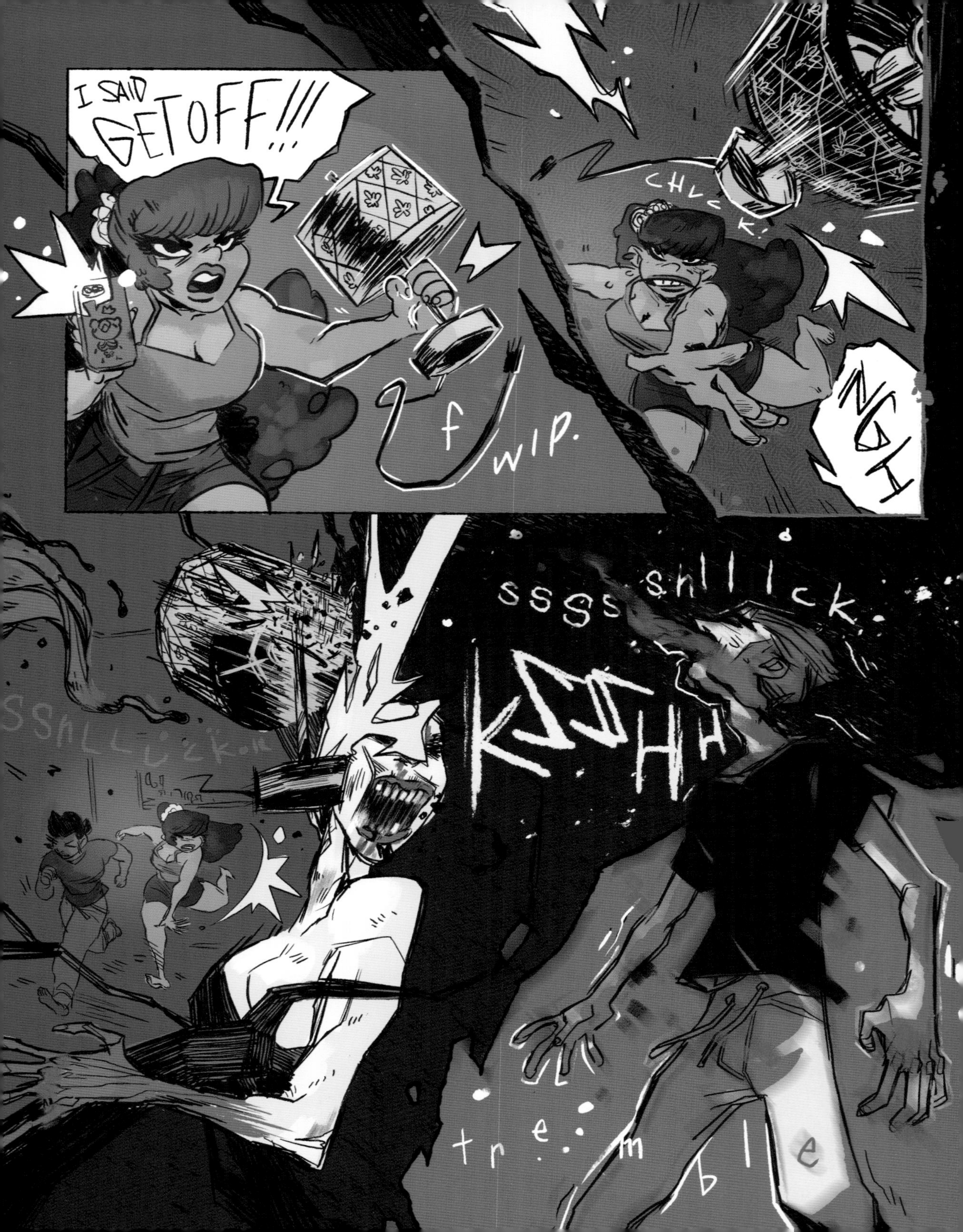
I SAID GETOFF!!!
f wip.
CHUCK!
NGH
SSSS shllick.
KSSH
SSHLLICK...
tremble

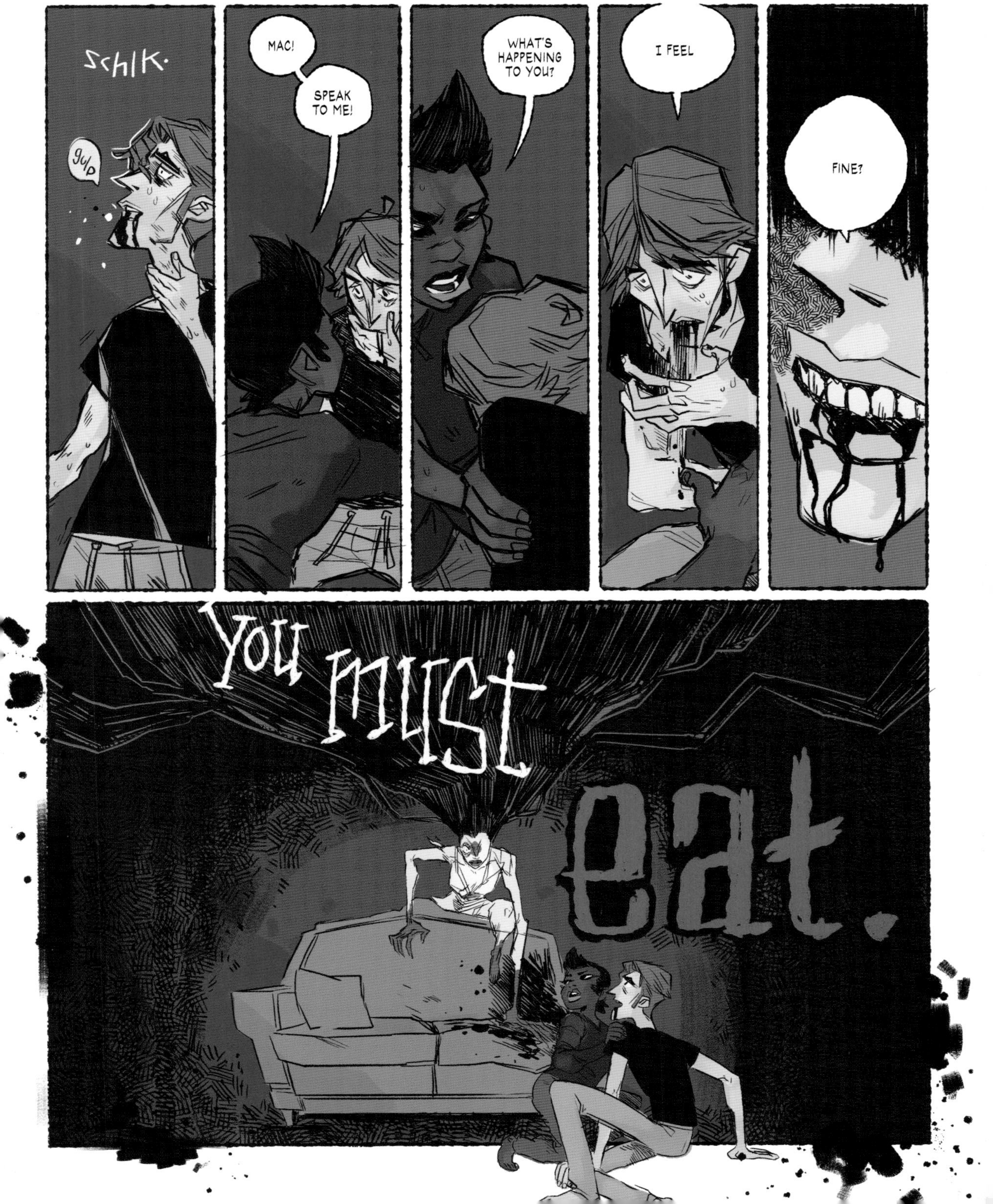
SCHLK.
gulp
MAC!
SPEAK TO ME!
WHAT'S HAPPENING TO YOU?
I FEEL
FINE?
YOU MUST
EAT.

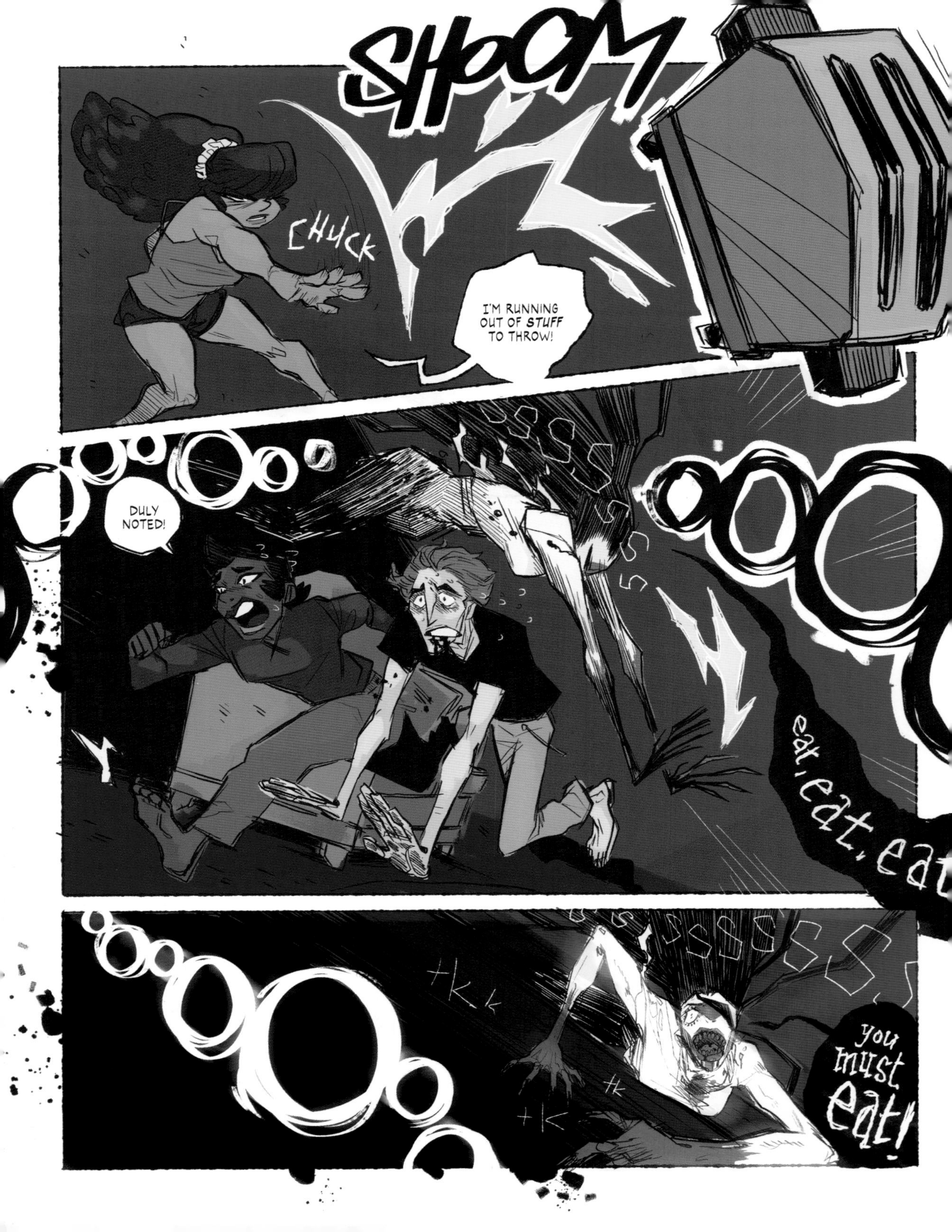
SHOOM
CHUCK
I'M RUNNING OUT OF STUFF TO THROW!
DULY NOTED!
eat, eat, eat
you must eat!

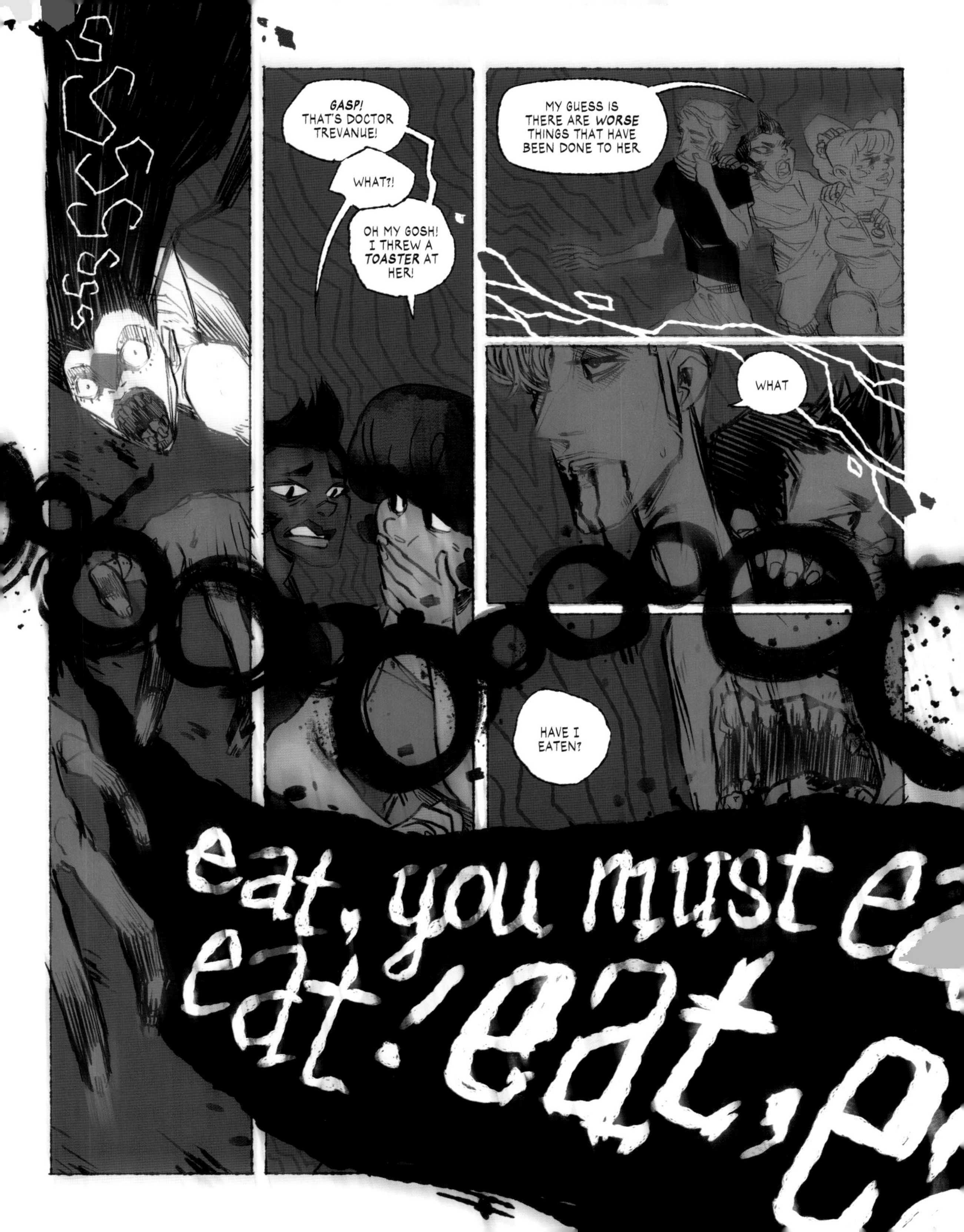
GASP! THAT'S DOCTOR TREVANUE!
WHAT?!
OH MY GOSH! I THREW A TOASTER AT HER!
MY GUESS IS THERE ARE WORSE THINGS THAT HAVE BEEN DONE TO HER
WHAT
HAVE I EATEN?
eat, you must e
eat. eat, e

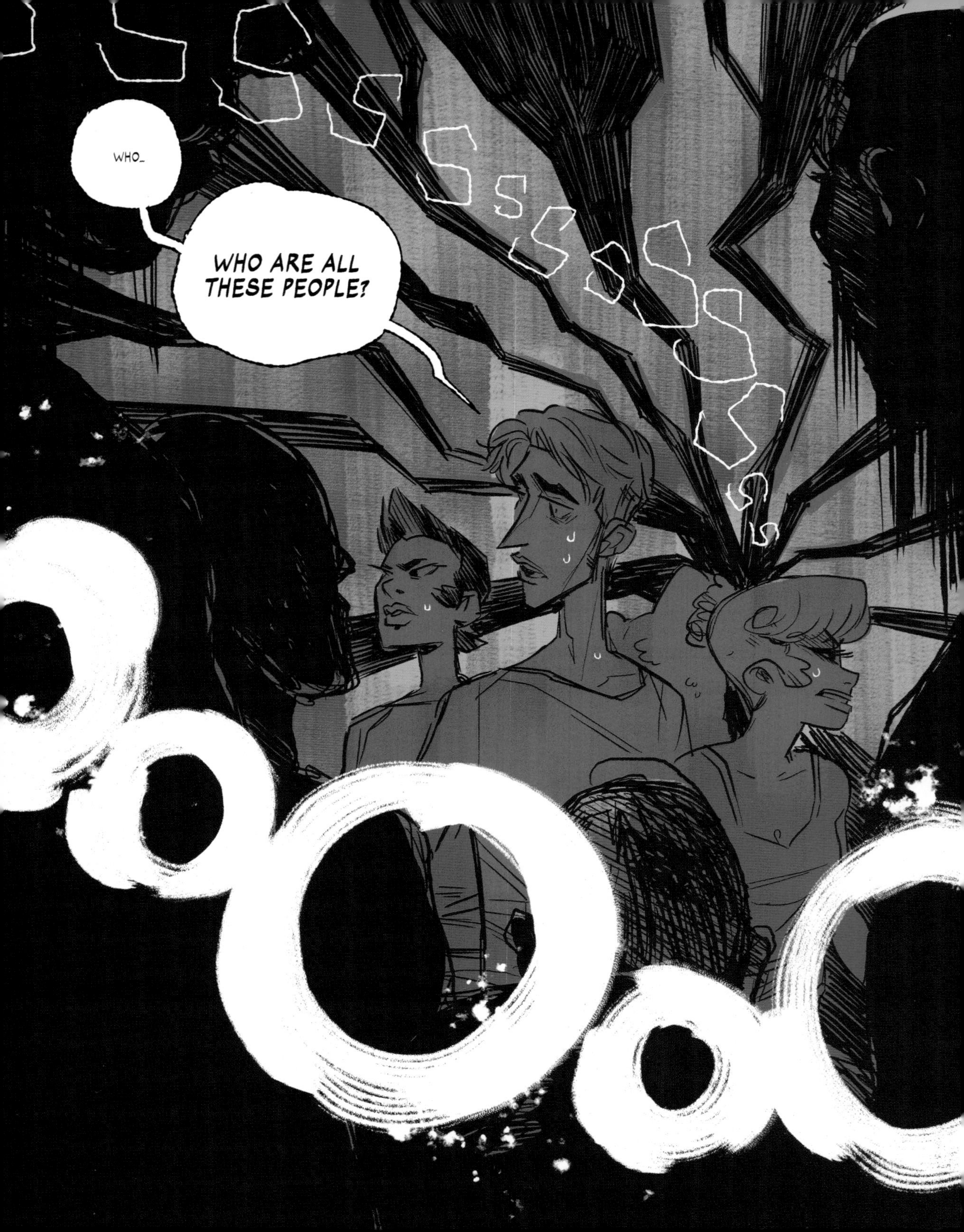
WHO...
WHO ARE ALL THESE PEOPLE?

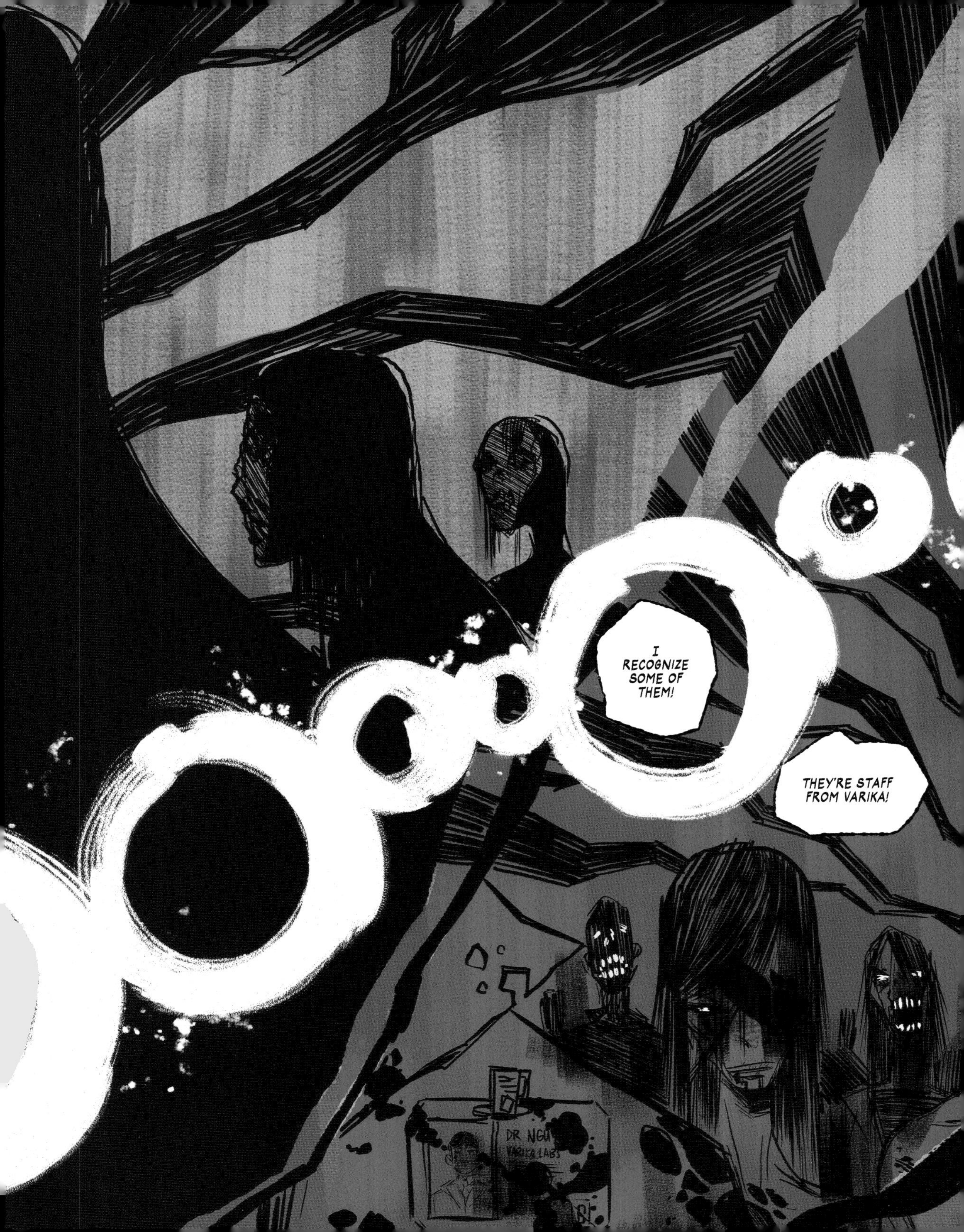
I RECOGNIZE SOME OF THEM!
THEY'RE STAFF FROM VARIKA!
VARIKA LABS

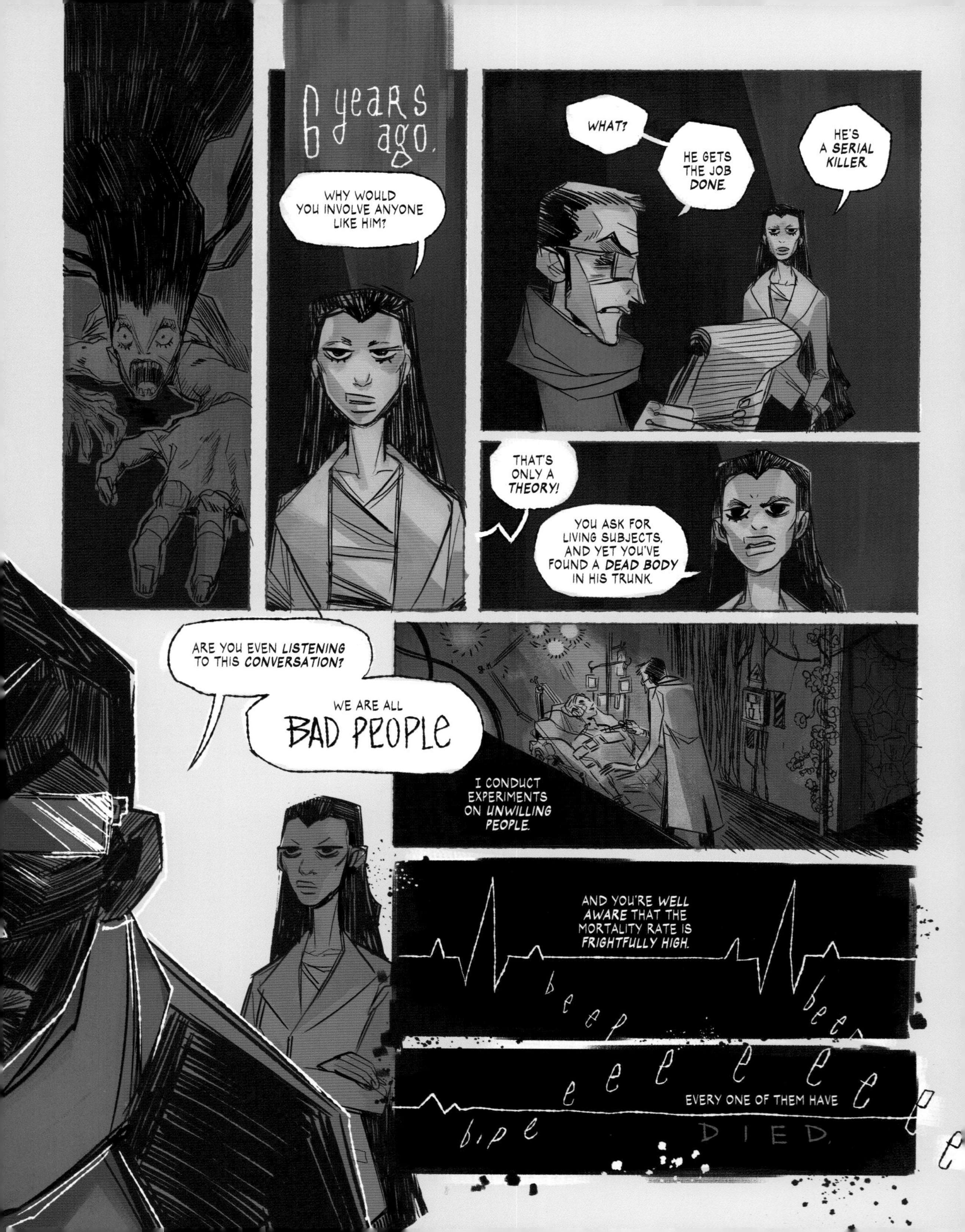
6 years ago.
WHY WOULD YOU INVOLVE ANYONE LIKE HIM?
WHAT?
HE GETS THE JOB DONE.
HE'S A SERIAL KILLER.
THAT'S ONLY A THEORY!
YOU ASK FOR LIVING SUBJECTS, AND YET YOU'VE FOUND A DEAD BODY IN HIS TRUNK.
ARE YOU EVEN LISTENING TO THIS CONVERSATION?
WE ARE ALL BAD PEOPLE
I CONDUCT EXPERIMENTS ON UNWILLING PEOPLE.
AND YOU'RE WELL AWARE THAT THE MORTALITY RATE IS FRIGHTFULLY HIGH.
beep
beep
EVERY ONE OF THEM HAVE
DIED.

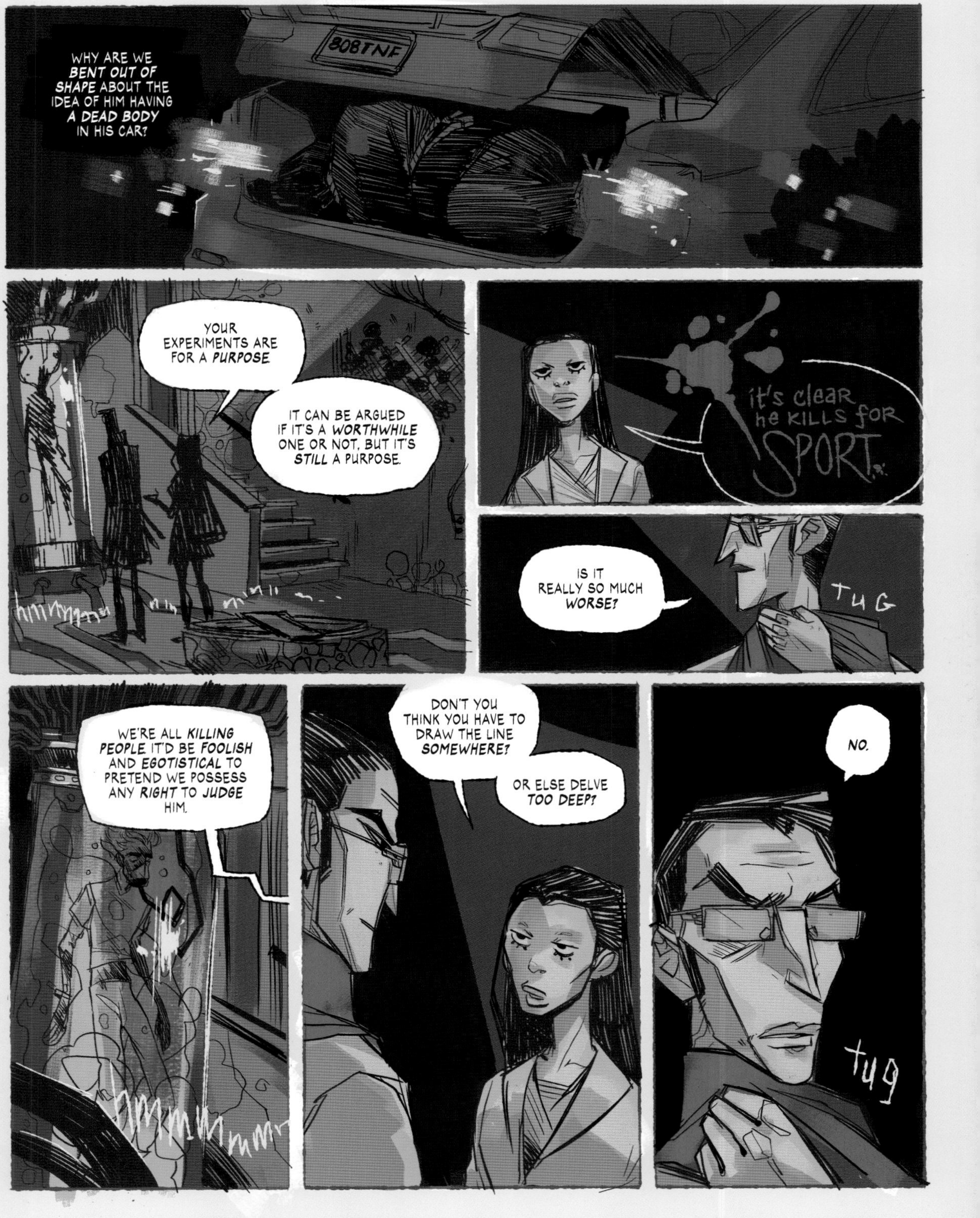

808TNF
WHY ARE WE BENT OUT OF SHAPE ABOUT THE IDEA OF HIM HAVING A DEAD BODY IN HIS CAR?
YOUR EXPERIMENTS ARE FOR A PURPOSE.
IT CAN BE ARGUED IF IT'S A WORTHWHILE ONE OR NOT, BUT IT'S STILL A PURPOSE.
hmmmm
it's clear he KILLS for SPORT.
IS IT REALLY SO MUCH WORSE?
TUG
WE'RE ALL KILLING PEOPLE. IT'D BE FOOLISH AND EGOTISTICAL TO PRETEND WE POSSESS ANY RIGHT TO JUDGE HIM.
hmmmmmmmm
DON'T YOU THINK YOU HAVE TO DRAW THE LINE SOMEWHERE?
OR ELSE DELVE TOO DEEP?
NO.
tug

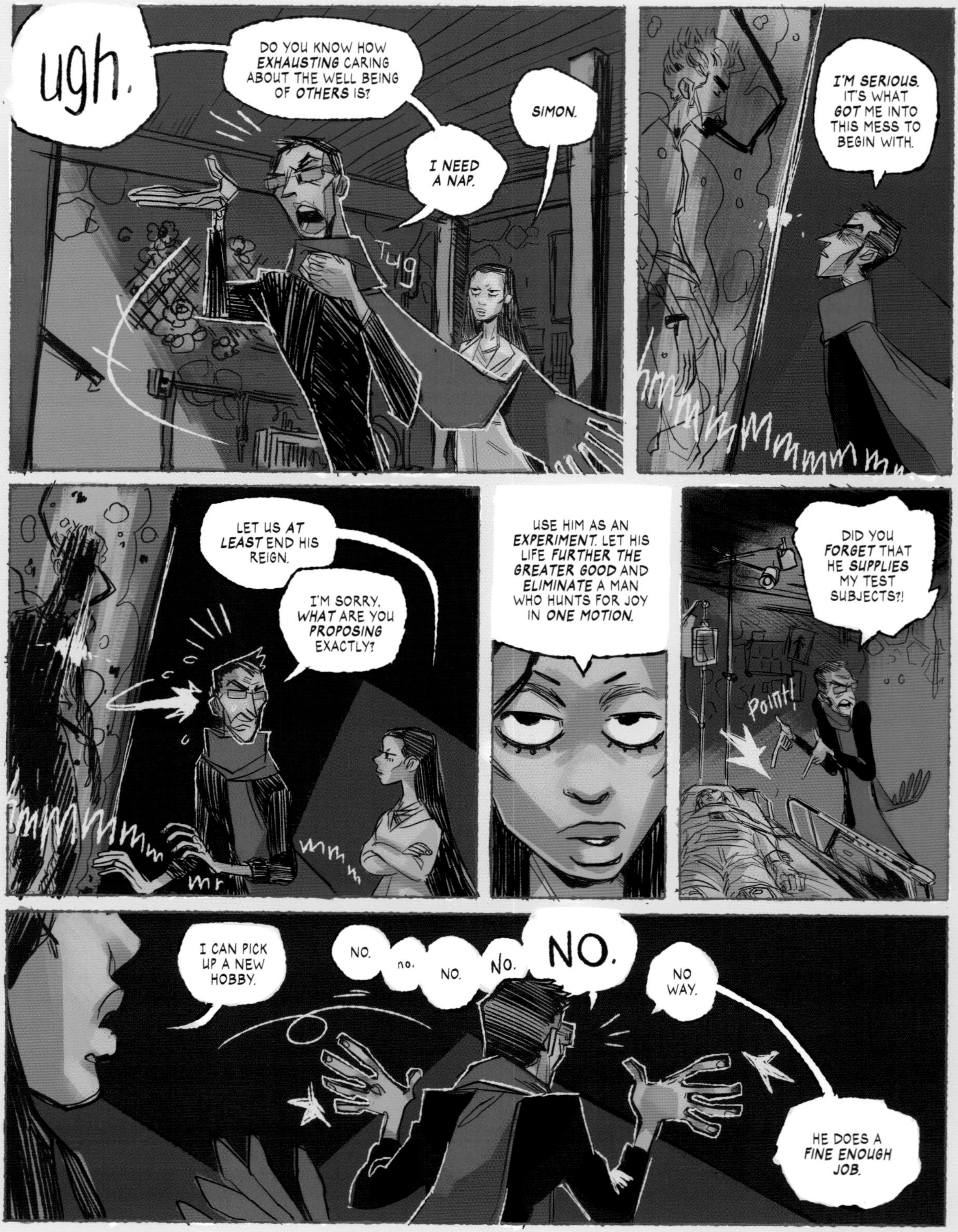

ugh.
DO YOU KNOW HOW EXHAUSTING CARING ABOUT THE WELL BEING OF OTHERS IS?
I NEED A NAP.
SIMON.
TUG
I'M SERIOUS. IT'S WHAT GOT ME INTO THIS MESS TO BEGIN WITH.
LET US AT LEAST END HIS REIGN.
I'M SORRY, WHAT ARE YOU PROPOSING EXACTLY?
USE HIM AS AN EXPERIMENT. LET HIS LIFE FURTHER THE GREATER GOOD AND ELIMINATE A MAN WHO HUNTS FOR JOY IN ONE MOTION.
DID YOU FORGET THAT HE SUPPLIES MY TEST SUBJECTS?!
POINT!
I CAN PICK UP A NEW HOBBY.
NO.
no.
NO.
NO.
NO.
NO WAY.
HE DOES A FINE ENOUGH JOB.

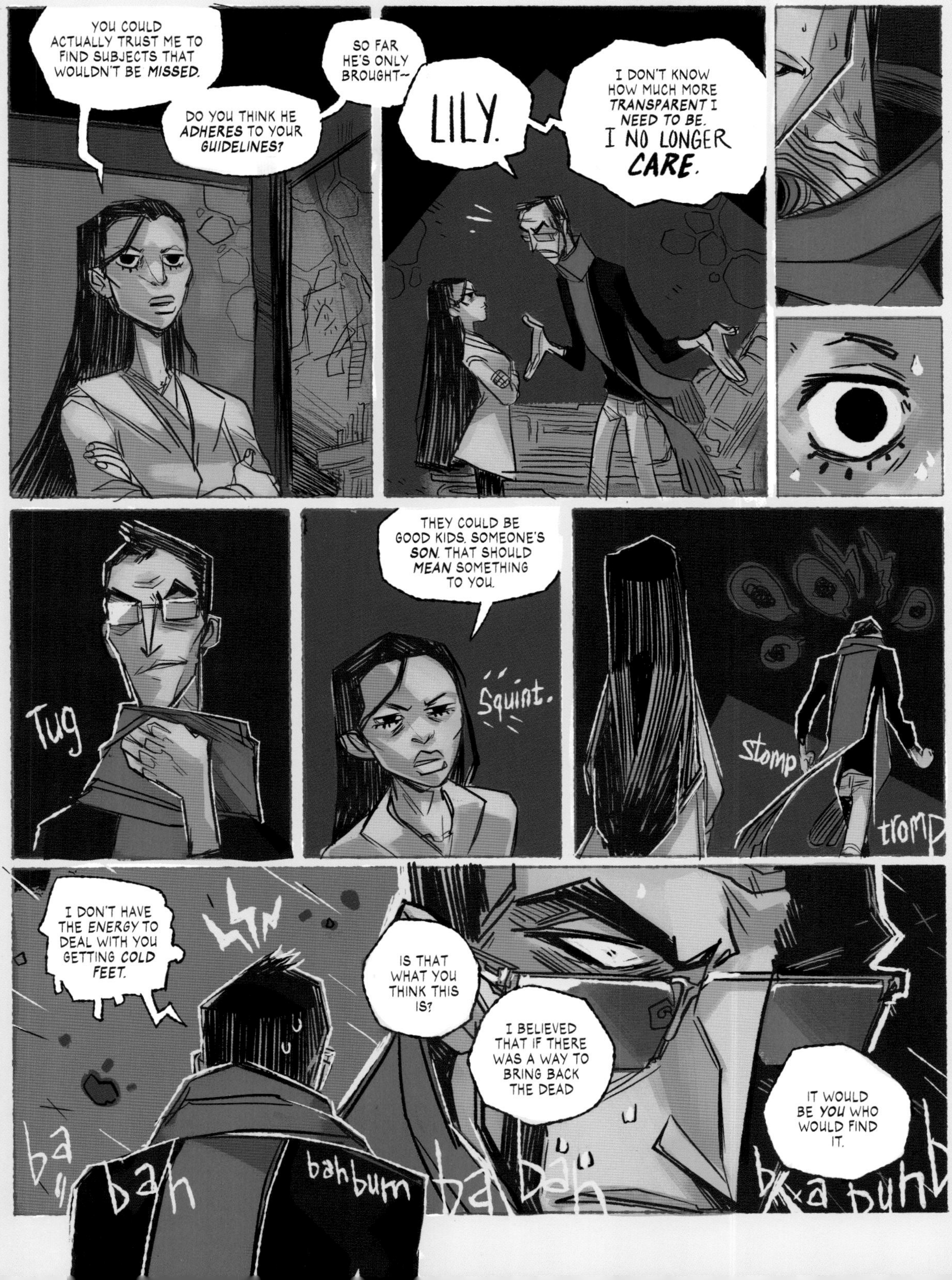
YOU COULD ACTUALLY TRUST ME TO FIND SUBJECTS THAT WOULDN'T BE MISSED.
DO YOU THINK HE ADHERES TO YOUR GUIDELINES?
SO FAR HE'S ONLY BROUGHT--
LILY.
I DON'T KNOW HOW MUCH MORE TRANSPARENT I NEED TO BE. I NO LONGER CARE.
Tug
THEY COULD BE GOOD KIDS. SOMEONE'S SON. THAT SHOULD MEAN SOMETHING TO YOU.
Squint.
stomp
tromp
I DON'T HAVE THE ENERGY TO DEAL WITH YOU GETTING COLD FEET.
IS THAT WHAT YOU THINK THIS IS?
I BELIEVED THAT IF THERE WAS A WAY TO BRING BACK THE DEAD
IT WOULD BE YOU WHO WOULD FIND IT.
ba bah
bahbum
ba Dah
b a bum

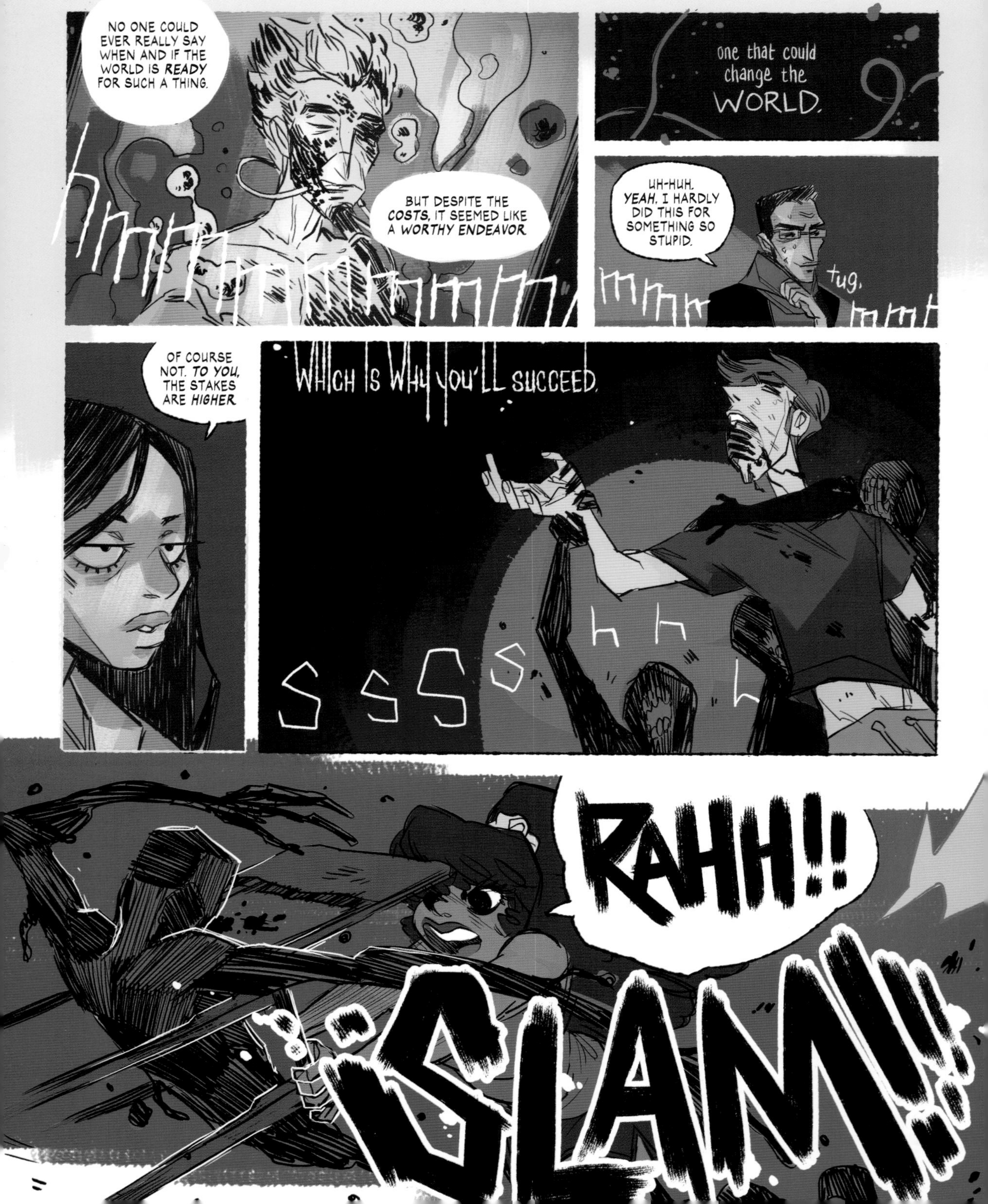
NO ONE COULD EVER REALLY SAY WHEN AND IF THE WORLD IS READY FOR SUCH A THING.
BUT DESPITE THE COSTS, IT SEEMED LIKE A WORTHY ENDEAVOR
hmmmmmmmm
one that could change the WORLD.
UH-HUH. YEAH, I HARDLY DID THIS FOR SOMETHING SO STUPID.
tug.
mmmmm
OF COURSE NOT. TO YOU, THE STAKES ARE HIGHER
WHICH IS WHY YOU'LL SUCCEED.
SSSShhhh
RAHH!!
SLAM!!

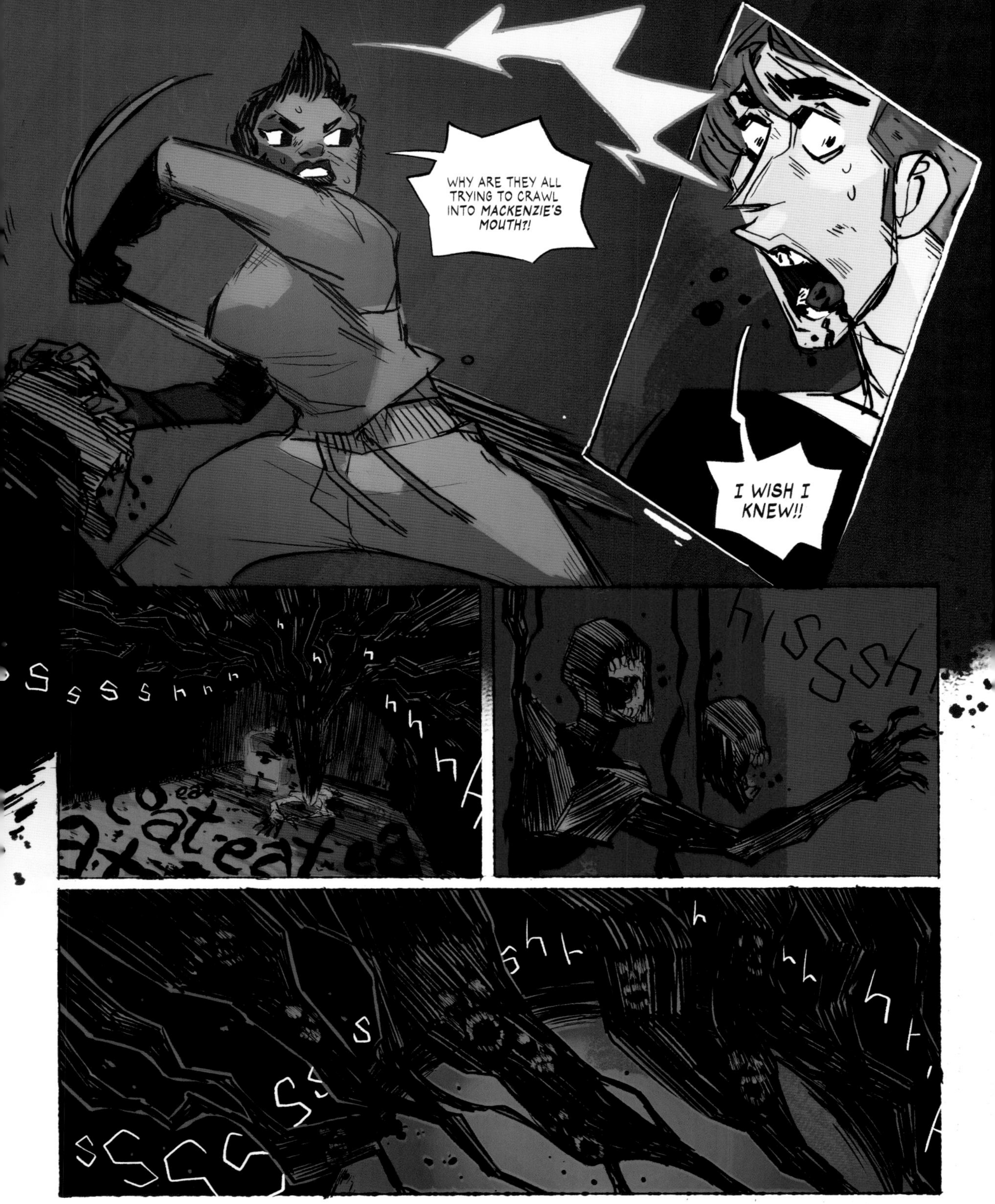

WHY ARE THEY ALL TRYING TO CRAWL INTO MACKENZIE'S MOUTH?!
I WISH I KNEW!!
SsSSShhhhhhhhA
eat eat eat
hiSSSh
sSSSSShhhhhhA

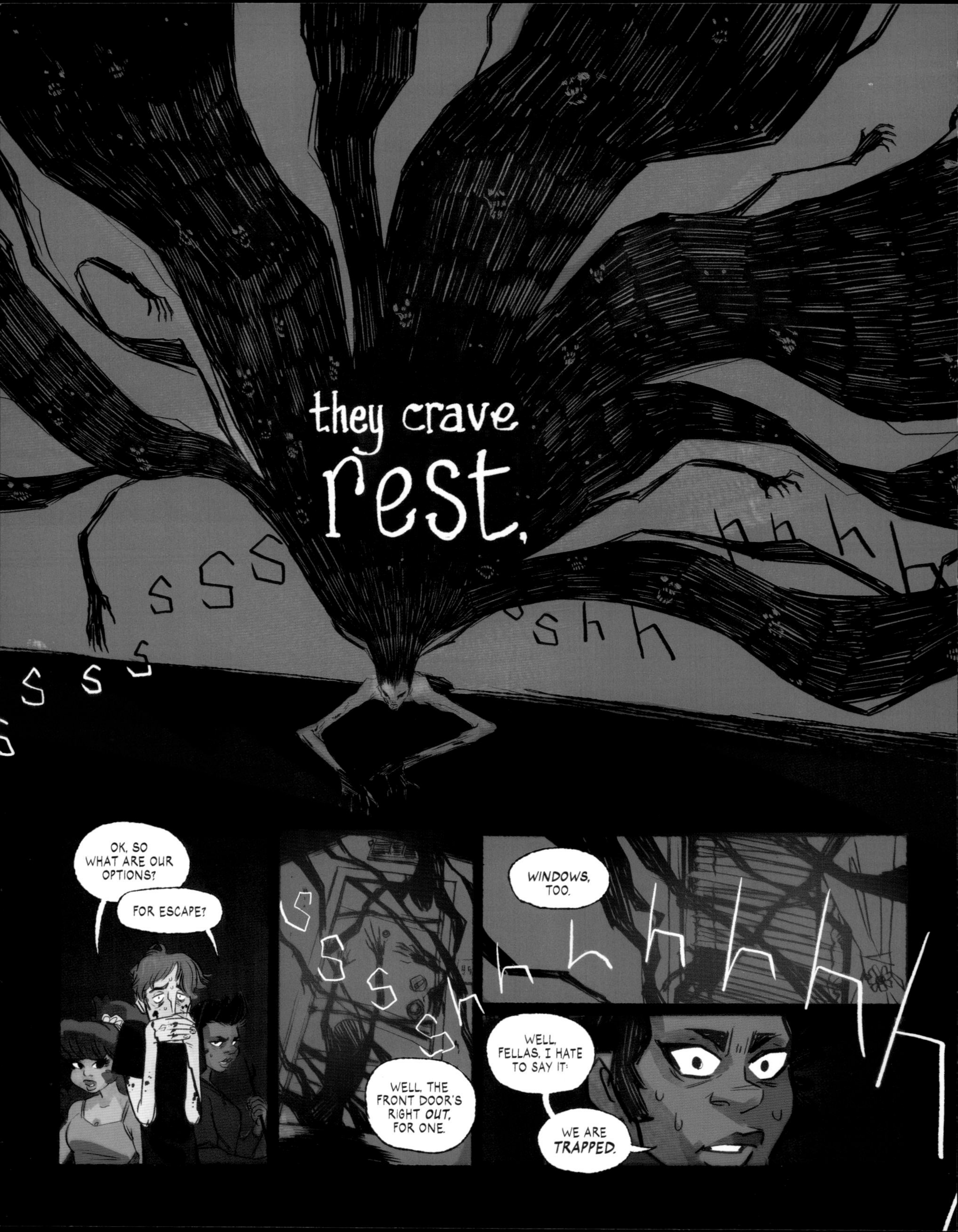
they crave
rest,
OK, SO WHAT ARE OUR OPTIONS?
FOR ESCAPE?
WELL, THE FRONT DOOR'S RIGHT *OUT*, FOR ONE.
WINDOWS, TOO.
WELL, FELLAS, I HATE TO SAY IT:
WE ARE *TRAPPED*.

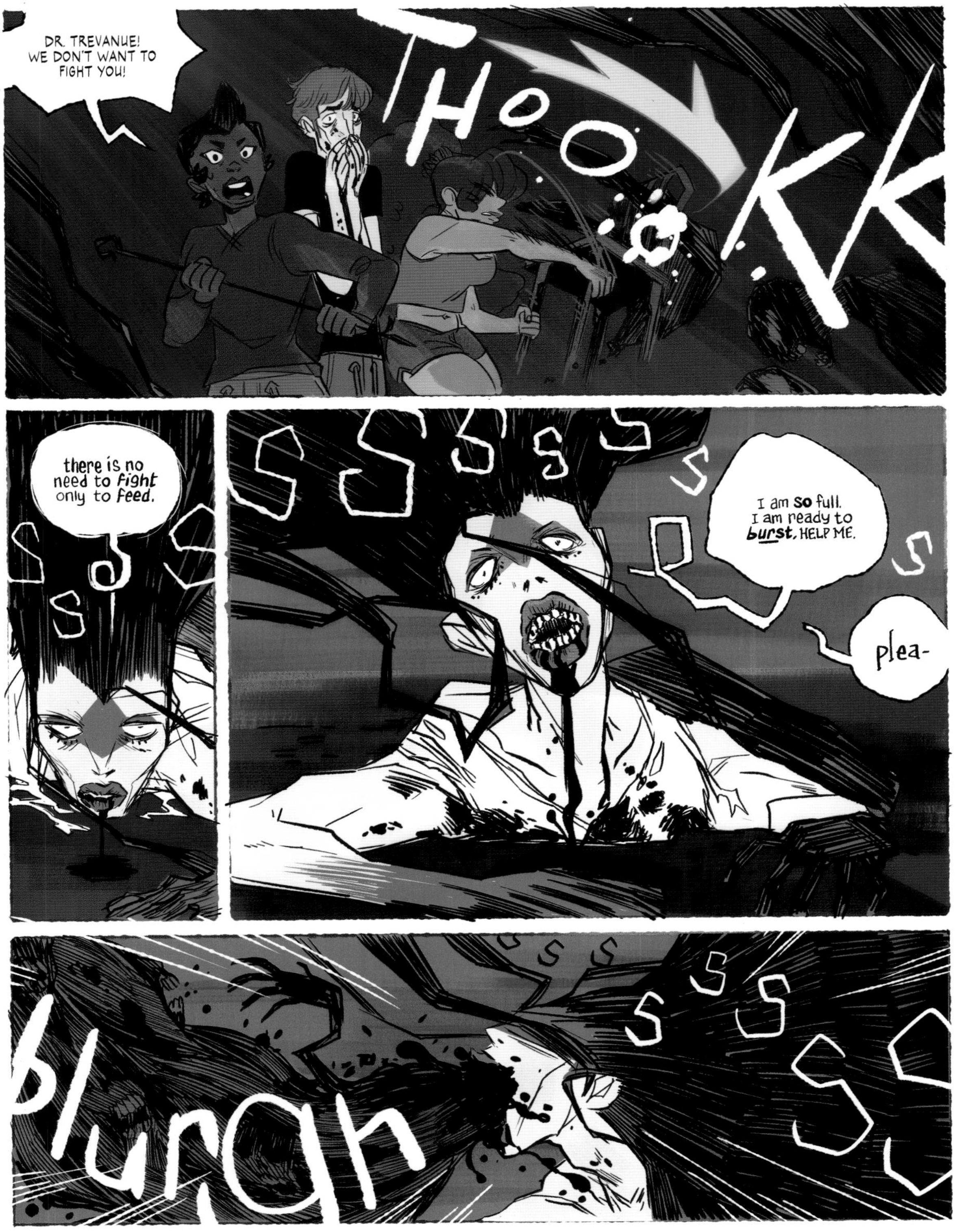
DR. TREVANUE! WE DON'T WANT TO FIGHT YOU!
THOOKK
there is no need to fight only to feed.
SSS
SSSSSSS
I am so full. I am ready to burst, HELP ME.
plea-
SSSSSS
blurah

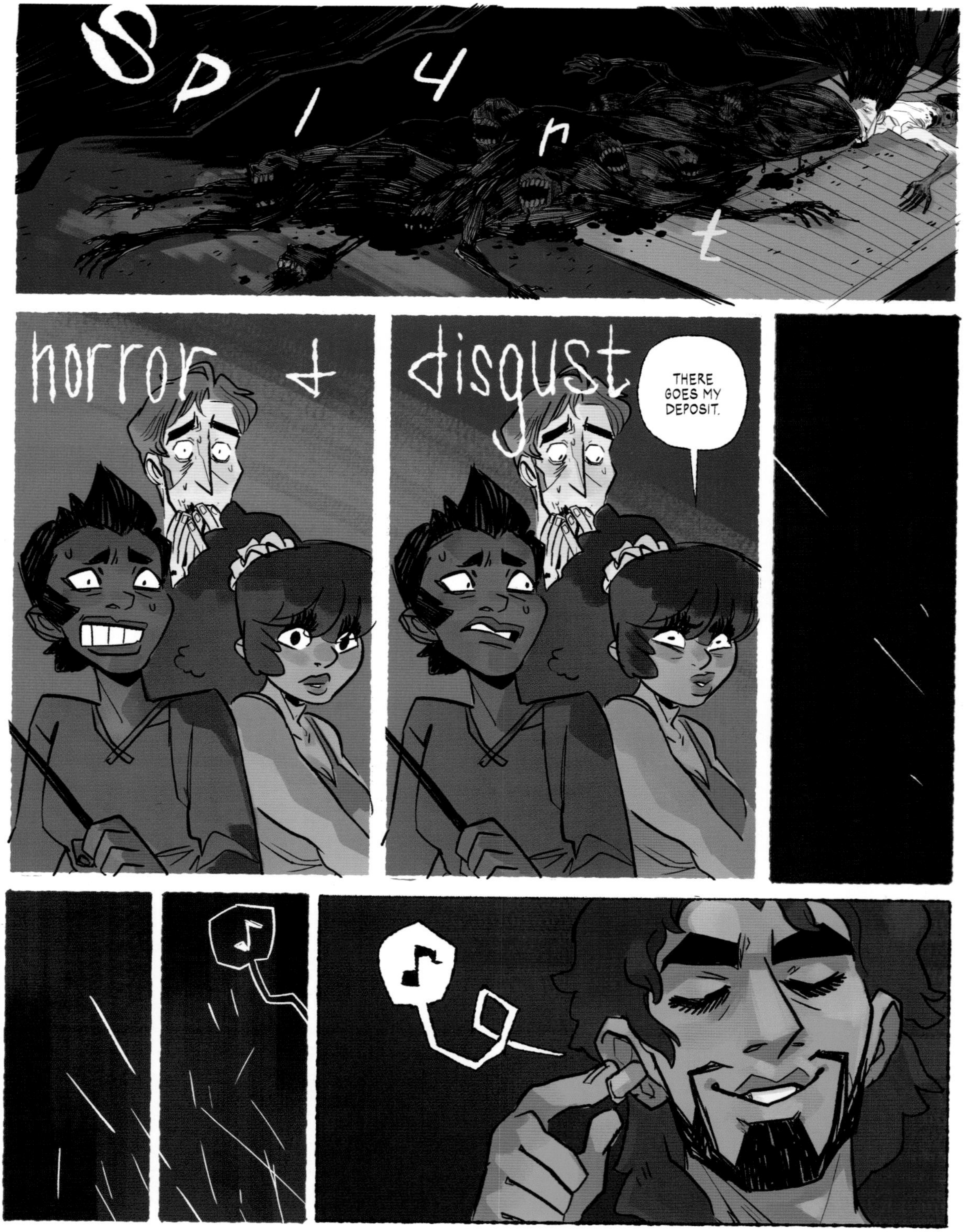
Splurt
horror & disgust
THERE GOES MY DEPOSIT.

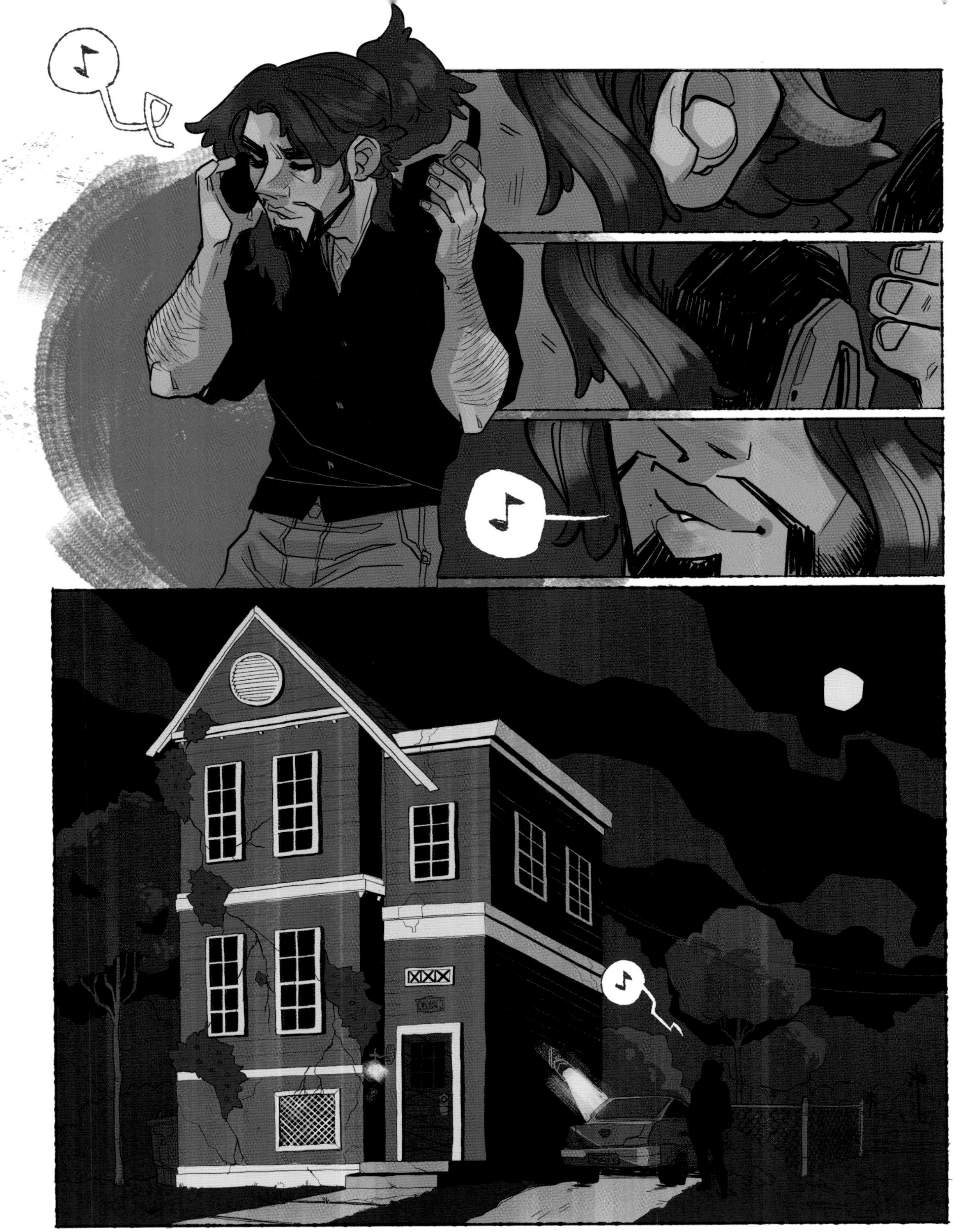

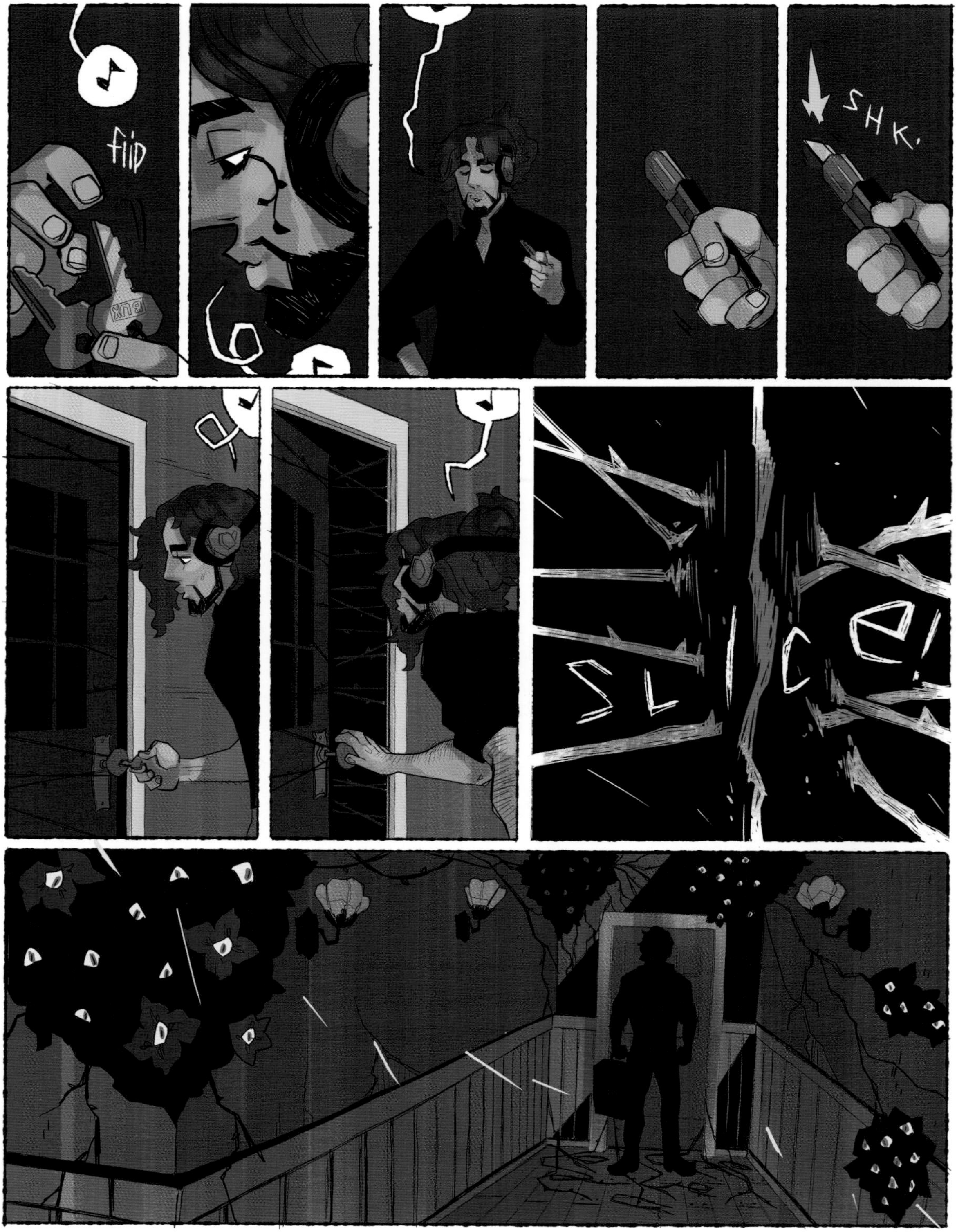

flip
SHK.
SLICE!

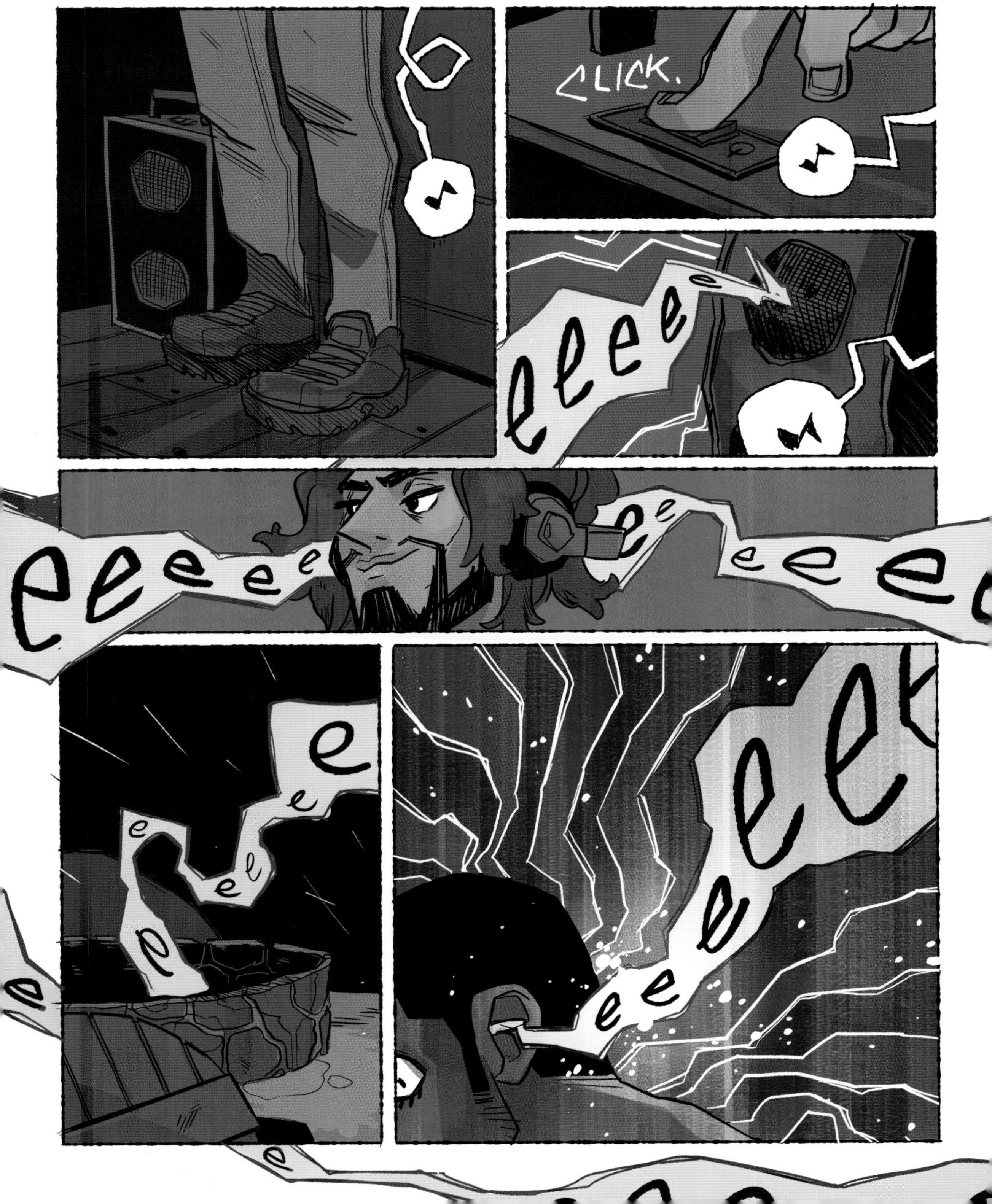
CLICK.
eeeeee
eeeeee
eeeeee
eeeeee
eeeeeeeee
e

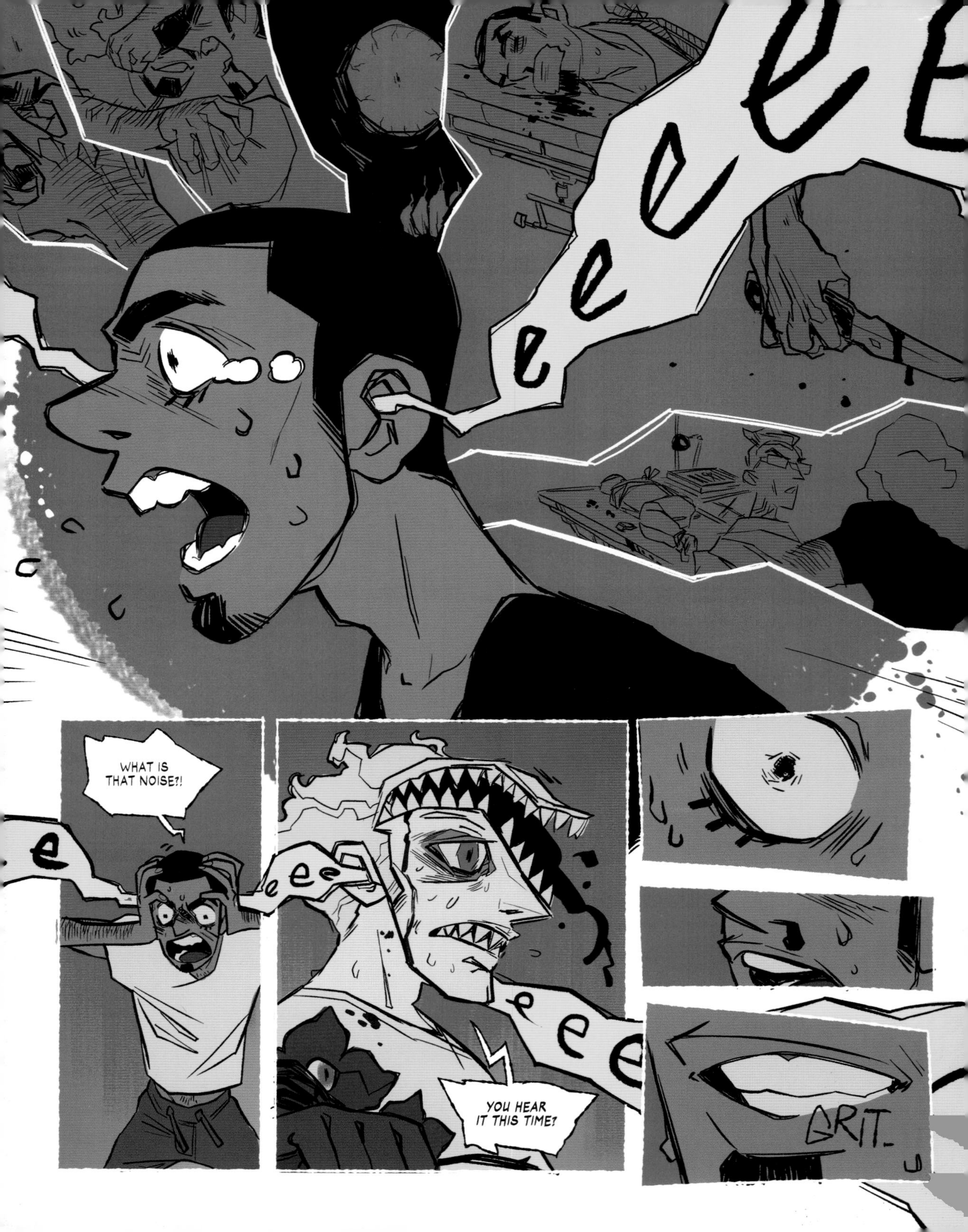

eeeeeeE
WHAT IS THAT NOISE?!
e
eee
eee
YOU HEAR IT THIS TIME?
GRIT.

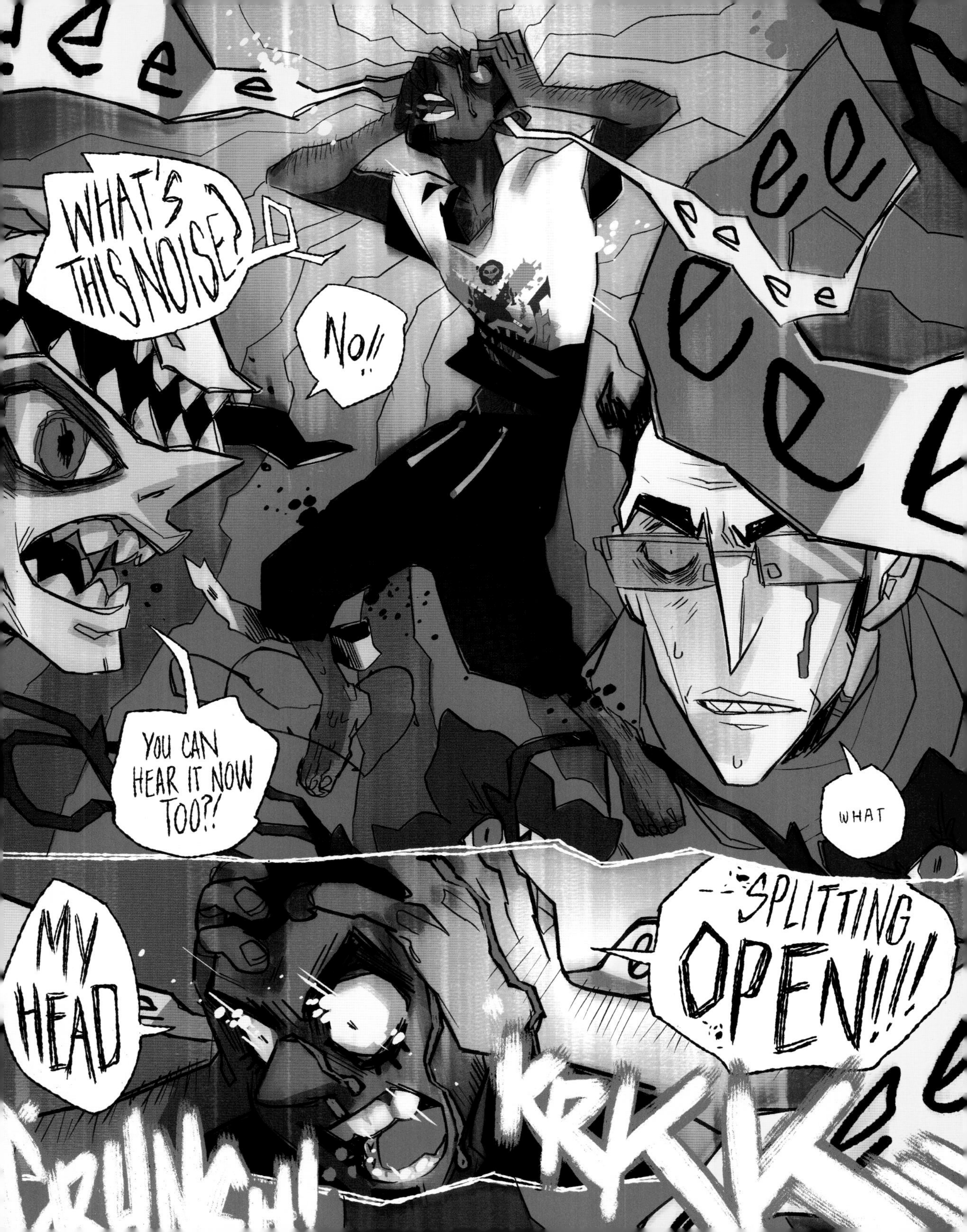
eeeee
eeeeeeeeee
WHAT'S THIS NOISE?
NO!!
YOU CAN HEAR IT NOW TOO?!
WHAT
MY HEAD
SPLITTING OPEN!!!
CRUNCH
KRK

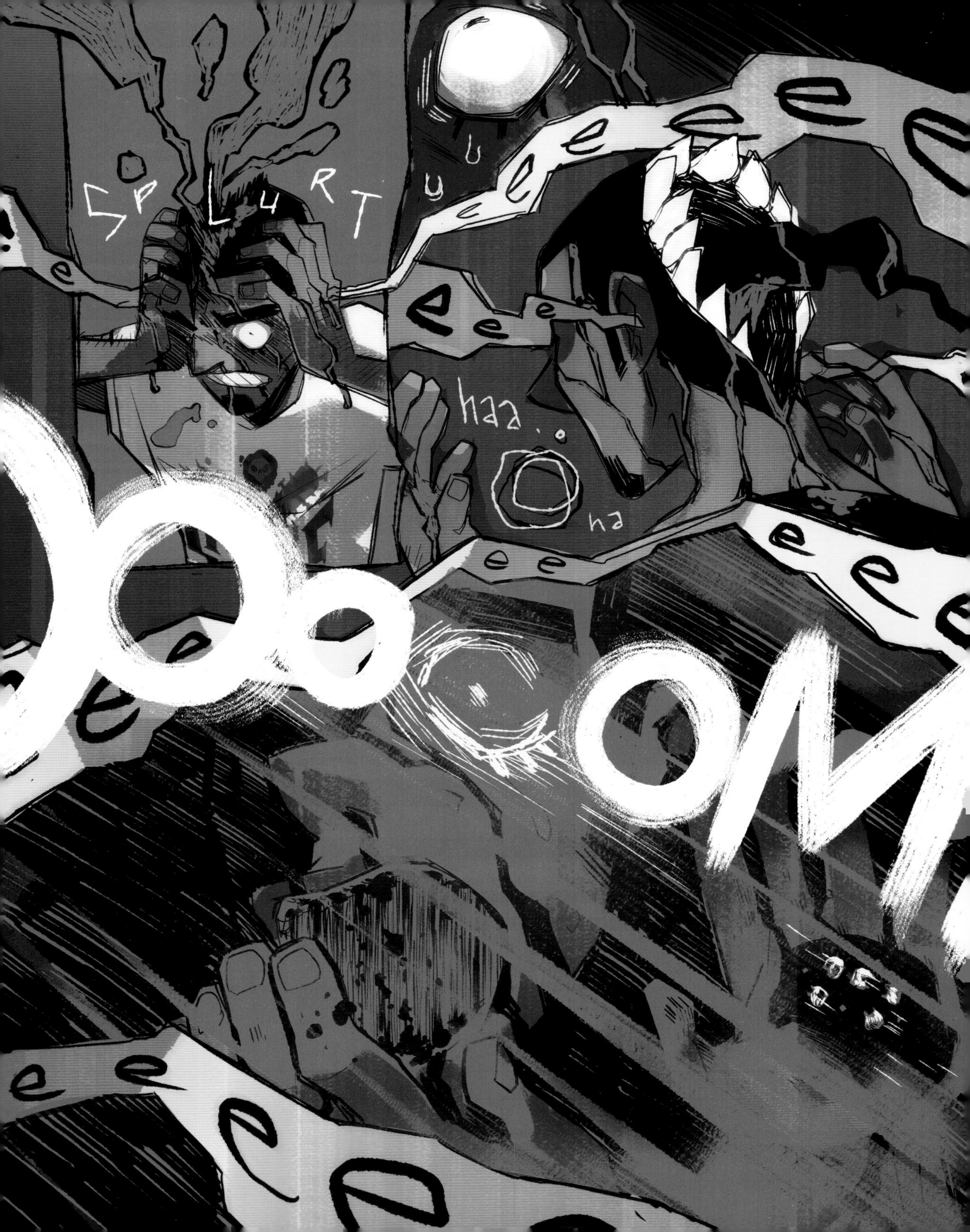
SPLURT
haa
ha
BOOOOM

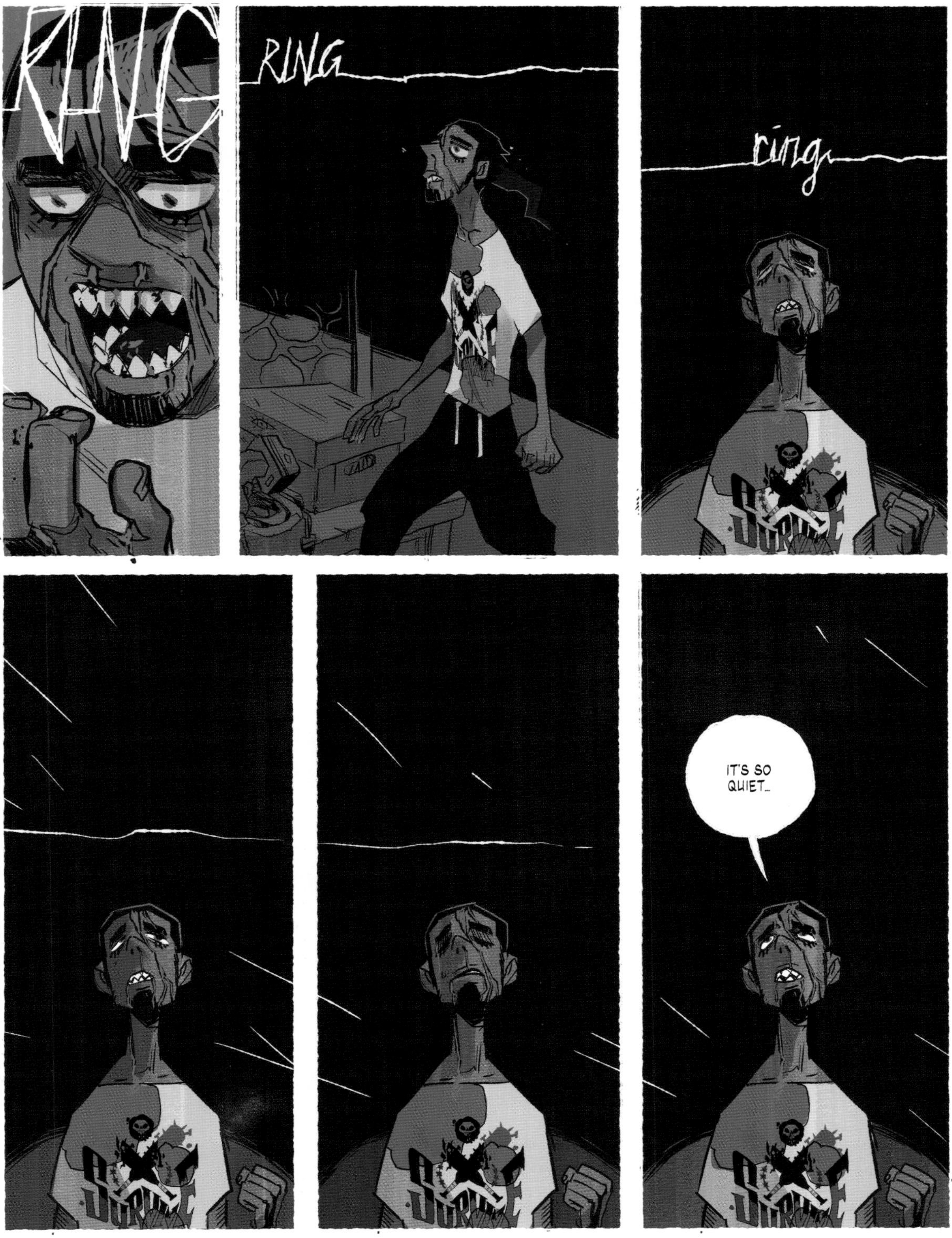
RING
RING
ring
IT'S SO QUIET...

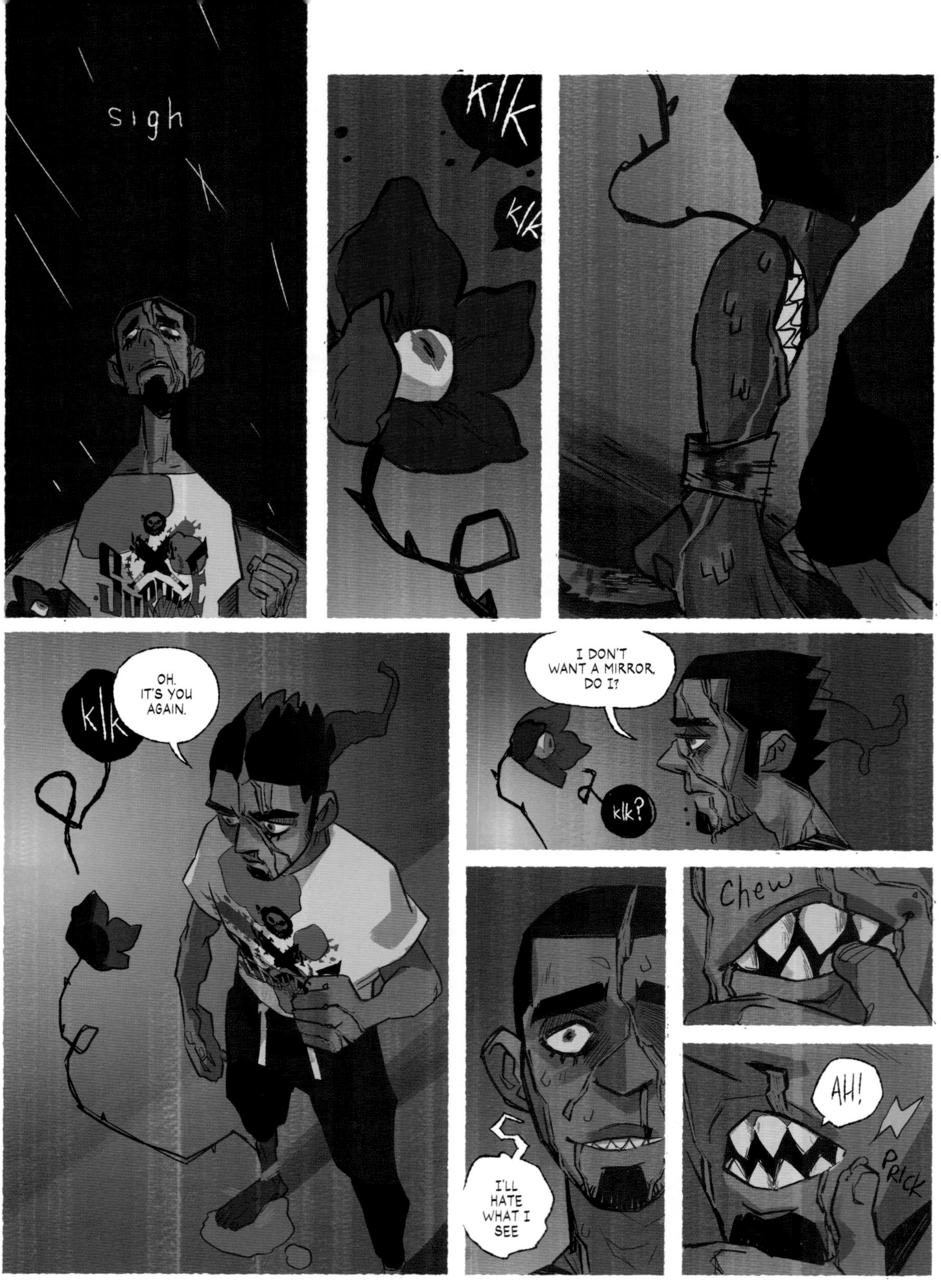
sigh
K/K
K/K
K/K
OH. IT'S YOU AGAIN.
I DON'T WANT A MIRROR, DO I?
K/K?
I'LL HATE WHAT I SEE
Chew
AH!
PRICK

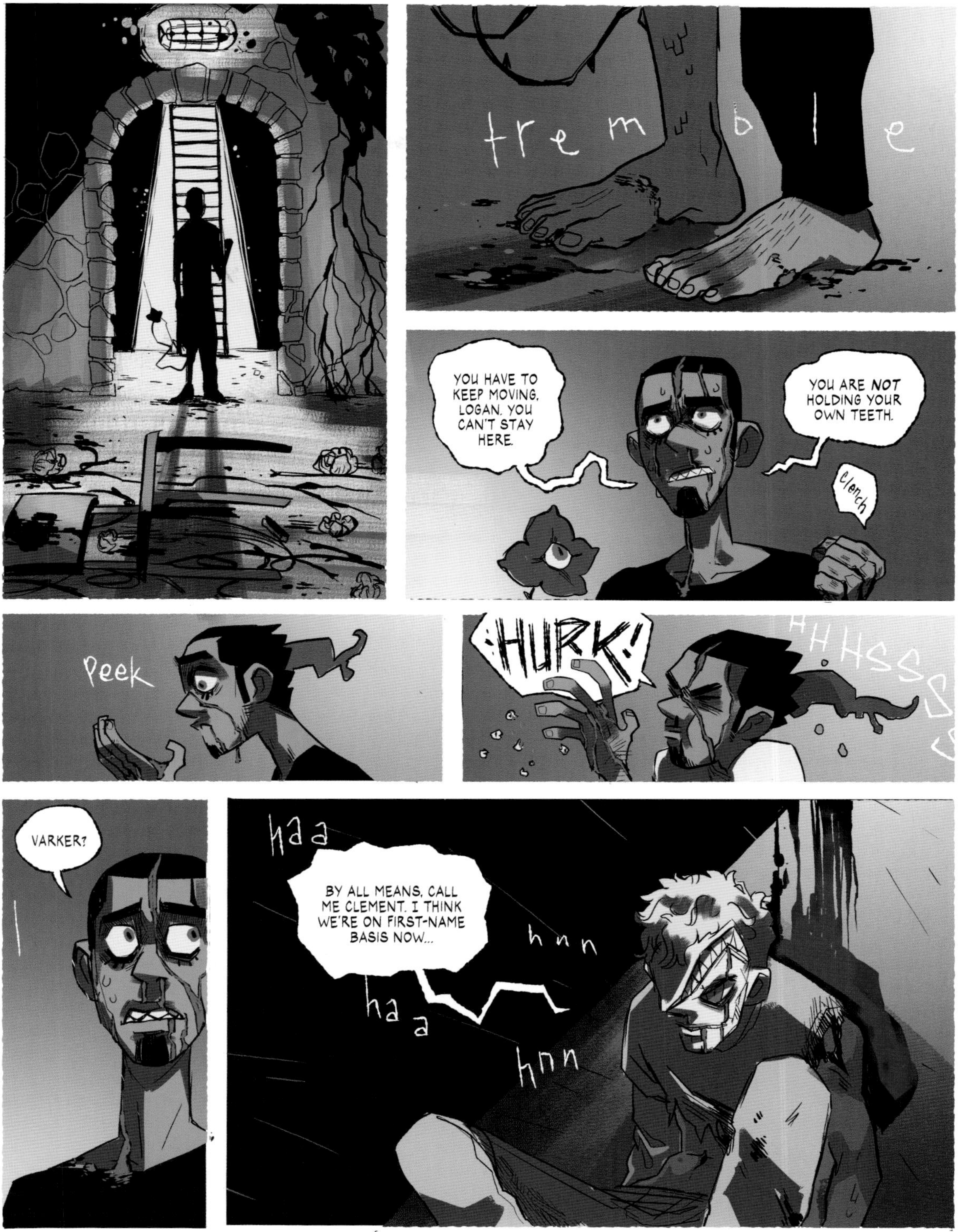
tremble
YOU HAVE TO KEEP MOVING, LOGAN. YOU CAN'T STAY HERE.
YOU ARE **NOT** HOLDING YOUR OWN TEETH.
clench
Peek
HURK!
HHHSSS
VARKER?
haa
BY ALL MEANS, CALL ME CLEMENT. I THINK WE'RE ON FIRST-NAME BASIS NOW...
hnn
haa
hnn

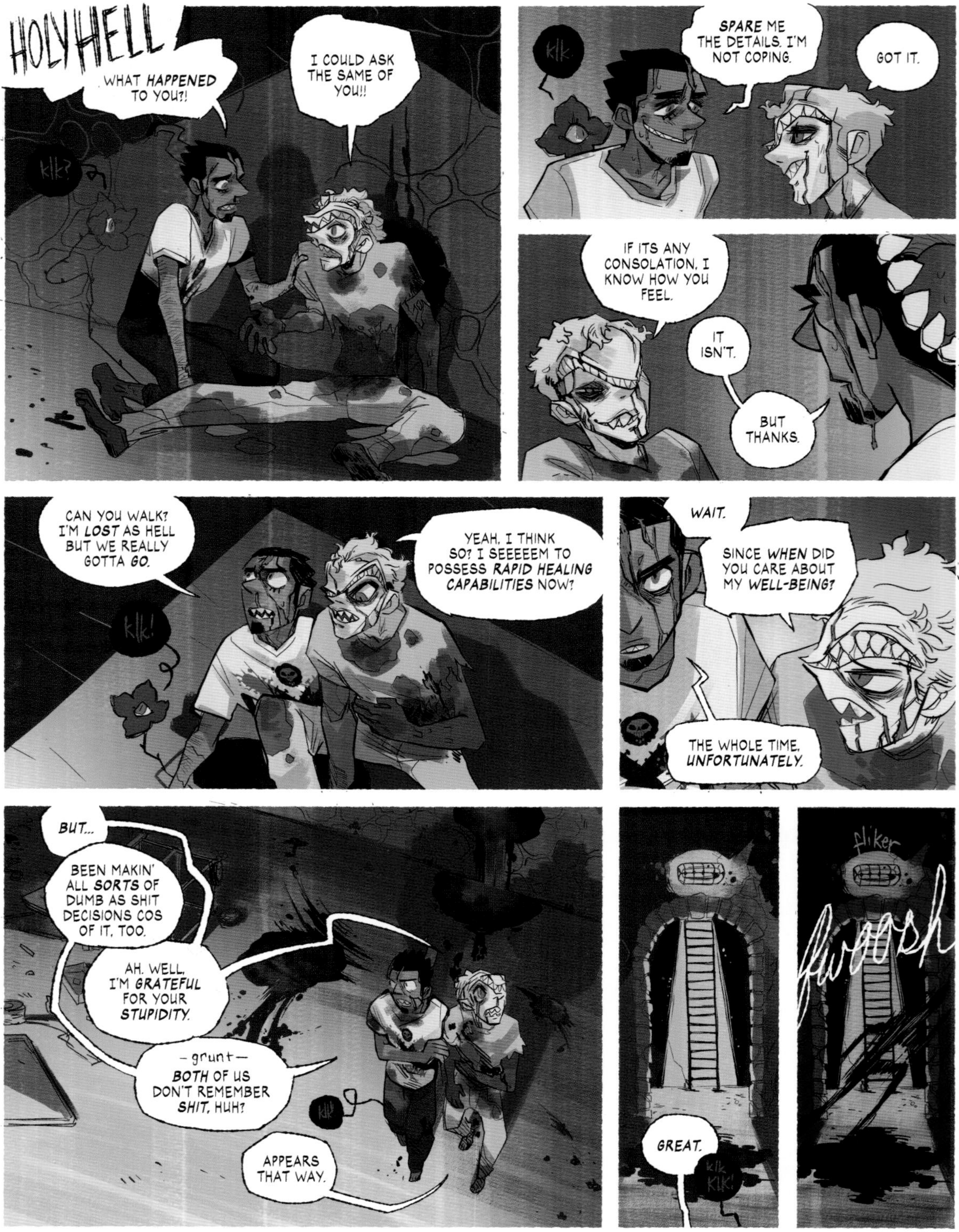
HOLY HELL
WHAT HAPPENED TO YOU?!
I COULD ASK THE SAME OF YOU!!
klk?
klk.
SPARE ME THE DETAILS. I'M NOT COPING.
GOT IT.
IF ITS ANY CONSOLATION, I KNOW HOW YOU FEEL.
IT ISN'T.
BUT THANKS.
CAN YOU WALK? I'M LOST AS HELL BUT WE REALLY GOTTA GO.
YEAH, I THINK SO? I SEEEEEM TO POSSESS RAPID HEALING CAPABILITIES NOW?
klk!
WAIT.
SINCE WHEN DID YOU CARE ABOUT MY WELL-BEING?
THE WHOLE TIME, UNFORTUNATELY.
BUT...
BEEN MAKIN' ALL SORTS OF DUMB AS SHIT DECISIONS COS OF IT, TOO.
AH. WELL, I'M GRATEFUL FOR YOUR STUPIDITY.
—grunt—
BOTH OF US DON'T REMEMBER SHIT, HUH?
klk
APPEARS THAT WAY.
GREAT.
klk KLK!
fliker
fwoosh

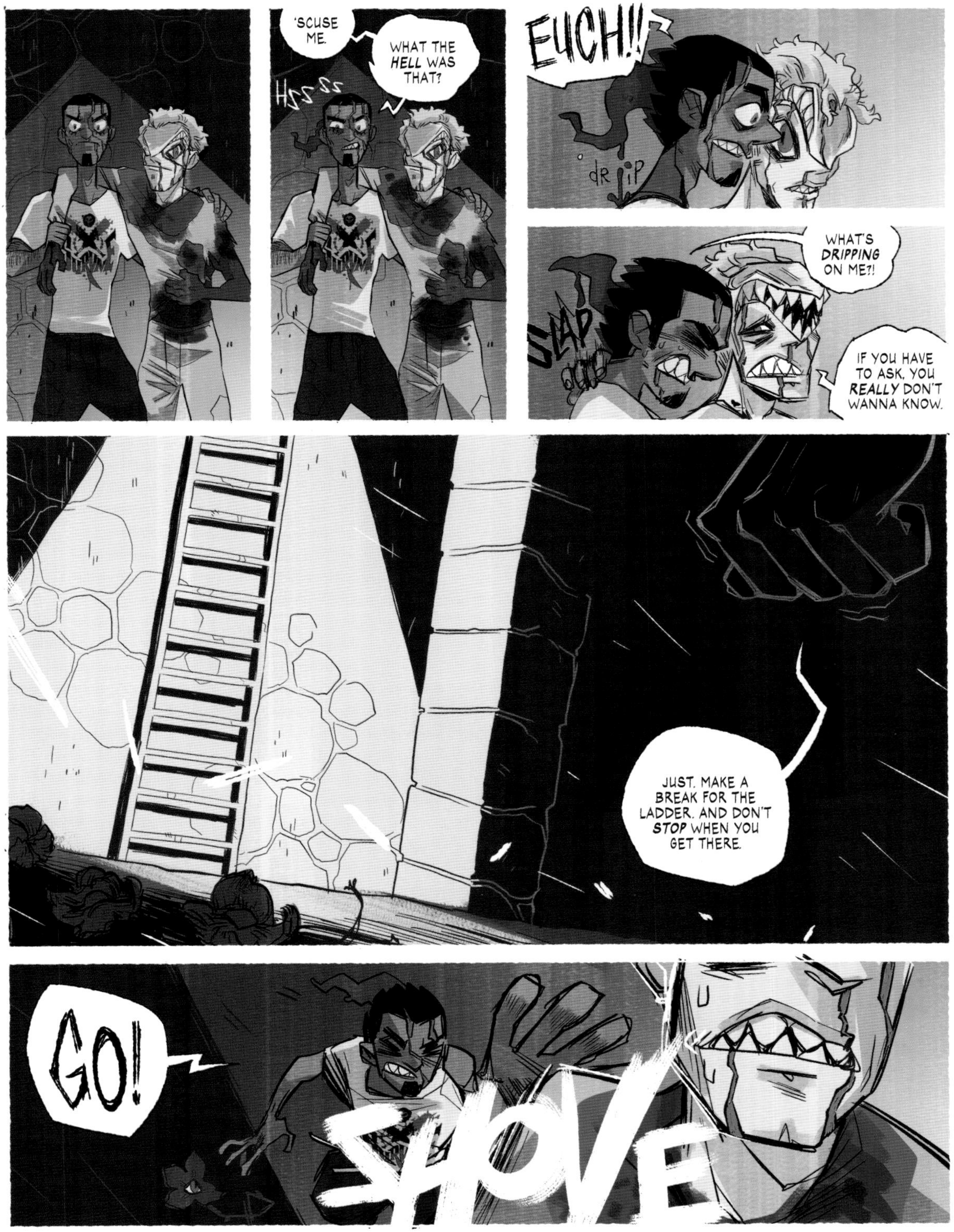
'SCUSE ME.
WHAT THE HELL WAS THAT?
HSZZZZH
EUCH!!
drip
WHAT'S DRIPPING ON ME?!
SLAP
IF YOU HAVE TO ASK, YOU REALLY DON'T WANNA KNOW.
JUST. MAKE A BREAK FOR THE LADDER. AND DON'T STOP WHEN YOU GET THERE.
GO!
SHOVE

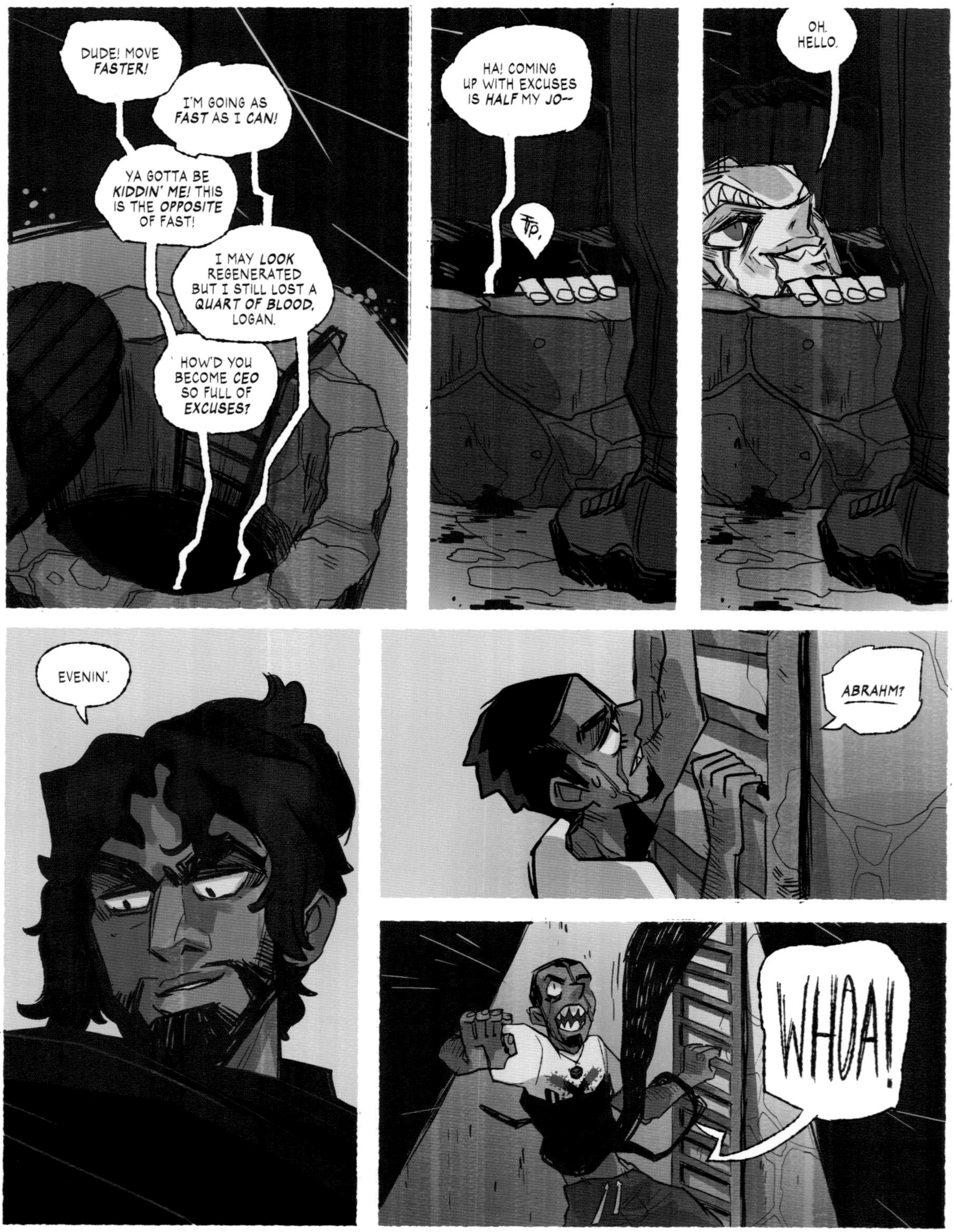
DUDE! MOVE FASTER!
I'M GOING AS FAST AS I CAN!
YA GOTTA BE KIDDIN' ME! THIS IS THE OPPOSITE OF FAST!
I MAY LOOK REGENERATED BUT I STILL LOST A QUART OF BLOOD, LOGAN.
HOW'D YOU BECOME CEO SO FULL OF EXCUSES?
HA! COMING UP WITH EXCUSES IS HALF MY JO--
OH. HELLO.
EVENIN'.
ABRAHM?
WHOA!

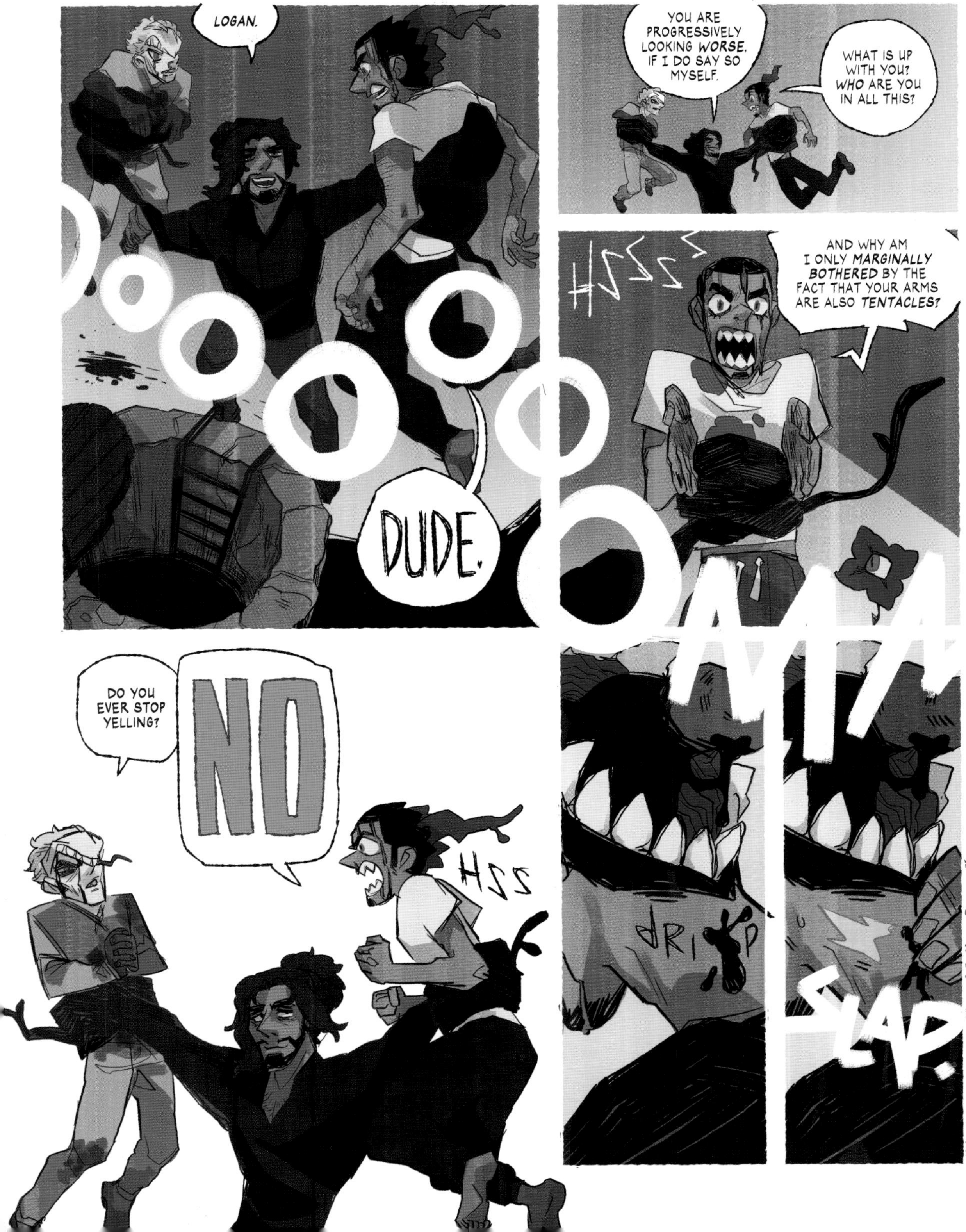
LOGAN.
DUDE.
YOU ARE PROGRESSIVELY LOOKING *WORSE*, IF I DO SAY SO MYSELF.
WHAT IS UP WITH YOU? *WHO* ARE YOU IN ALL THIS?
AND WHY AM I ONLY *MARGINALLY BOTHERED* BY THE FACT THAT YOUR ARMS ARE ALSO *TENTACLES*?
DO YOU EVER STOP YELLING?
NO
HSS
drip
SLAP.

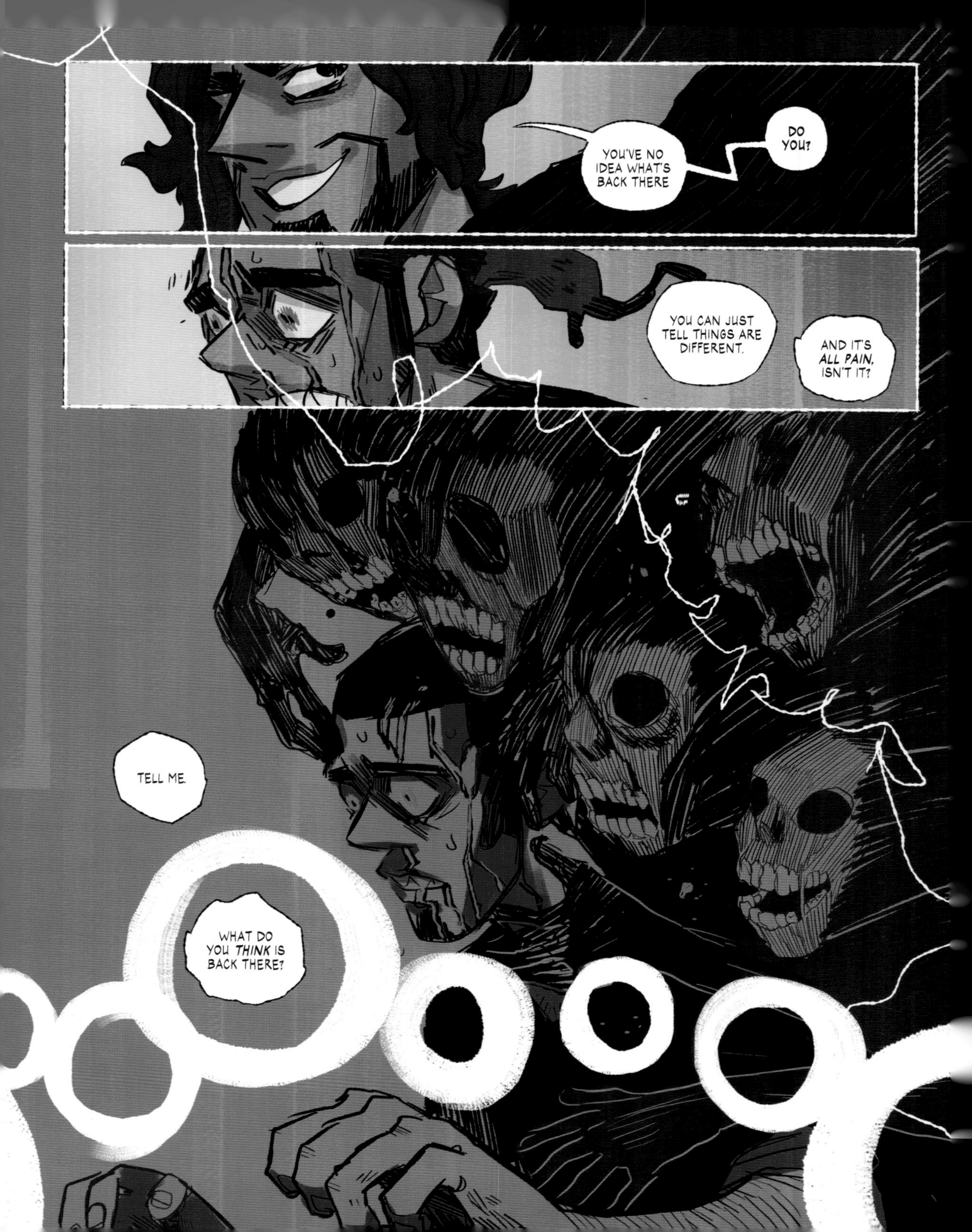
YOU'VE NO IDEA WHAT'S BACK THERE
DO YOU?
YOU CAN JUST TELL THINGS ARE DIFFERENT.
AND IT'S *ALL PAIN,* ISN'T IT?
TELL ME.
WHAT DO YOU *THINK* IS BACK THERE?

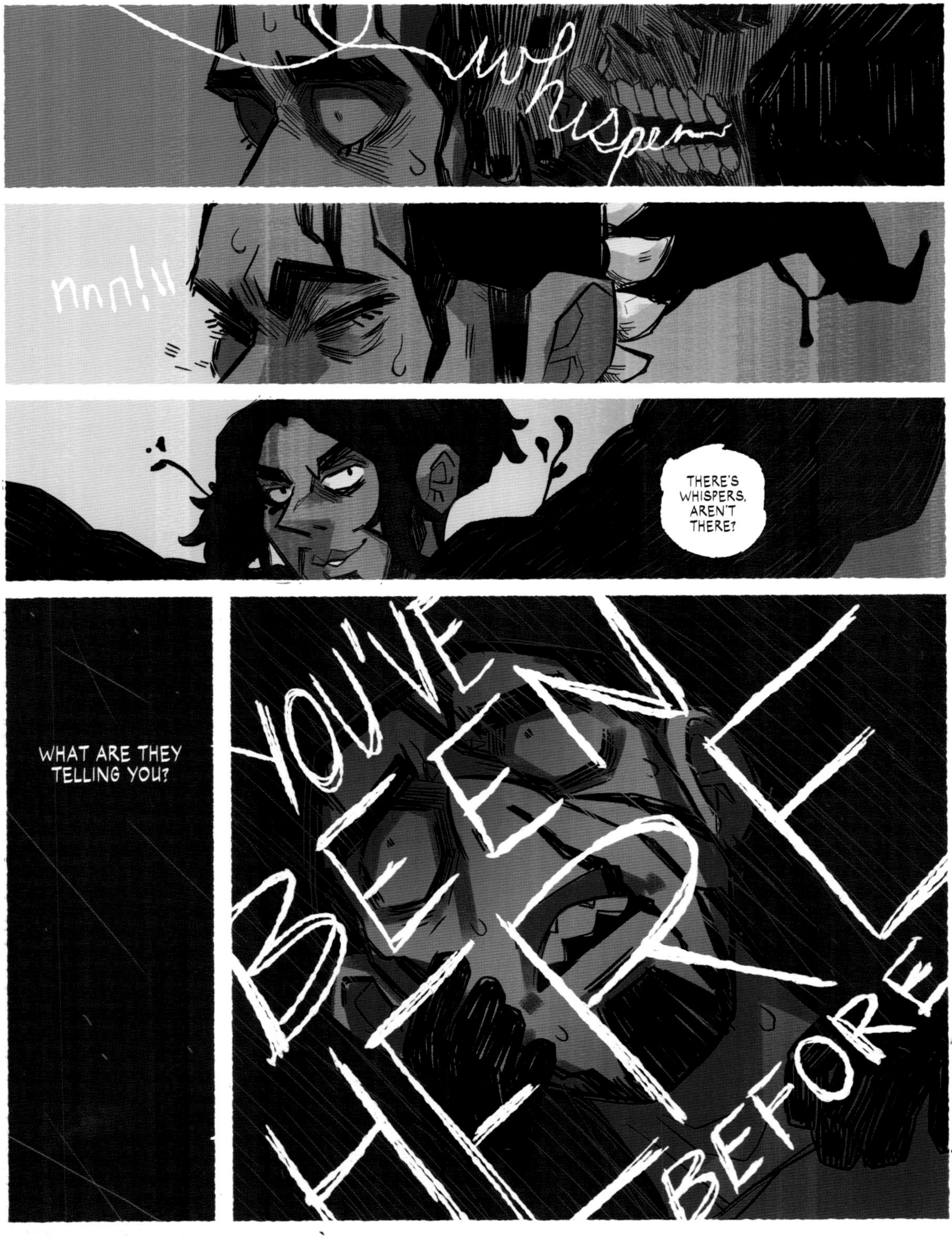
whisper
nnn!!
THERE'S WHISPERS, AREN'T THERE?
WHAT ARE THEY TELLING YOU?
YOU'VE BEEN HERE BEFORE

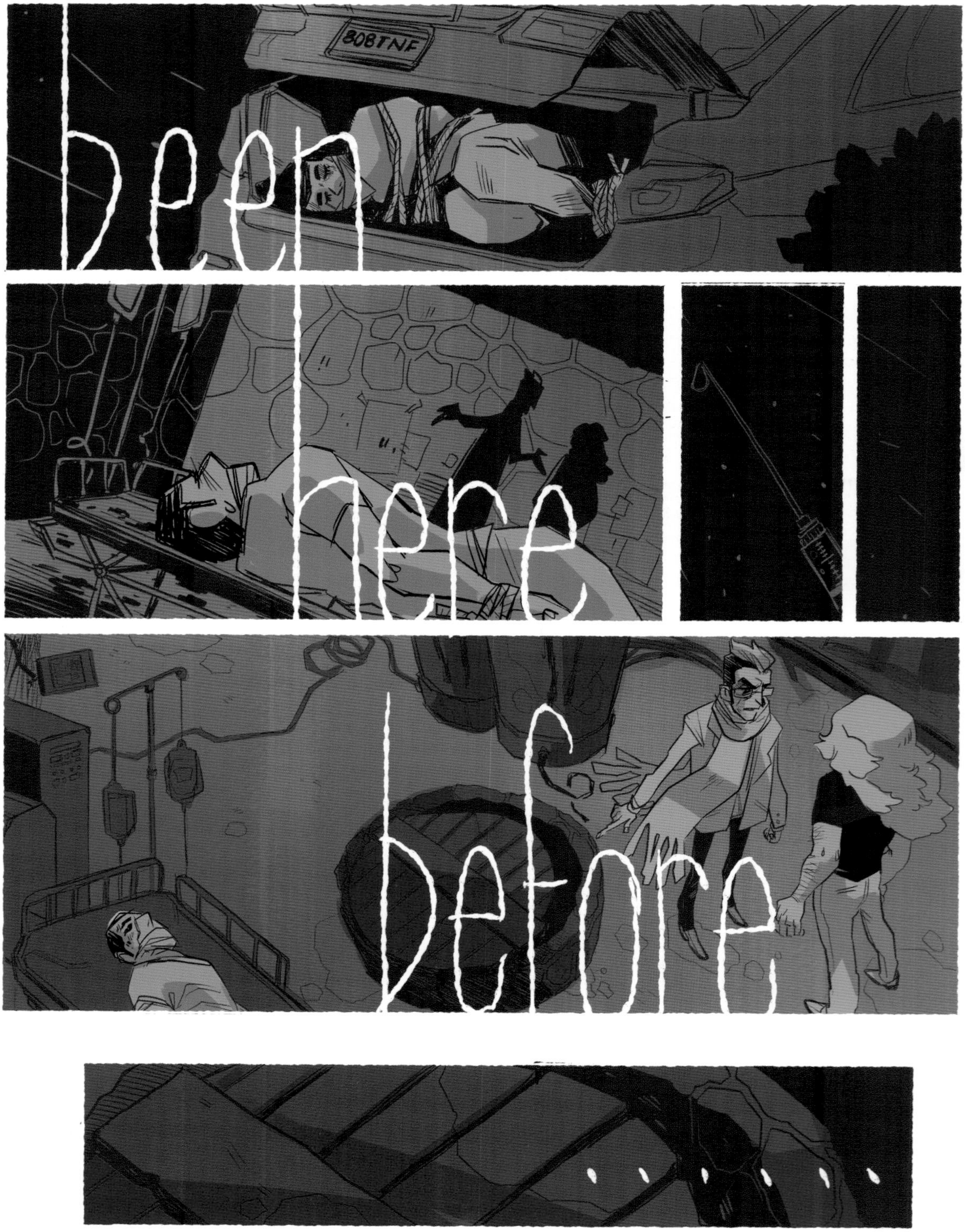

8OBTNF
been
here
before
. . . . . .

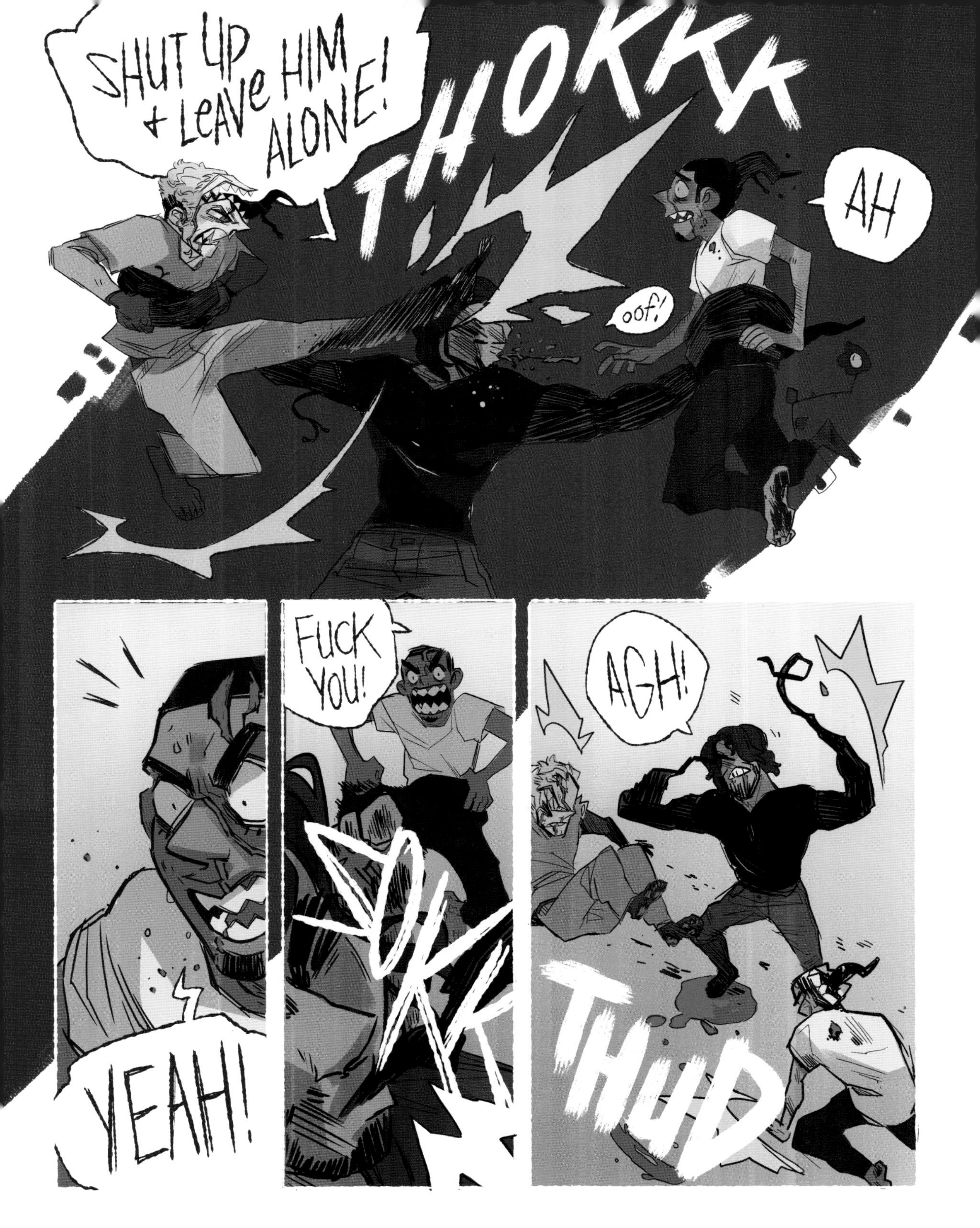
SHUT UP + LEAVE HIM ALONE!
THOKKK
AH
oof!
YEAH!
FUCK YOU!
AGH!
THUD

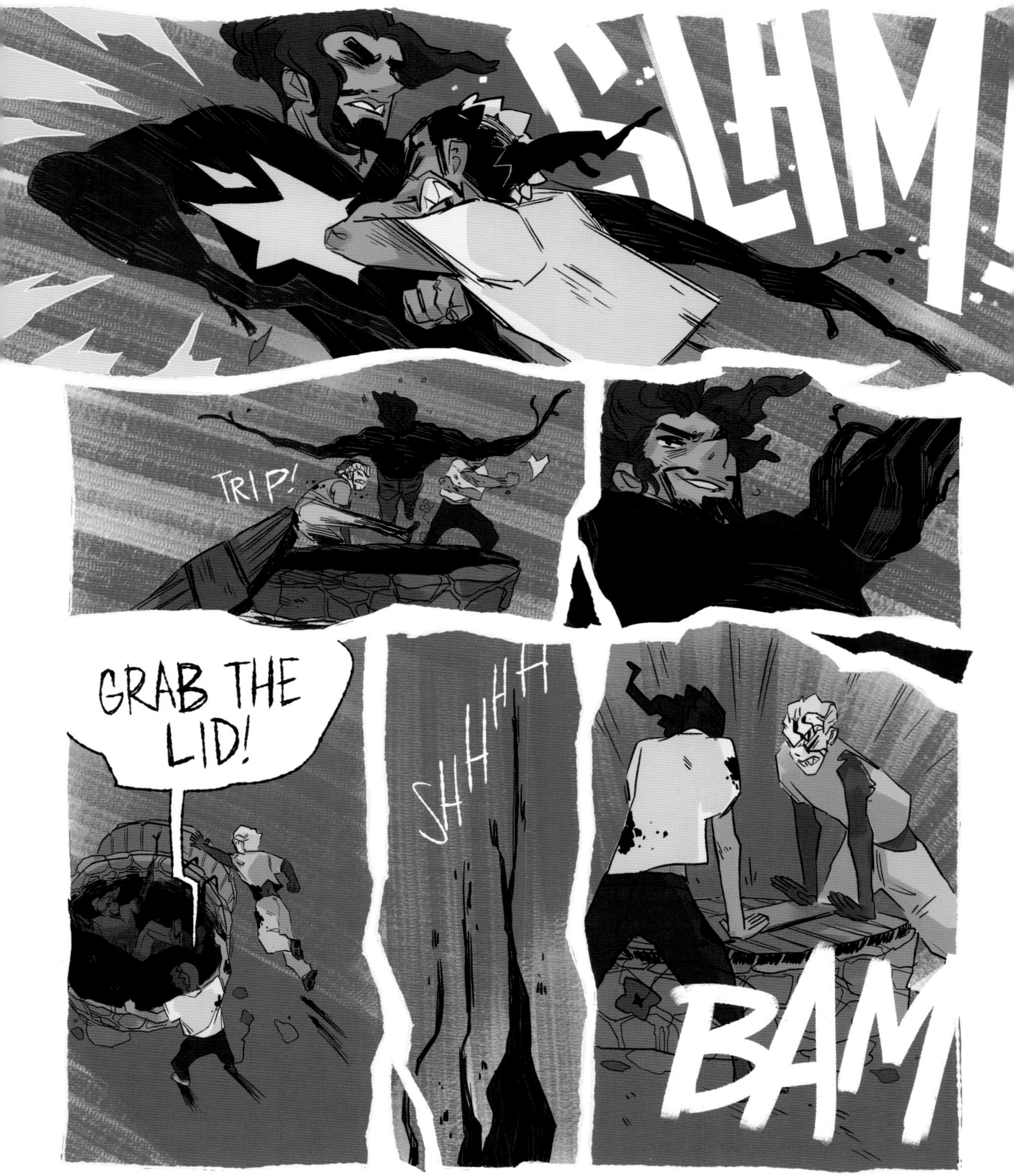
SLAM!
TRIP!
GRAB THE LID!
SHHHHH
BAM

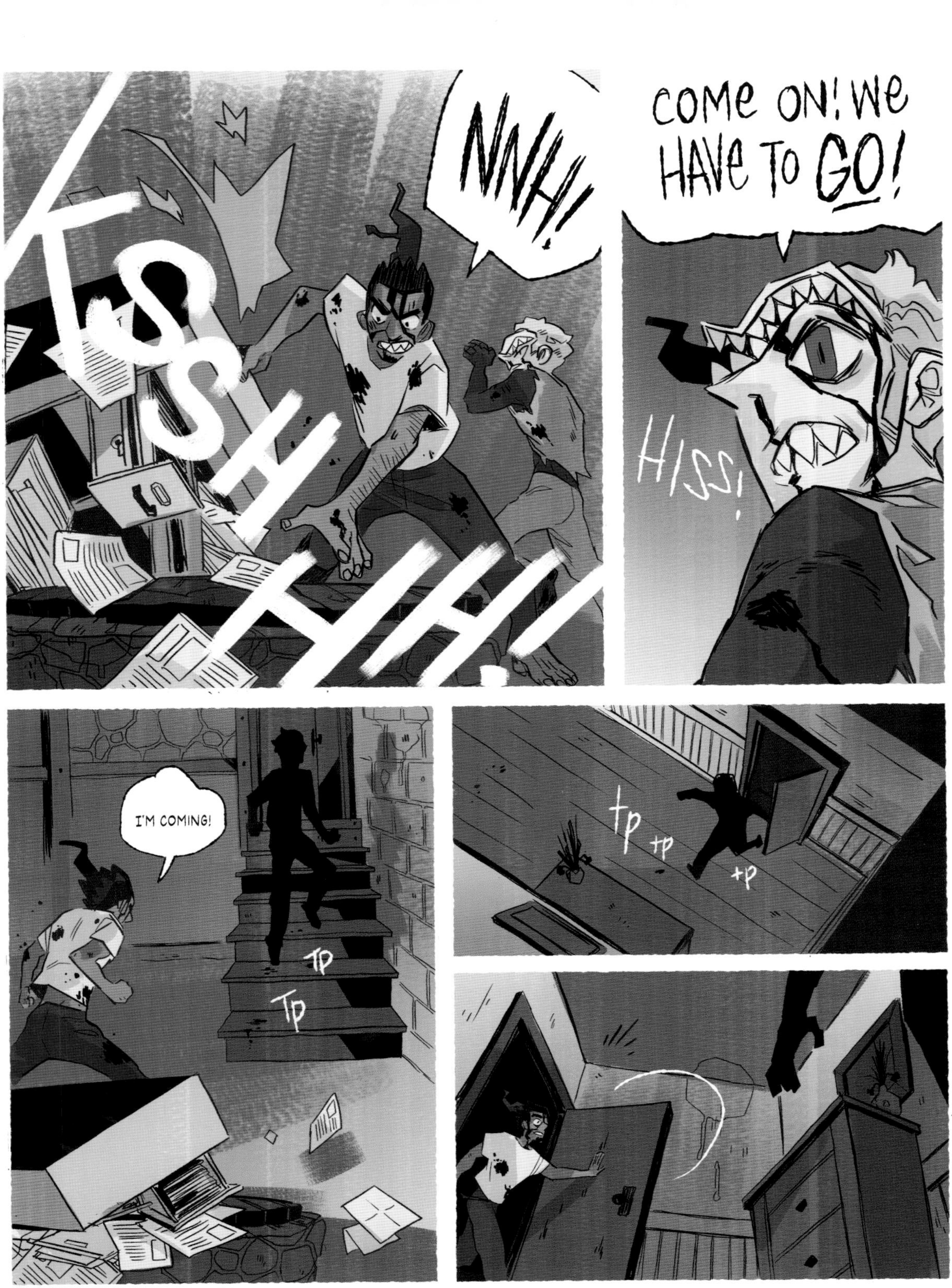
KSSHHH!
NNH!
COME ON! WE HAVE TO GO!
HISS!
I'M COMING!
TP
TP
tp
tp
+p

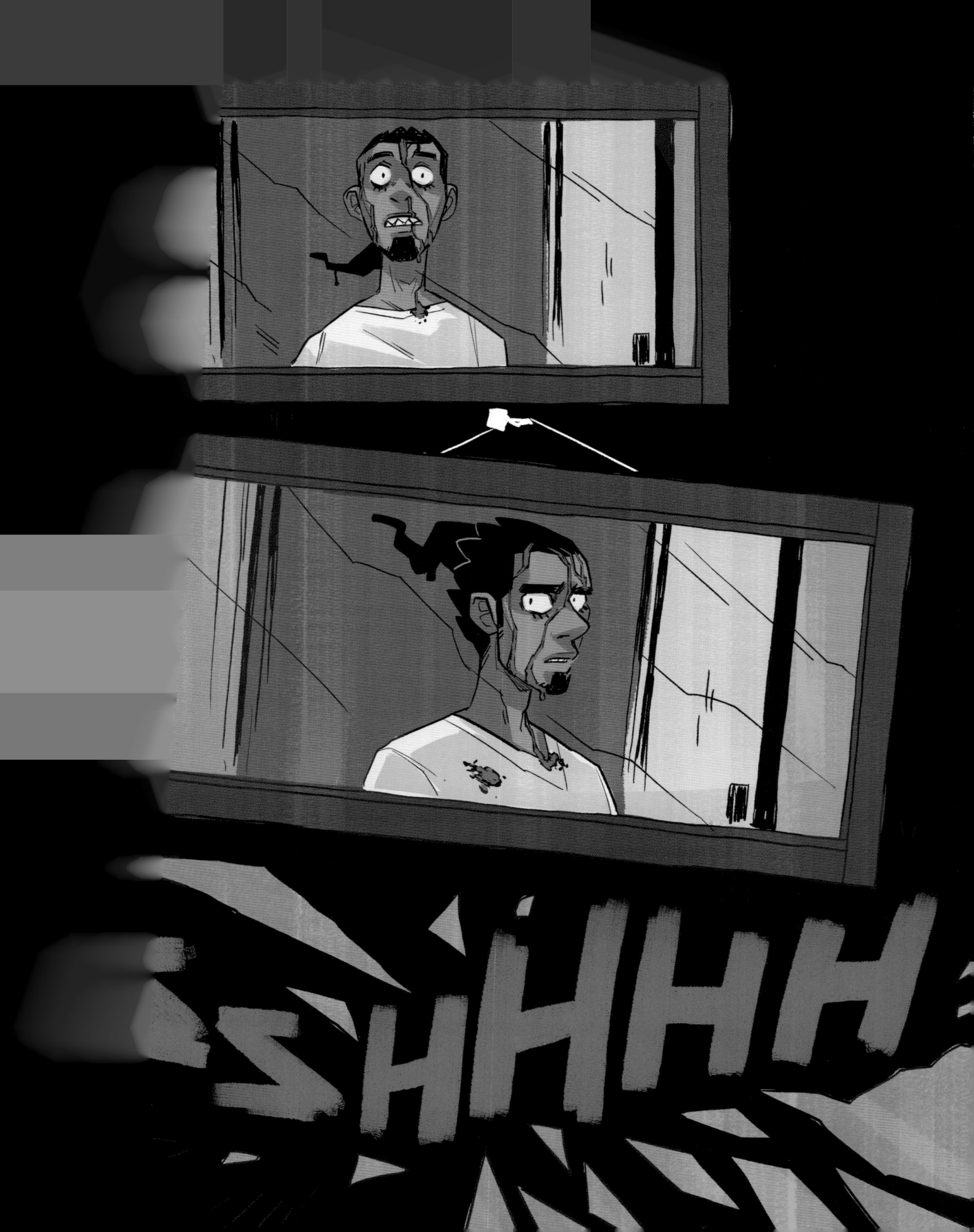
SHHHH

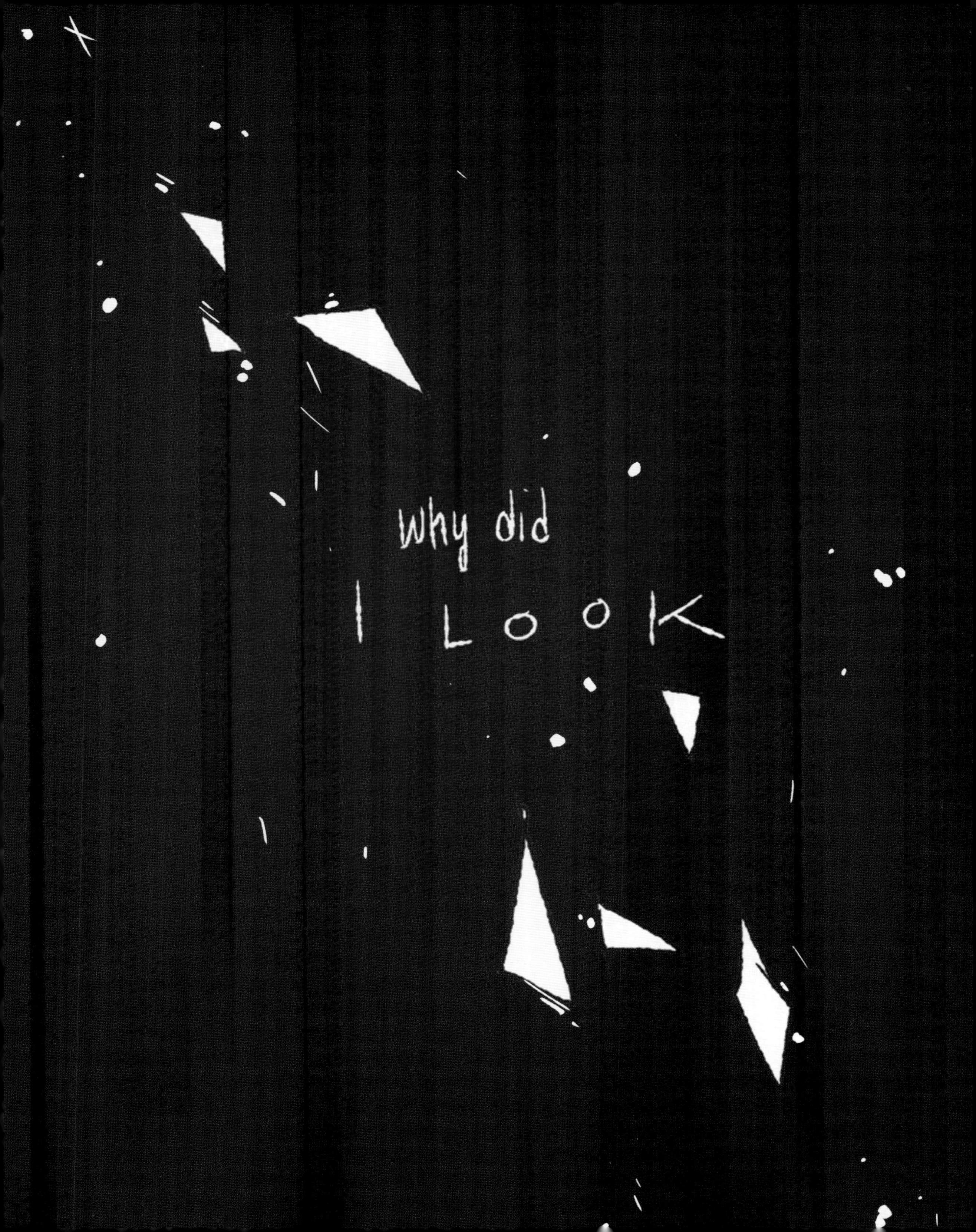
why did
I LOOK

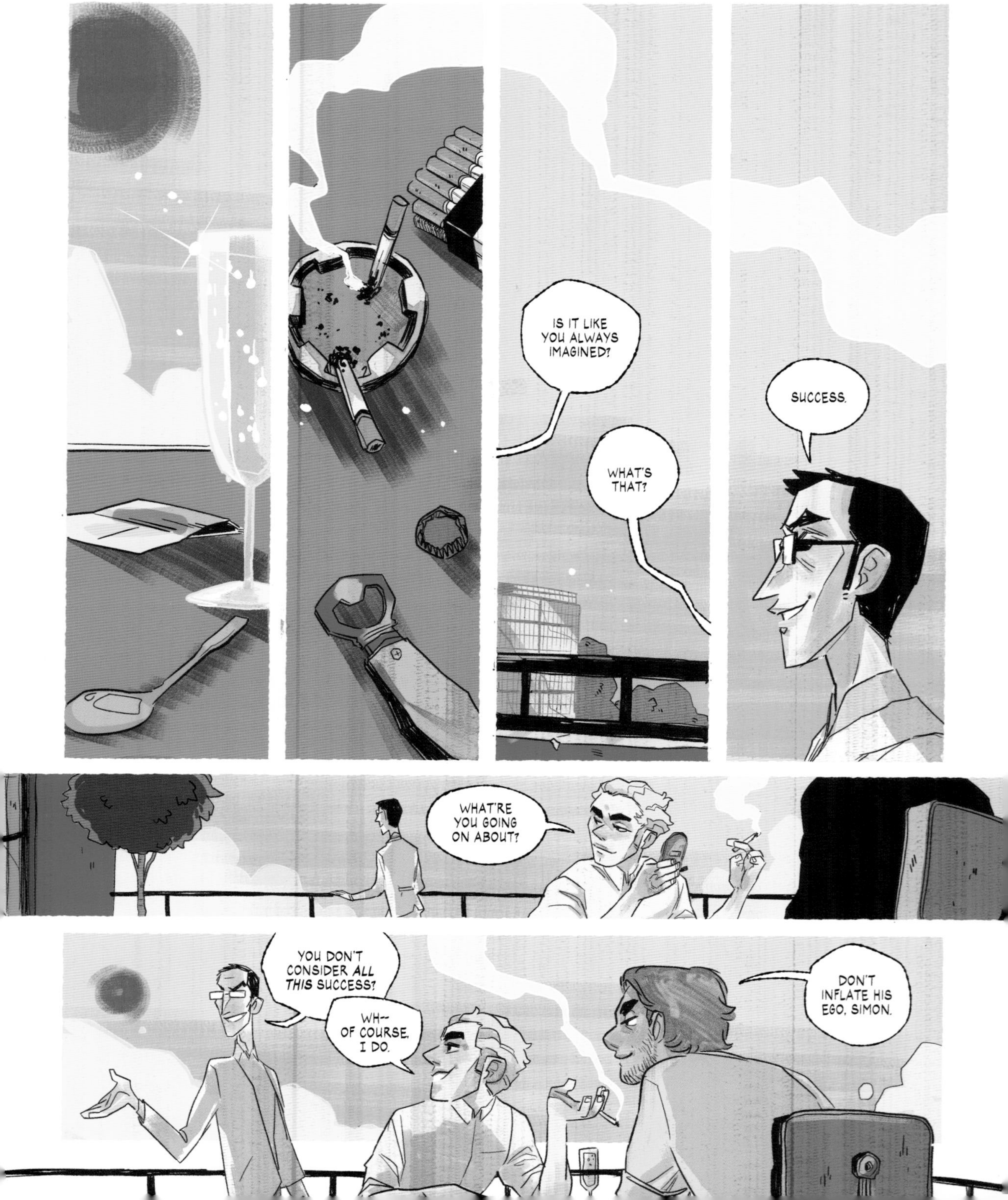
IS IT LIKE YOU ALWAYS IMAGINED?
WHAT'S THAT?
SUCCESS.
WHAT'RE YOU GOING ON ABOUT?
YOU DON'T CONSIDER *ALL THIS* SUCCESS?
WH-- OF COURSE, I DO.
DON'T INFLATE HIS EGO, SIMON.

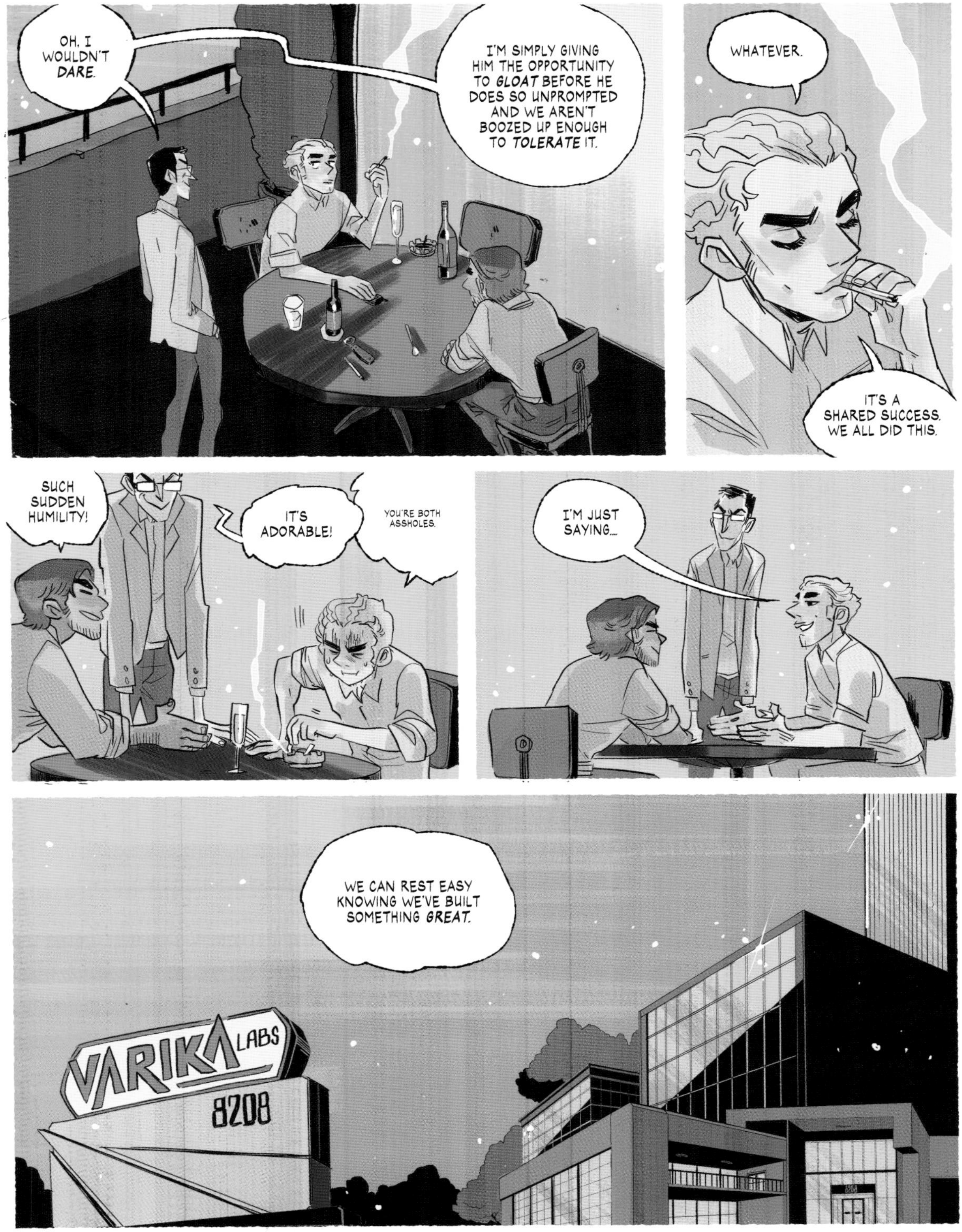
OH, I WOULDN'T *DARE*.
I'M SIMPLY GIVING HIM THE OPPORTUNITY TO *GLOAT* BEFORE HE DOES SO UNPROMPTED AND WE AREN'T BOOZED UP ENOUGH TO *TOLERATE* IT.
WHATEVER.
IT'S A SHARED SUCCESS. WE ALL DID THIS.
SUCH SUDDEN HUMILITY!
IT'S ADORABLE!
YOU'RE BOTH ASSHOLES.
I'M JUST SAYING....
WE CAN REST EASY KNOWING WE'VE BUILT SOMETHING *GREAT*.
VARIKA LABS
8208

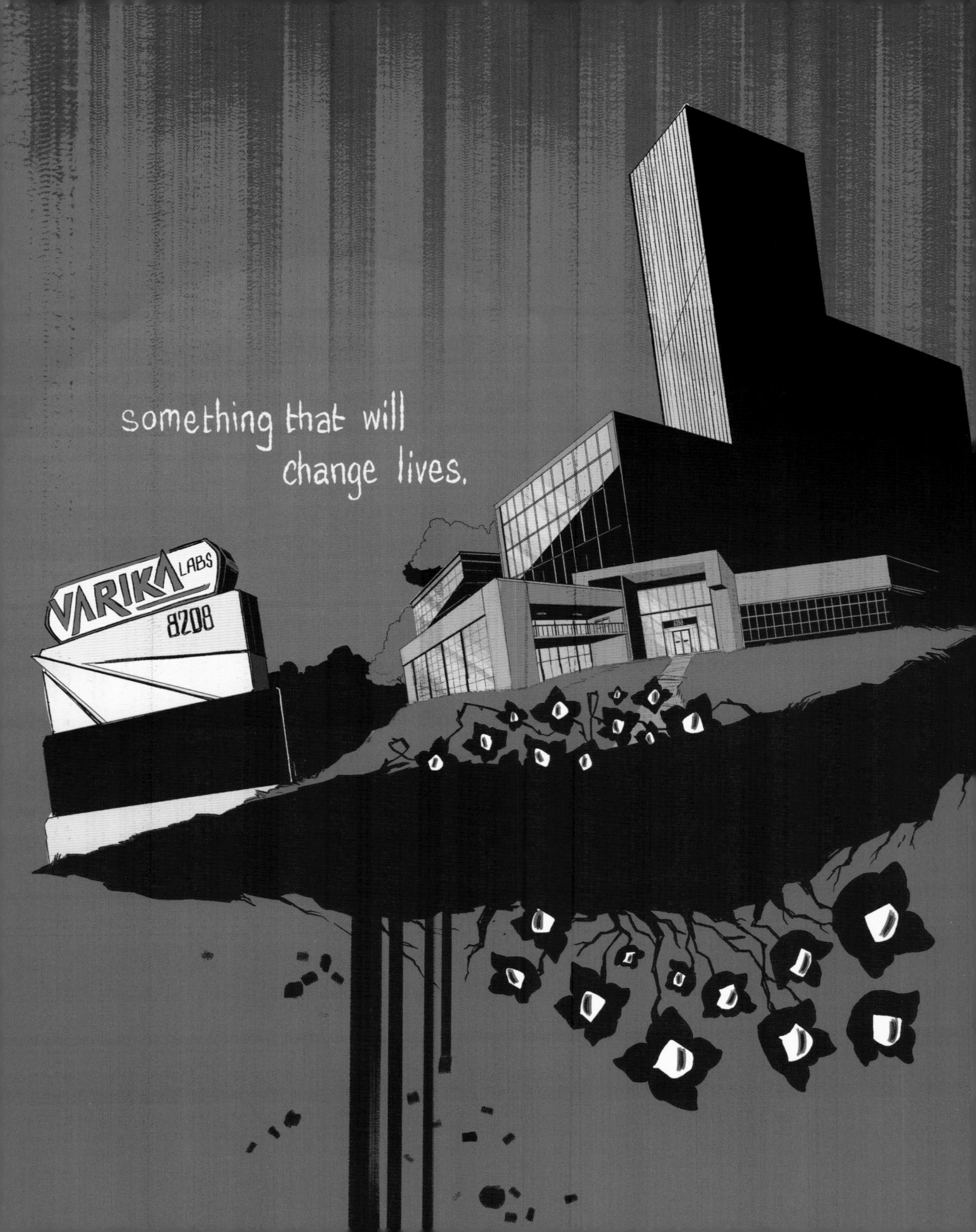

something that will change lives.
VARIKA LABS
8208

end of

BOOK TWO

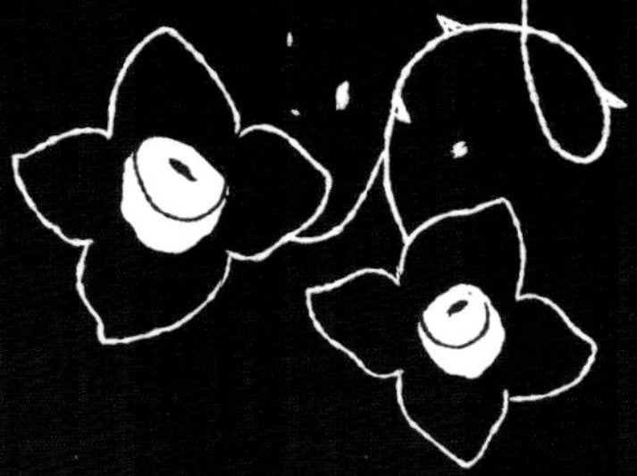

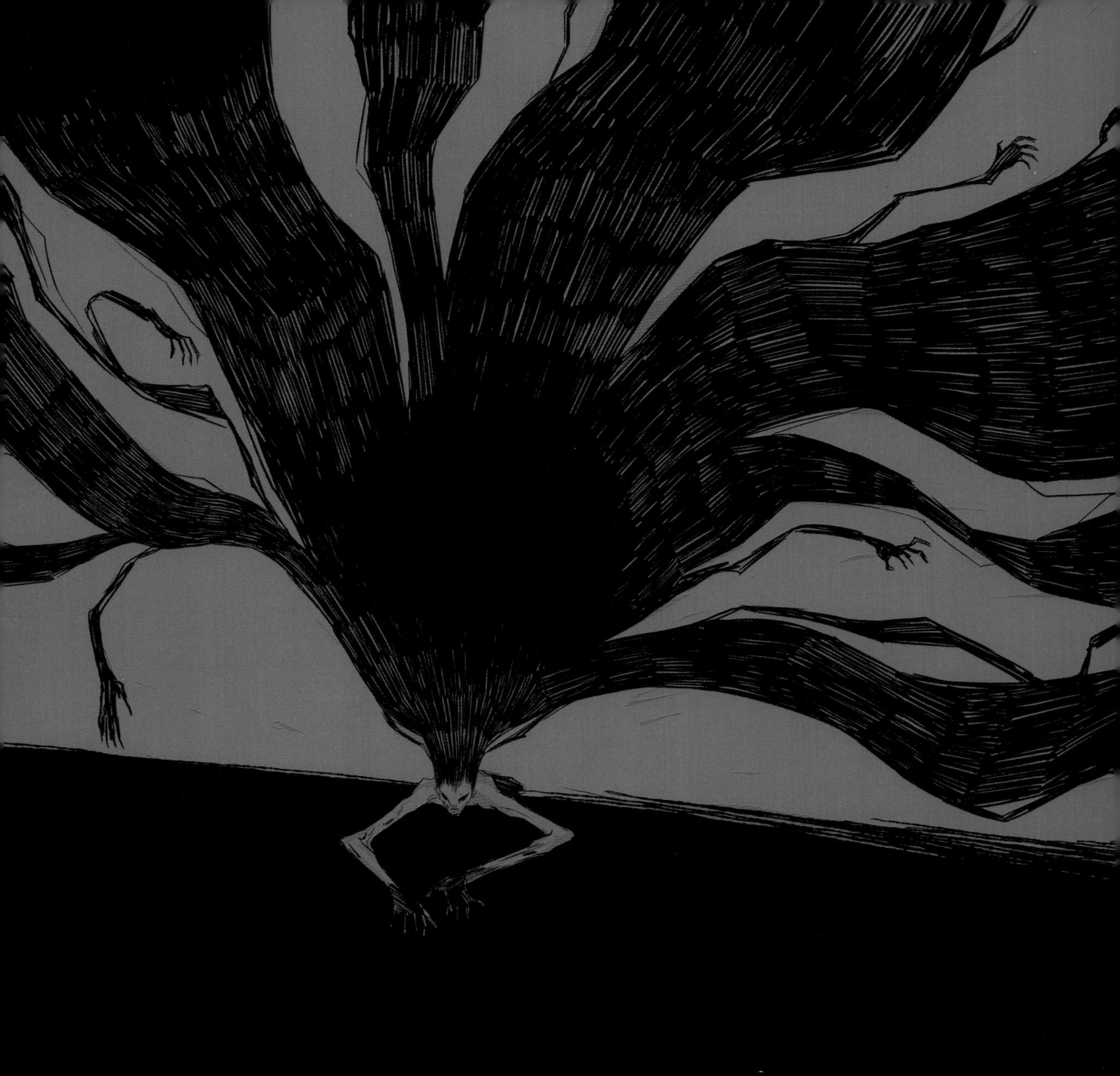

BONUS CONTENT

BIRKOV WAS ALWAYS A LITTLE OFF

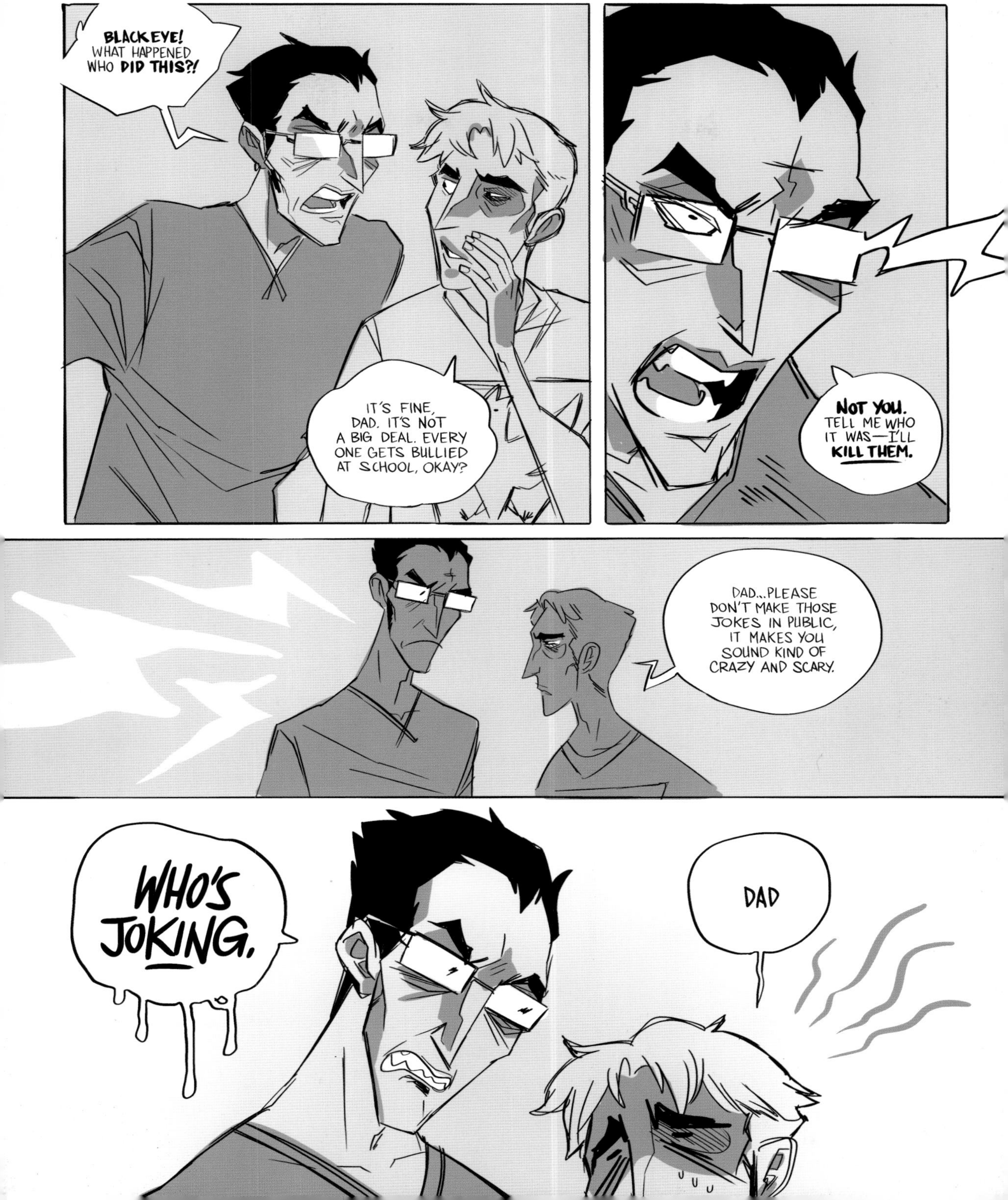
BLACK EYE! WHAT HAPPENED WHO DID THIS?!
IT'S FINE, DAD. IT'S NOT A BIG DEAL. EVERY ONE GETS BULLIED AT SCHOOL, OKAY?
NOT YOU. TELL ME WHO IT WAS—I'LL KILL THEM.
DAD...PLEASE DON'T MAKE THOSE JOKES IN PUBLIC, IT MAKES YOU SOUND KIND OF CRAZY AND SCARY.
WHO'S JOKING.
DAD

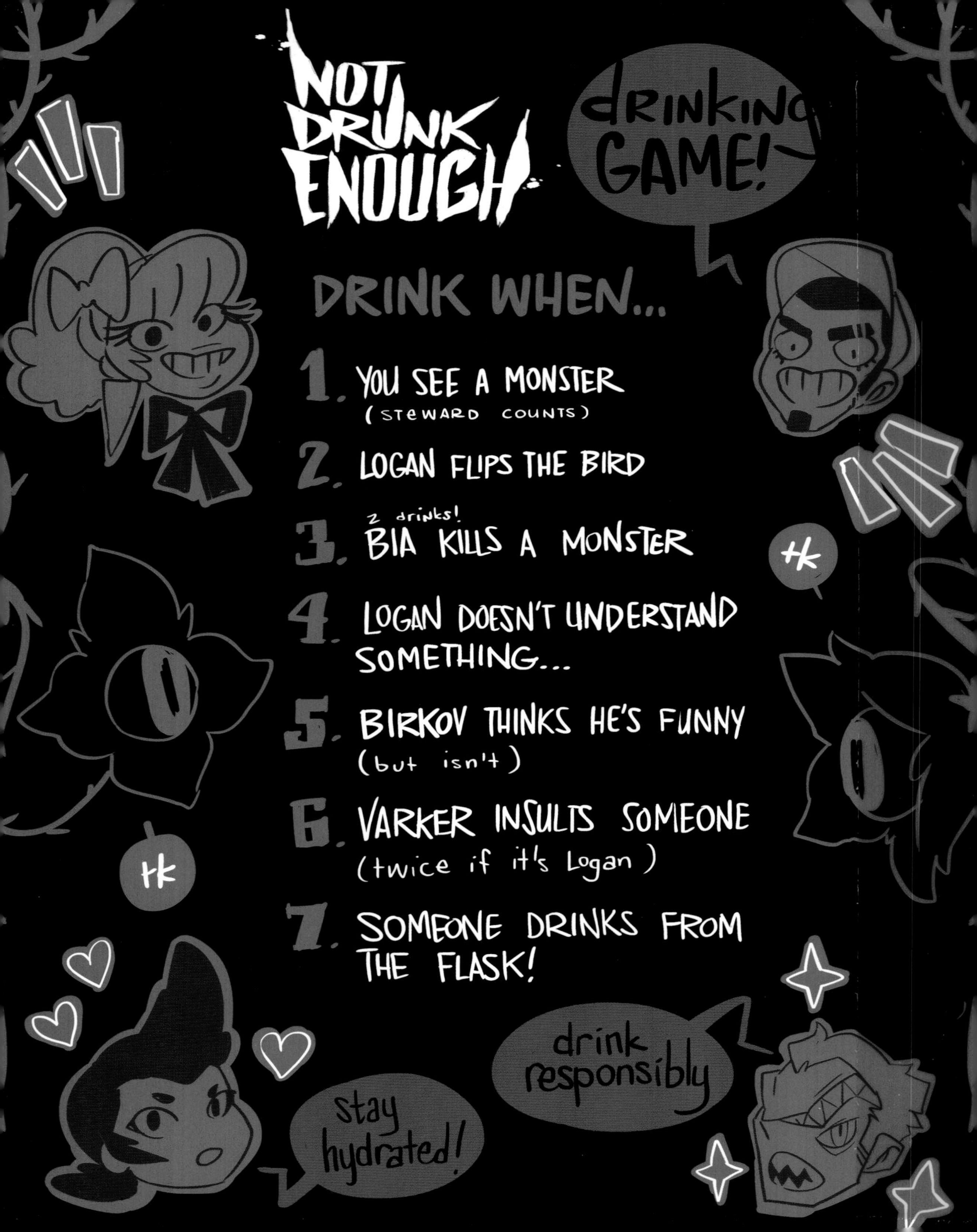
NOT DRUNK ENOUGH
drinking GAME!
DRINK WHEN...
1. YOU SEE A MONSTER
(STEWARD COUNTS)
2. LOGAN FLIPS THE BIRD
3. BIA KILLS A MONSTER
2 drinks!
4. LOGAN DOESN'T UNDERSTAND SOMETHING...
5. BIRKOV THINKS HE'S FUNNY
(but isn't)
6. VARKER INSULTS SOMEONE
(twice if it's Logan)
7. SOMEONE DRINKS FROM THE FLASK!
tk
tk
drink responsibly
stay hydrated!

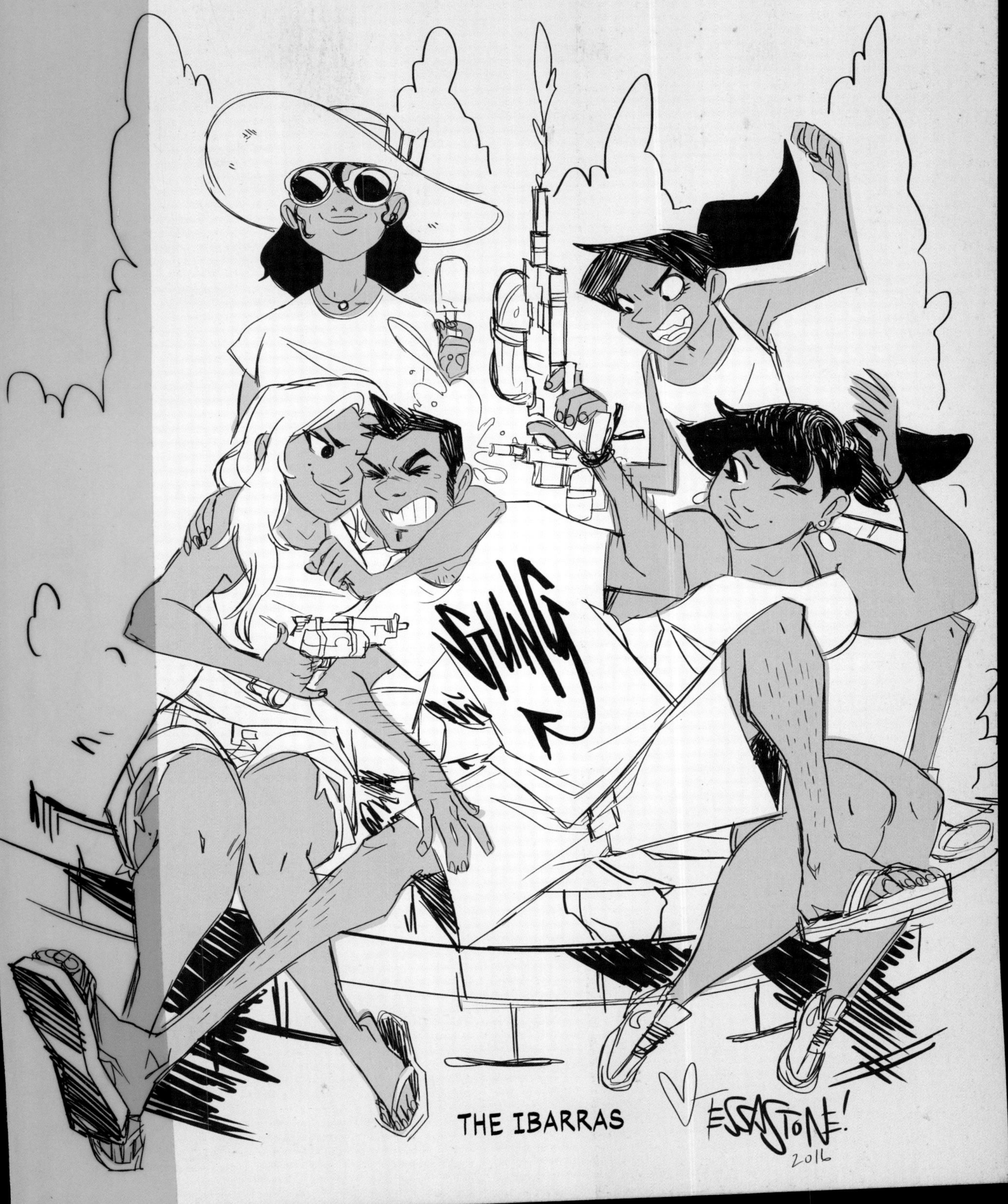
STUNG
THE IBARRAS
TESSASTONE!
2016

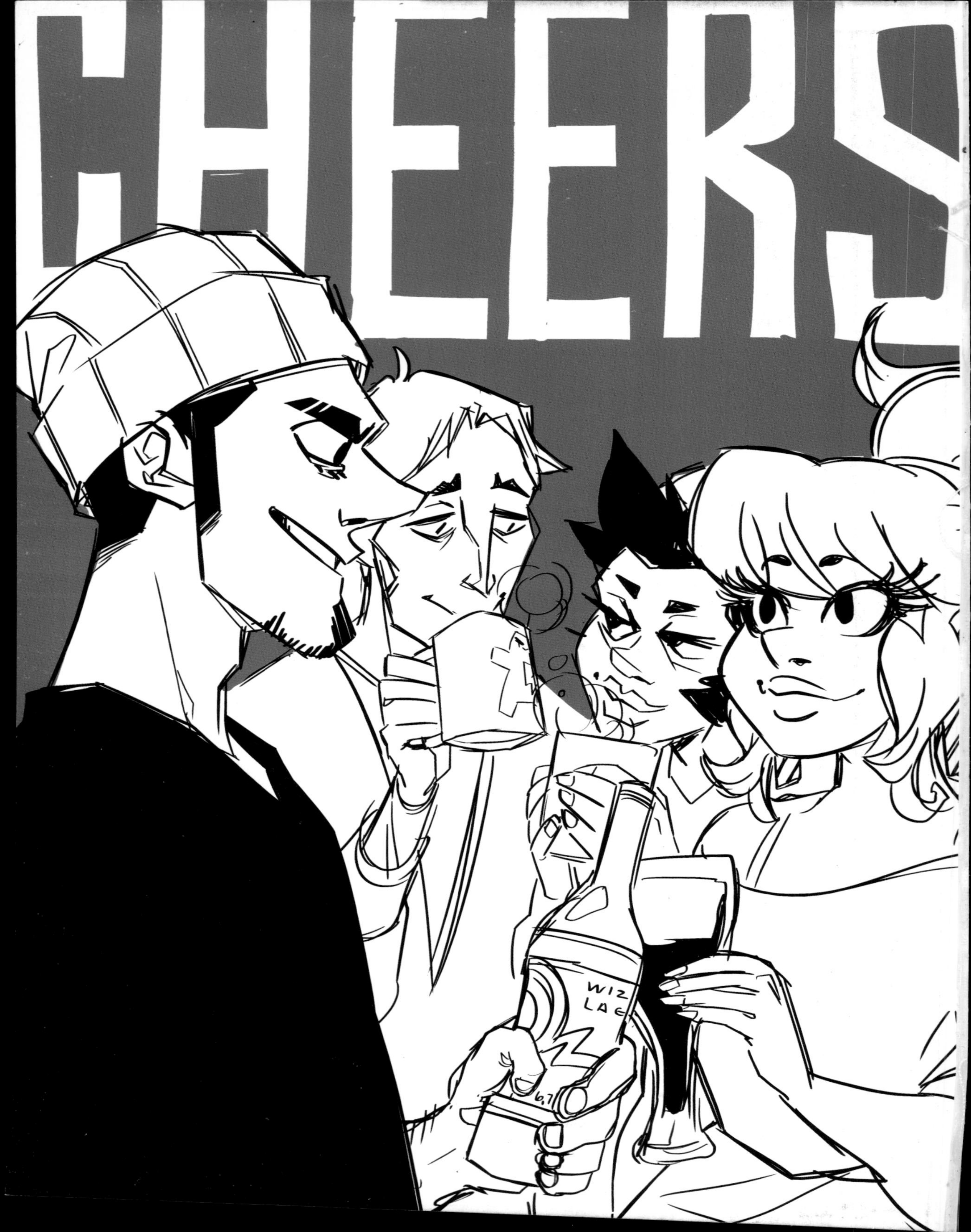
HEERS
WIZ
LAG
6.7